Global Inequalities

Sociology for a New Century

A PINE FORGE PRESS SERIES

Edited by Charles Ragin, Wendy Griswold, and Larry Griffin

Sociology for a New Century brings the best current scholarship to today's students in a series of short texts authored by leaders of a new generation of social scientists. Each book addresses its subject from a comparative, historical, and global perspective and, in doing so, connects social science to the wider concerns of students seeking to make sense of our dramatically changing world.

- *Global Inequalities*   York W. Bradshaw and Michael Wallace
- *How Societies Change*   Daniel Chirot
- *Cultures and Societies in a Changing World*   Wendy Griswold
- *Crime and Disrepute*   John Hagan
- *Gods in the Global Village: The World's Religions in Sociological Perspective*   Lester R. Kurtz
- *Waves of Democracy: Social Movements and Political Change* John Markoff
- *Development and Social Change: A Global Perspective*   Philip McMichael
- *Constructing Social Research*   Charles C. Ragin
- *Women and Men at Work*   Barbara Reskin and Irene Padavic
- *Cities in a World Economy*   Saskia Sassen

Forthcoming:

- *Social Psychology and Social Institutions*   Denise and William Bielby
- *Schools and Societies*   Steven Brint
- *The Social Ecology of Natural Resources and Development* Stephen G. Bunker
- *Ethnic Dynamics in the Modern World*   Stephen Cornell
- *The Sociology of Childhood*   William A. Corsaro
- *Economy and Society*   Mark Granovetter
- *People and Populations: Demography and the Human Experience* Dennis P. Hogan
- *Racism in the Modern World*   Wilmot G. James
- *Health and Societies*   Bernice Pescosolido
- *Organizations in a World Economy*   Walter W. Powell

Global Inequalities

York W. Bradshaw
Michael Wallace
Indiana University

PINE FORGE PRESS
Thousand Oaks, California • London • New Delhi

For information, address:

 Pine Forge Press
A Sage Publications Company
2455 Teller Road
Thousand Oaks, California 91320
(805) 499-4224
E-mail: sdr@pfp.sagepub.com

Sage Publications Ltd.
6 Bonhill Street
London EC2A 4PU
United Kingdom

Sage Publications India Pvt. Ltd.
M-32 Market
Greater Kailash I
New Delhi 110 048 India

Production: Scratchgravel Publishing Services
Designer: Lisa S. Mirski
Typesetter: Scratchgravel Publishing Services
Cover: Lisa S. Mirski
Production Manager: Rebecca Holland

Printed in the United States of America

05 06 07 08 09 10 13 12 11 10 09 08

Library of Congress Cataloging-in-Publication Data

Bradshaw, York W., 1960– .
    Global inequalities / York W. Bradshaw, Michael Wallace.
        p. cm. — (Sociology for a new century)
    Includes bibliographical references and index.
    ISBN 0-8039-9060-X (pbk. : alk. paper)
        1. Economic history—1945– . 2. Regional economic disparities.
    I. Wallace, Michael, 1954– . II. Title. III. Series.
    HC59.B664   1996
    330.9—dc20
                                   95-49168
                                     CIP

Contents

ABOUT THE AUTHORS

York W. Bradshaw is Associate Professor of Sociology and African Studies at Indiana University. He received his Ph.D. in 1987 from Northwestern University, where he learned the value of traveling abroad to discover new cultures and ways of life. He has continued to travel, research, and teach in a variety of countries around the world. His publications focus on topics that concern the developing world, including urbanization patterns, economic development, and health and education issues. He is editor of a forthcoming book titled *Education in Comparative Perspective: New Lessons from Around the World,* and he is co-editor of the *International Journal of Comparative Sociology.* Outside of his academic work, he conducts seminars for businesses and not-for-profit organizations on how to enhance teamwork in situations of cultural diversity.

Michael Wallace is Professor of Sociology at Indiana University. He received his Ph.D. from Indiana University. His past work has dealt with issues of labor markets, organization of work, and other topics in social stratification. He edited the book *Deindustrialization and the Restructuring of American Industry* and is currently editor of the annual volume *Research in Social Stratification and Mobility.* His current research interests include analyses of the labor movements in Canada and Western Europe.

ABOUT THE PUBLISHER

Pine Forge Press is a new educational publisher, dedicated to publishing innovative books and software throughout the social sciences. On this and any other of our publications, we welcome your comments, ideas, and suggestions. Please call or write to:

Pine Forge Press
A Sage Publications Company
2455 Teller Road
Thousand Oaks, California 91320
(805) 499-4224
Fax (805) 499-7881
E-mail: sdr@pfp.sagepub.com

Illustrations

Tables

Foreword

Sociology for a New Century offers the best of current sociological thinking to today's students. The goal of the series is to prepare students, and—in the long run—the informed public, for a world that has changed dramatically in the last three decades and one that continues to astonish.

This goal reflects important changes that have taken place in sociology. The discipline has become broader in orientation, with an ever-growing interest in research that is comparative, historical, or transnational in orientation. Sociologists are less focused on "American" society as the pinnacle of human achievement and more sensitive to global processes and trends. They also have become less insulated from surrounding social forces. In the 1970s and 1980s sociologists were so obsessed with constructing a science of society that they saw impenetrability as a sign of success. Today, there is a greater effort to connect sociology to the ongoing concerns and experiences of the informed public.

Each book in this series offers in some way a comparative, historical, transnational, or global perspective to help broaden students' vision. Students need to comprehend the diversity in today's world and to understand the sources of diversity. This knowledge can challenge the limitations of conventional ways of thinking about social life. At the same time, students need to understand that issues that may seem specifically "American" (for example, the women's movement, an aging population bringing a strained social security and health care system, racial conflict, national chauvinism, and so on) are shared by many other countries. Awareness of commonalities undercuts the tendency to view social issues and questions in narrowly American terms and encourages students to seek out the experiences of others for the lessons they offer. Finally, students need to grasp phenomena that transcend national boundaries—trends and processes that are supranational (for example, environmental degradation). Recognition of global processes stimulates student awareness of causal forces that transcend national boundaries, economies, and politics.

Global Inequalities, by York W. Bradshaw and Michael Wallace, provides a comprehensive introduction to global inequalities between and within major world regions. The book presents general theoretical arguments and then applies them to four areas: Africa, Asia, Europe, and the Americas. The strength of the book is that it mixes academic material with lively stories and examples from around the globe. Bradshaw and Wallace discuss global success stories as well as criticize needless patterns of inequality. In the final chapter the authors present suggestions for creating positive social changes throughout the world. Bradshaw and Wallace have given us a comprehensive, rigorous, and eminently readable treatment of an issue of global significance.

Larry Griffin

Preface

Forty years ago, there would have been little demand for this book in the United States. Colleges offered few courses on international studies, and the general public did not know or care very much about global issues. Aside from concerns over communism and war, few people were even interested in what happened around the world. And there was virtually no interest in poor countries and where they fit into the global puzzle.

The situation is much different today. Savvy college students can select from a variety of courses in international economics, politics, and cultures, and they may learn a foreign language or two. Students can take specialized courses in Asia, Africa, Europe, or Latin America, and they may even volunteer for the Peace Corps upon graduation. Business students, and businesspeople in general, are also taking a greater interest in global issues as financial markets stretch far beyond U.S. borders. Moreover, students, businesspeople, and the general public are traveling more today than ever before, generating considerable interest in other cultures and countries. Without broad knowledge of global issues, people will miss out on a wide array of career, educational, and travel opportunities.

This book offers a general introduction to important issues throughout today's world. We examine a wide variety of topics, from global economic trends to ethnic conflicts, in four major regions: Africa, Asia, Europe, and the Americas. Our primary goal is to introduce people to these areas, providing a theoretical framework that helps readers understand the regions better. Every region has its unique features, but each also exhibits features that are common across regions, countries, and cultures. By studying all of these characteristics, people can learn more about other countries while also learning more about their own nations.

Our principal focus throughout the book is on inequality at several different levels. Two points are important in considering inequality. First, there are substantial economic and political inequalities between and within different regions and countries. For instance, Asia is widely viewed as an emerging economic giant, certainly more powerful than Africa and threatening to surpass both Europe and the Americas. Such inequalities have implications for each region as well as for the countries and individuals within the regions. Second, inequalities change over time, reshuffling the economic and political fortunes of regions, countries, and communities. Brutally racist regimes turn democratic (for example, South Africa), leading global powers lose strength (Britain), superpowers break up and face economic crisis (the Soviet Union), and communist giants open their markets to capitalist development (China). Change is an enduring feature of the world, and it is a constant theme throughout this book.

This book presents a combination of academic works, lively stories and examples, and reports from newspapers and other popular press outlets. An understanding of current events is essential for anyone interested in global issues. At the same time, academic models and theories help us make sense of current events and place them in an appropriate context. Stories and examples not only illustrate major points, they are also fun to read and fun to tell. We enjoy relating the many examples and stories that we have gathered in years of research around the world.

Although this book covers a lot of territory, we do not try to cover every country, every issue, or every theoretical model. To the contrary, we are selective in each respect, trying to present a variety of major issues and topics. Readers can use our presentation as a starting point and then focus on additional countries, issues, and theories that interest them. The world is so dynamic and diverse that we will never run out of topics to investigate and ponder.

We have benefited enormously from the assistance of many people while writing this book. Bruce Heilman and Julie Kmec were the primary research assistants throughout the project, and they did a truly outstanding job. We are very grateful for their efforts. Ophra Leyser, David Brady, John Gnida, Suzanne Goodney, and Carla Shirley also provided able research assistance at different points in the project. Stephen Ndegwa (College of William and Mary), Jie Huang (Ohio State University), Cynthia Woolever (Midway College), Jeanne Hurlbert (Louisiana State University), and Craig Jenkins (Ohio State University) read the manuscript and offered superb suggestions for revision. The book would not be nearly as coherent without their insightful comments. A group of wonderful graduate students also read and commented on the book draft, including Claudia Buchmann, Njeri Gikonyo, Rita Noonan, Sabine Rieble, and Agostino Zamberia. Their excellent suggestions made us rethink, revise, and reconsider our arguments. One of the true pleasures of being a professor is to work closely with graduate students and to watch the students become the teachers. Faculty and student participants in Indiana

University's Program in Comparative International Studies also provided an enthusiastic and critical audience for many of our early ideas.

Where would international researchers and teachers be without maps? Many maps in this book were drawn by John Hollingsworth. His precision, careful attention to detail, and overall dedication are much appreciated.

Special thanks are reserved for a few people. Larry Griffin read several versions of our manuscript and provided his "usual" set of comments, which, quite frankly, were nothing short of extraordinary. Larry has commented on much of our work through the years, and it is always a privilege to learn from him. He has the rare ability to make unusually incisive comments in a very constructive and supportive manner. Victoria Nelson offered excellent suggestions about how to reorganize an early draft and to make the overall manuscript more readable. Steve Rutter of Pine Forge Press is the best publisher that one could possibly hope to encounter. He has read several versions of the manuscript and done a superb job of synthesizing comments from other reviewers and then offering his own suggestions. Moreover, Steve has shown great patience and encouragement throughout the project, as we tried to finish this book amid too many other deadlines. We are extraordinarily grateful for his efforts. Finally, we express our gratitude to Charles Ragin and Wendy Griswold for editing the Pine Forge series along with Larry Griffin.

In Chapter 1 we discuss an African proverb: "It takes a whole village to raise a single child." Reflecting on the generous support and assistance that we have received while writing this book, we might paraphrase that statement as "It takes a whole village of scholars to write a single book." Using the most widely spoken language in Africa, Swahili, we say *Asante sana.* (Thank you very much.)

York W. Bradshaw
Michael Wallace

1

The Reality of Inequality:
Stories from Around the World

A Global Village?

In the spring of 1989, several thousand Chinese college students gathered in Beijing's Tiananmen Square to demonstrate for democracy. It was a remarkable event for a country that has never embraced dissent and open protest. As many as one million students and their supporters occupied the square for six weeks, often chanting "Long Live Freedom, Long Live Democracy." They erected a thirty-foot "Goddess of Democracy" modeled after the American Statue of Liberty. But weeks later the spirited protest ended when the Chinese communist government lost patience and ordered the demonstration crushed—literally. Soldiers surrounded the square, tanks rolled down the Avenue of Eternal Peace, and tear gas canisters screamed through the air. On June 4, 1989, at least 1,000 fleeing students were murdered. Thousands more were arrested and many of them were quietly executed.

One of the world's most lasting images of this failed uprising was the heroic gesture of Wang Weilin, a 19-year-old Chinese student, who stood in front of a column of tanks, delaying for six minutes their arrival into the square. Both the soldiers and the youth knew well that the outcome was inevitable: Weilin was forcibly removed, the tanks rolled into the square, and the uprising was crushed. The world does not know what fate befell young Weilin, but nobody could mistake the impact of his singular act of courage. Captured by television cameras and beamed throughout the world, this chilling image signaled to tyrants everywhere the tenacious resolve of ordinary citizens to achieve democracy.

The Chinese government tried to censor news reports of the Tiananmen massacre, in China and abroad. In earlier times, the government could have effectively suppressed unfavorable coverage because it had held exclusive control of national news sources. But by 1989, new technologies were able to eclipse the clumsy strategies of the aging dictators. International television, led by CNN, was one such technology. But there were others. Armed with fax machines, students and their sympathizers transmitted pictures and written accounts of the carnage throughout the world. In turn, sympathizers in other countries (especially Chinese students studying in the United States) were able to fax information back to the demonstrators in China. This "instant" form of communication was partly responsible for the swift denunciation of China by foreign governments and other global institutions. If the events at Tiananmen Square were to occur today, electronic mail (E-mail) messages would further increase the speed and volume of communication between China and other countries in the global village.

But is the world really a "global village"? The answer is clearly "yes" in many respects: Economies are interconnected, computers and fax machines link people across oceans, new diseases ignore national boundaries, and environmental destruction in one part of the world profoundly affects other parts of the world. For example, the Calophyllum lanigerum tree that grows in the rain forests of Malaysia produces a substance that, according to the U.S. National Cancer Institute, destroys HIV cells. This means that the Malaysian rain forests *may* offer a cure for AIDS. Unfortunately, loggers are fighting with international researchers, pharmaceutical companies, and the Malaysian government to continue cutting the rich forests. If loggers succeed in this remote area, the resulting heavy cutting may have repercussions throughout the world, but not just for AIDS research. Many of the world's medicines come from plants in numerous rain forests. The cure for AIDS, cancer, and many other diseases may already have been deforested today (Shenon 1994).

The global village is dynamic, even chaotic at times, exhibiting good and bad features. It contains hunger and famine, wars and other forms of violence, and growing despair in many regions. But it also contains extraordinary acts of kindness and courage, medical breakthroughs, new technologies, and hopes for a better future. This book tries to explain and interpret the changing fortunes of different regions, countries, communities, and people around the world. Although we discuss theories, present data, and tell lively stories, we constantly focus attention back on people. The world is full of people who work, struggle, and attempt to enjoy their communities and families. They—and we—are all part of the global village.

A Few of the Players

The most striking feature of the global village might be summed up in one word: disparity. Disparities, large and small, run through and across every human community on this planet, often producing tension and polarity. Inequality has a human face. The following four lives embody some of these extremes: in family structure, personal and international economics, cultural expectations, violence, hope, and despair. The stories come from Africa, Asia, the Americas, and Europe, the regions we emphasize in this book.

Paul Habyarimana

Paul Habyarimana is only five years old, but throughout the last several months he has experienced more hardship than most people see in a lifetime. It started in the spring of 1994, when the small African country of Rwanda erupted in warfare. One ethnic group went on a rampage against a rival group, the group to which Paul belongs. Paul has seen hundreds of people knifed, shot, and beaten to death; he has seen babies sliced in half; he has seen women raped; he has experienced the hunger, disease, and intense fear that stalk refugees of war; and he has viewed thousands of decaying bodies along the road.

After surviving several weeks of hell, Paul followed hundreds of thousands of other refugees across the Rwandan border into Goma, Zaire. Within a short time, fleeing refugees caused this small city to swell to nearly one million people. With little food, no running water, and no toilet facilities in the area, an epidemic of cholera quickly broke out. This deadly intestinal disease, which spreads rapidly when human waste is not disposed of in a sanitary manner, killed several thousand refugees.

Somewhere along the path to Zaire, Paul's parents were killed. He does not want to talk about it with the humanitarian relief workers or reporters who descended on Goma. Paul has joined the thousands of war orphans that are now present in this relief camp. The nations of Africa are totally unprepared for orphans. They do not have the resources to establish orphanages and, in fact, orphanages are incompatible with indigenous African culture. An African proverb says, "It takes a whole village to raise a single child." Traditionally, African children are raised and nurtured not just by loving parents but by a robust system of extended families (grandparents, aunts, uncles, cousins) and other village members. But this web of support breaks down in times of war, when families are separated and entire villages can be wiped out. Paul and his fellow orphans face a bleak future.

Paul has seen a growing number of white faces in the squalid refugee camp in recent days. French, American, and German relief workers give him food and medicine. The white soldiers in camp break up fights, dig water wells, and distribute food, blankets, and other necessities. And, perhaps most fascinating of all, he sees people carrying television cameras and microphones around the camp, recording sickness, disease, and death. One group of white men stop and point the camera at him and a group of about ten other children.

But Paul will not see the white faces for very long. Television cameras will leave when American viewers have numbed to the tragedy. French soldiers will leave when a political solution seems impossible. A few committed relief workers will stay behind until the ethnic fighting overtakes the makeshift city. In a short time, the fighting and killing will fade from the headlines. In fact, only two things are clear after eighteen months of fighting in Rwanda: (1) As many as one million Rwandans are already dead, and (2) most of the world has largely forgotten about this forsaken corner of the global village.

Paul Habyarimana is too young to know anything about history. If he knew history, he might be confused. Following Adolf Hitler's annihilation of 6 million Jews during World War II, the new Jewish state of Israel, the United States, and other countries (including Germany) proclaimed "never again": Never again would sadistic madmen like Hitler be allowed to commit genocide against innocent people. But what happened?: a million killed in Rwanda, a million slaughtered in the "killing fields" of Cambodia (1970s), hundreds of thousands killed in both Uganda (1970s) and the former Yugoslavia (1990s), and the list goes on. What is going on in the global village?

To increase educational awareness, the states of Illinois, Florida, and New Jersey have passed laws that require schools to teach students about "THE Holocaust," as if there were only one! Remember the adage: Those who don't learn history are bound to repeat it. Well, "never again" has turned into "again and again." You only need three things for a holocaust: a group that commits genocide, a group that is victimized by genocide, and a group that stands by and allows it to happen.

Sadisah

Sadisah (the only name on her pay stub) is a Nike employee in the developing country of Indonesia, located in the South Pacific. (Some of the basic facts for this story are based on Ballinger 1993.) Nike is a large corporation headquartered in Portland, Oregon, and ranks among the 200 largest U.S. firms in market value. In 1994, it grossed about $4.1 billion in sales and made a profit of about $323 million (Bongiorno 1995, 112). Philip Knight, Nike's colorful chief executive officer, averaged more than $1 million in compensation for each year during the period 1992 through 1994 (Byrne 1995, 116). Nike's huge profits are possible largely because foreign workers like Sadisah make shoes for a very cheap wage. During Nike's growth surge in the 1980s, the United States lost more than 65,000 jobs in shoe manufacturing industries to low-wage foreign workers. Nike now makes most of its shoes in Indonesia, China, Malaysia, Thailand, and Taiwan. The company used to make shoes in South Korea, but pressure to increase wages in that country prompted the shoemaker to move some of its facilities to other, poorer countries. In Indonesia, for instance, wages are about one-seventh the South Korean rate.

Sadisah grew up in a rural area with little money or opportunity. She is the oldest of seven children. Her parents make a meager living by farming and doing odd jobs, and all but Sadisah's youngest sister work to support the family. Sadisah attended school sporadically for a few years and, at the age of fifteen moved to Jakarta, Indonesia's capital city, in hopes of finding a better life. After three years as a Nike employee, Sadisah earns only enough money to eat and rent a small apartment in a shantytown. Her dwelling does not have running water or electricity. Still, it is a solid structure and represents a better quality of life than that lived by many of Jakarta's poor families.

Sadisah's working conditions at Nike are bleak by U.S. standards. She works 10½ hours a day, six days a week. She earns about fourteen cents an hour, with a slight bonus (two additional cents an hour) for overtime work. Using machinery, she makes nearly fourteen pairs of Nike shoes each day. The work is hard: physically demanding, monotonous, and hot. Most of Sadisah's coworkers are young women in their teens or early twenties, and most have no more than an elementary school education. She is frightened by the prospect that most of her coworkers are dismissed by the time they are in their late twenties.

Sadisah makes enough money to survive, but certainly not enough to buy a pair of Nike shoes. Many of the shoes that she manufactures cost about eighty dollars in the United States, while the labor costs in Indonesia to make each pair of shoes is about twelve cents! Even after figuring in additional costs for things like advertising and transportation, this is a very healthy profit margin. One of Nike's most famous advertisements features Michael Jordan, who makes several million dollars a year endorsing the company's shoes. Sadisah has never seen a picture of Michael Jordan and does not know anything about the Chicago Bulls. We might also safely assume that Michael Jordan knows little about the conditions under which Sadisah and her coworkers toil to produce the Nike shoes that he promotes. By the way, Sadisah would have to work for 44,492 *years* to equal Michael Jordan's multiyear, multimillion dollar endorsement contract with Nike. This is simply another reality of today's global village.

Russell Tanner

Russell Tanner is a 46-year-old former autoworker who used to be employed by General Motors (GM) in Norwood, Ohio, a working-class suburb of Cincinnati. For almost a decade GM had negotiated with the local unions of the Norwood plant and a sister plant in Van Nuys, California, both of which manufactured Camaros and Firebirds, to get greater concessions from its unionized workers. This management practice, known as whipsawing, allows employers to play one local union off against the other in order to lower the overall costs of labor in both plants. In 1987, GM finally determined that only one plant was needed to meet the demand for these two car lines; the Norwood plant became one of twelve GM plant shutdowns that idled 29,000 workers nationwide. Ironically, about the same time, GM opened several new plants in Mexico—where American unions could be avoided altogether.

Russell, the third generation in his family to work in the Norwood plant, grew up with the idea that the plant would be there to provide a stable and secure place of employment throughout his lifetime. Hired at the plant the day after he graduated from high school, Russell was very good at his job and had performed most of the jobs in the GM plant, but the skills he had learned at GM were not in great demand by employers in the changing economy. He had twenty-one years of seniority at the plant when it closed, not enough to retire with full retirement benefits but enough to qualify him for two years of supplemental unemployment benefits (what GM workers refer to as "SUBpay"). These benefits paid Russell about 90 percent of his weekly pay as an autoworker. He also participated in a joint company-union training program, learning how to repair air conditioners, a trade he hoped to fall back on if he could not find other work.

Unable to find permanent work, Russell worked at a few odd jobs "off the record" while he continued to draw his subpay. His wife, Loretta, took an evening job as a waitress in addition to her day job as a receptionist to supplement the family's income. The family began to cut back on expenses, foregoing such luxury items as movies, vacations, and eating out at restaurants. Because Russell lost his health insurance benefits through GM and because neither of Loretta's employers provided a family health plan, the family's health care situation became much more precarious.

Russell stayed at home more and tried to deal with the psychological trauma of not being the main provider for his family. The role reversals caused severe strain in his marriage and in his relationships with the children. The situation also worsened Russell's drinking problem, placing an even greater strain on the family. Despite this crisis, the family has remained together, at least so far. They contemplated moving to another city to find employment, but where would they go? Who would buy their house, relieving the Tanners of their thirty-year mortgage obligation? The closing of the GM plant had marked Norwood, once a bustling community with numerous factories, as a city in decline. Norwood had become what one city official referred to as an "industrial ghost town," a place into which few families wanted to move.

The experience of Russell Tanner and his family is similar to that of thousands of other blue-collar workers in the United States whose jobs and skills are being undermined by dramatic transformations in the global economy. The shift to a post-industrial, service-based economy, while creating new opportunities for many, has in its wake left thousands of workers whose skills no longer fit the jobs in the new economy. The typical middle-class dream of a secure job and stable income, a house of one's own, and a good education for one's children has, for many, become a dream deferred. Increasingly, more U.S. workers are understanding that their fates are interconnected with those of workers in distant countries who will work harder, for less pay, while making no demands for input into managerial decisions about production. Many U.S. working-class families like the Tanners seem the unlikely victims of a global competition that they do not fully comprehend and cannot control.

Regina Müller

When 24-year-old Regina Müller was asked recently to reflect on the last five years of her life she replied, "Up and down." From her apartment in Leipzig, Germany, Regina talked about the incredible events of 1989, the revolutionary year that all East Europeans will remember forever. East Europeans (like her) demonstrated for democracy, demanded an end to communism, and actually drove long-time tyrants out of office. "They even shot that butcher in Romania," she remembered, referring to the Romanian army's execution of Nicolae Ceausescu, the dictator who had established a secret police force to spy on, imprison, torture, and kill Romanians who opposed his regime. And, of course, Regina most fondly remembered how East Germans drove out Eric Honecker, their own tyrant. He fled to South America to avoid being imprisoned, or worse.

Shortly after Honecker fell from power, the Berlin Wall was torn down in a festive celebration. The wall had stood since 1961, separating the communist East from the free West. "Sure I was there," Regina recalled enthusiastically, "it was like a giant party." The crowd sang, drank, and chanted as the most visible sign of the Iron Curtain was demolished, enabling people from the East and West to visit each other freely. Families that had been separated for decades were reunited. East Germans were especially excited for another reason: They would become part of a united Germany, meaning that their standard of living should increase appreciably since West Germany was an economic powerhouse. Regina looked forward to a better job, better housing, and more opportunity.

"It hasn't happened yet, but we are still hoping," Regina shrugged. She and many others moved west to Frankfurt, Germany's largest city, but found it too expensive. The unified German economy was slowing down and unemployment was growing. Reunification was more expensive and draining than many had calculated because East German factories had to be modernized, East German housing had to be improved, and East German social services had to be brought up to West German standards. This upset some West Germans because they had to pay higher taxes to finance such improvements. ("They sometimes resent us because of those taxes," Regina related.) East Germans are also upset because, as soon as the wall fell, they had expected their quality of life to improve.

Although Regina's life has not improved as much as she had hoped, it is still better than five years ago. She no longer fears a secret police force and she is pleased with the large investment that the government is making in eastern Germany. Still, she has the same job she held five years ago (working as a seamstress) and her wages have not improved under the new capitalist system. The promise of capitalism remains in eastern Germany and other parts of Eastern Europe, but Regina wonders when this promise will become a reality.

Using Sociology to Study Global Inequalities

Sociology is the study of human societies, both large and small. Some sociologists study interaction between two or three people, others focus on institutions or neighborhoods, and still others examine communities or cities. The vast majority of American sociologists study these phenomena in the United States. A small—but growing—number of sociologists are also examining other countries and societies in an effort to explain similarities and differences around the world. Why can some countries provide advanced medical care while others cannot prevent even basic diseases like measles? Why do some societies suffer from high levels of obesity while others face chronic food shortages? Why do some countries suffer from civil wars that kill thousands of innocent people while others live in peace? Why do some countries destroy their forests and natural resources while others guard theirs? Why do some countries initiate constructive policies that help people while others seem to encourage suffering? These are but a few of the questions that interest internationally oriented sociologists.

Some of these questions also interest students and other citizens in economically developed countries. They will find this book interesting. By contrast, some students and citizens may have little interest in these issues, perhaps asking, "Why should I pay any attention to global issues?" Thank you for asking. We propose three basic reasons. First, as noted earlier, the world is becoming increasingly interconnected. For example, businesses are much more global in scope than ever before, with millions of Americans working for foreign companies in both the United States and abroad. In this new global environment, employers put a premium on people who speak at least two languages and are knowledgeable about other cultures. Books like *Riding the Waves of Culture* (Trompenaars 1994), *Managing Cultural Differences* (Harris and Moran 1991), *Voices of Diversity* (Blank and Slipp 1994), and many others are being snatched up by savvy businesspeople. Moreover, the American workforce is becoming increasingly diverse and multicultural. In fact, the U.S. workforce is undergoing incredible changes: More nationalities, races, ethnic groups, and women are joining the labor force. By the year 2000, more than 85 percent of labor force entrants will be female, African American, Asian American, Latino, or new immigrants (Blank and Slipp 1994, 3). Workers who do not understand the experiences and cultures of diverse groups of people will not function well. And, effective managers and executives will undoubtedly have the knowledge and skills to build bridges among different groups in a changing world.

Second, we need to learn about global problems if we are ever going to solve them. Violence, environmental destruction, inequality, unemployment, and disease are all global issues that affect nations, communities, and individuals. For instance, the best-selling book *The Hot Zone* (Preston 1994) presents an especially frightening scenario that *may* be occurring in different parts of the world: Unknown and terrifying "new" viruses may be emerging from deforested areas and infecting human populations. Many of these viruses remained dormant in tropical regions for centuries or, at worst, were active in very localized areas. No longer, argues the book. The Ebola virus, the Marburg virus, and even the human immuno-deficiency virus (HIV) have emerged from forests and made their way into increasingly broader segments of the animal and human populations. Most frightening of all, some scientists and doctors believe that a few of these viruses (though not HIV) can mutate and become *airborne*, meaning that large populations can die terrible deaths by just breathing the air. Not everyone agrees with the book (Gladwell 1995), but it raises a possibility that all citizens should at least consider.

Third, learning about global issues is interesting and fun, especially when done on a firsthand basis. Some people are fortunate to travel abroad on business; an even larger number of people elect to travel abroad to learn, vacation, and relax. In fact, the international travel and tourism industry is booming. More people than ever before are traveling, airplanes are becoming bigger and faster, and some airport hubs have all the at-tributes of minicities (Cole 1995). Incredibly, it is estimated that nearly 11 percent of the international labor force works in the travel or tourism in-dustry (Naisbitt 1994, 104). One of the most popular travel opportunities is in the area of "ecotourism." You can travel to the world's most beautiful regions—like the Galapagos Islands, Ecuadoran cloud forests, Mount Kenya, wild game preserves—and learn about their environmental and cultural significance. Some of the costs go to protect the region you visit.

In conclusion, learning about global issues is important for those who want to make a better living, create positive changes, learn about exciting new cultures, and have fun. Regardless of your college major, we hope this book broadens your academic and personal views of the world. College students in the United States and other countries will shape the world in significant ways. They have the chance to avoid past mistakes and chart new futures for us all. Dynamic changes can occur when people look at the world in bold new ways.

Questioning Assumptions

Many things shape our view of reality: family, life experiences, school, friends, church, media, travel, and the list goes on. Some of these phe-nomena have influenced us in positive ways. At the same time, they may have encouraged us to accept certain points of view without really think-ing about them. Many dynamic people in business, academics, law, medi-cine, and other fields have a common quality: They constantly *challenge current perspectives of reality*. They look for new (and better) ways to do things. They are not comfortable with easy assumptions that others take for granted.

Let's think about this issue by looking at two maps of the world. One of the most popular maps in the United States is based on the so-called Mercator Projection and is found in many schools and homes across the country (see Map 1.1). Because it is a popular and respected map, most people assume that it contains a reasonably accurate representation of the world. Does it?

Take a close look at the map. What qualities jump out at you? Of course, the map places the United States in the center of the world. It splits Asia (and the vilified former Soviet Union) in half to ensure that the United States fits in the middle of the map. (How would you feel if the United States were cut in half to highlight another country?) Even more important, we tend to define everything according to the placement of the United States: "North" is Canada and above; "South" is Mexico and below. The "Middle East," a widely accepted term, is hardly "east" to many countries in the world. In fact, we might argue that this area should simply be called the "Middle Center," because it is where Europe, Asia, and Africa come together. It is also a region that contains an incredible amount of human history. And the "Far East"? It is only "far" and "east" to the United States and selected other countries.

People have adopted these terms and perspectives without really questioning the assumptions upon which they are based. In fact, what happens when we define the world from another perspective, one that places, say, Africa in the center of the world? Let's look at the second map, based on the Peters Projection, which does just this. In Map 1.2, "North" is now Europe, "South" is Antarctica, the "Middle East" is around China, and the "Far East" is the Pacific Ocean and the United States. As you read this book, we challenge you to look at the world (and global situations) from several perspectives; avoid the temptation to automatically place your view in the center of the universe.

We can learn more from these maps. Map 1.1 badly distorts the size of different regions of the world. Let's compare this map to Map 1.2, which is one of the most accurate in the world. In the first map the equator, which is supposed to divide the world in half, is nearly two-thirds of the way down the map, thereby greatly exaggerating the northern half of the world. Look at it. Europe is portrayed as larger than South America (Map 1.1), when, in fact, South America is almost twice the size of Europe (Map 1.2). North America is portrayed as larger than Africa (Map 1.1), when, in fact, Africa is much larger than North America (Map 1.2). And Greenland is portrayed

MAP 1.1 Mercator Projection of the World

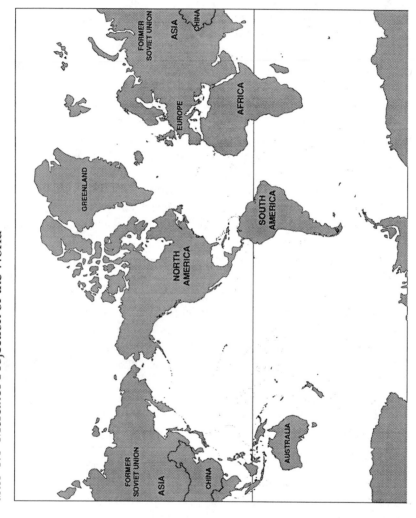

MAP 1.2 Peters Projection of the World

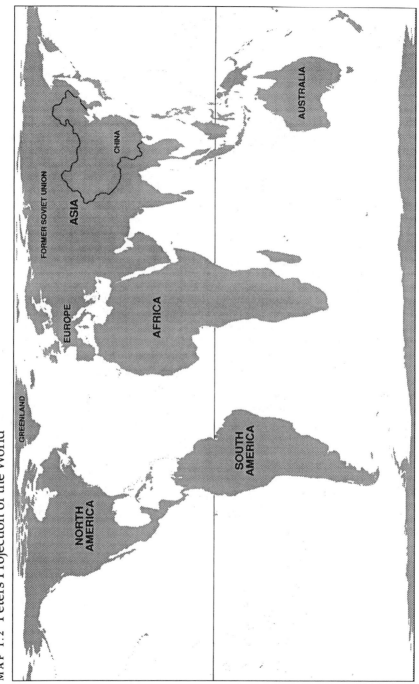

as a geographic behemoth, larger than China (Map 1.1), when, in fact, China is much bigger than Greenland (Map 1.2). The world's mapmakers have always been from Europe and North America, leading them to accentuate the size and importance of their own regions over the poorer regions of Africa and Asia.

Finally, we might ask why these two maps are so different. It is because the first map is based on projections made in 1569—more than 425 years ago! Yet, this old map has shaped the views of millions of people about the size, shape, and location of different areas of the world. Imagine basing other facets of our life on 400-year-old technology and views! We hope this book informs you about important issues around the world and in your own country. No one can afford to be out of date in today's changing world.

How This Book Is Organized

Chapter 2 examines different types of inequality throughout the world. It also discusses several trends that influence many of us in the global system. Chapter 3 discusses two popular (and competing) explanations of global inequality and then proposes a new way to look at international phenomena. We do not propose a new theory, but we do try to improve upon and integrate earlier views. Chapters 4, 5, 6, and 7 look at different regions of the world, including Africa, Asia, Europe, and the Americas, from a substantive and theoretical perspective. This survey does not exhaust every region of the world, but it does examine most major areas of the globe. Finally, Chapter 8 summarizes the book and discusses how to make positive changes in the world.

The Swahili word *safari* means journey; we envision this project as a safari to different areas and countries of the world. We hope you enjoy the trip.

2

An Unequal World

The Death of Children

Imagine that you turn on the news one evening and hear the following headline: "Thirty-five thousand people died today as a series of tornadoes swept across the United States." This calamitous news would dominate the attention of the country for weeks and months to come. Night after night the news media would revisit the devastated areas, showing funerals and interviewing relatives, friends, and neighbors of the victims. *Nightline* and other news programs would provide unceasing coverage of such an incredible natural disaster.

Although it does not receive much attention, each *day* around the world more than 35,000 children die, not from tornadoes or other natural disasters but from *preventable* or easily *treatable* diseases. In just two days, more children die around the world from these causes than the total number of Americans who died over a decade of combat in Vietnam (58,000). Figure 2.1 shows the six leading causes of child death around the world for 1983 and 1992. Although increases in medication and immunization decreased the number of deaths during this decade, the numbers are still extremely high.

The biggest killer is now pneumonia, an acute respiratory disease that can be treated easily with medication and proper shelter. Second is diarrhea, caused by bacteria contained in water, food, and the general environment. Most life-threatening diarrhea in the developing world could be eliminated if people had access to clean water and proper sanitation. Measles, the third biggest killer, can be prevented with immunization. The next, malaria, is transmitted by the female anopheles mosquito. After engorging itself with the blood of an infected person, the mosquito spreads the disease by biting another person. Malaria can be prevented through the use of medication, mosquito nets, and clothing that covers all skin. Tetanus, fifth on the list, is a viral disease that can be prevented through immunization or treated with medication. Whooping cough is an acute respiratory disease that can be prevented and treated.

FIGURE 2.1

The Six Leading Diseases That Kill Children, 1983, 1992

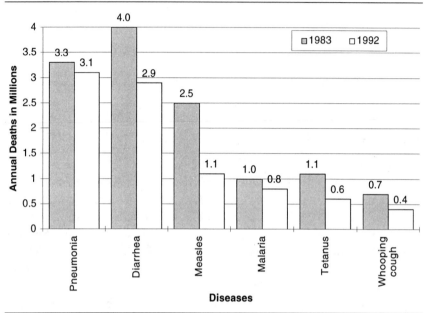

Source: UNICEF 1994a.

The most dramatic improvements in Figure 2.1 have been for diseases that can be prevented through a series of vaccinations. Measles deaths, for instance, have been substantially reduced because of the high percentage of young children now vaccinated around the world. Figure 2.2 shows the incredible increase in the percentage of children vaccinated since 1984, a figure that is almost 80 percent today. By contrast, although there is an oral prophylaxis (tablet) to prevent malaria, it is effective for only two weeks at a time and is also much too expensive for the vast majority of poor people in developing countries. Until there is a real vaccine for malaria, it will remain one of the most intractable killers across underdeveloped regions. For Africans, in fact, the most dangerous "animal" on the continent is not the buffalo, rhinoceros, or lion, but the mighty mosquito.

History was made on Sunday, September 30, 1990, when the desperate plight of children finally attracted the attention of world leaders. Seventy-one presidents and prime ministers met in New York at the first United Nations World Summit for Children. This meeting, at that time the largest single gathering of international leaders in history, produced a document that promised the world's children a better and brighter future. The promise included a "10-point program to protect the rights of children and to improve their lives" (UNICEF 1991, 55–56), including better health care, availability of clean water, more educational opportunities, increased status for women, stronger families, freedom from war, and other laudable objectives. The conference stressed that children represent the most vulnerable and innocent segment of society, requiring special attention by governments, international organizations, and other institutions. Although some of the conference's objectives are currently unrealistic, this gathering of global leaders helped to raise the consciousness of the world about its children.

Perhaps there is no better indicator of global inequality than the different levels of child survival in poor and rich countries. Because of the diseases and conditions previously discussed, children in developing countries have poor "life chances." Look at the rather startling statistics displayed in Figure 2.3, which show the number of children who die before age five for every 1,000 children born. In the 42 poorest countries of the world, an average of 166 children die before age five for every 1,000 children born; in 67 middle-income countries, the figure is 47 children; and in the 23 richest countries, the number declines to 9 children. Among rich countries, the United States is slightly worse than average at 10 deaths; the lowest death rate in the world is Finland's 5 deaths per 1,000 births. Map 2.1 shows the distribution of child mortality around the world. In general,

FIGURE 2.2

Percent Immunized Against Measles, Worldwide, 1984–1993

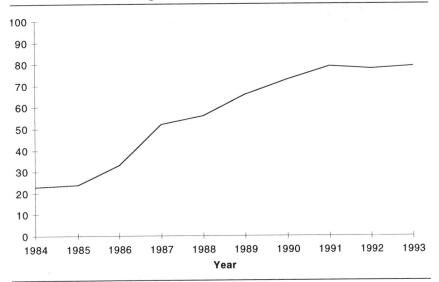

Source: UNICEF 1995.

FIGURE 2.3

Number of Children Dying Before Age Five per 1,000 Births, 1992

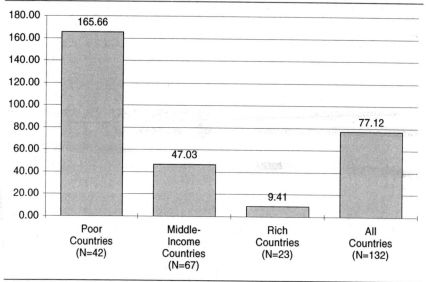

Source: World Bank 1994, 1995a.

the richer countries of the world have low mortality rates and the poorer countries have very high rates.

The incredible gap in life chances between rich and poor countries could be narrowed with a relatively small expenditure of resources. In fact, it would cost very little to prevent the killers of Third World children. The United Nations International Children's Emergency Fund (UNICEF) estimates that a child can be fully immunized for about $1.50; a child dying from acute diarrhea can be treated with packets of oral rehydration salts that cost $.10 each (the salts are mixed with water and then given to the child); and a child suffering from pneumonia can be treated successfully with antibiotics that cost about $1.00 (Adamson 1990; UNICEF 1991). A coordinated program to control the major childhood diseases, reduce child malnutrition by half, bring safe water and sanitation to every community, provide basic education for all children, and make family planning universally available would cost only about $25 billion a year. Is this a lot of money? Consider these facts: U.S. citizens spend $31 billion on beer each year and Europeans spend $50 billion on cigarettes each year (UNICEF 1993, 7).

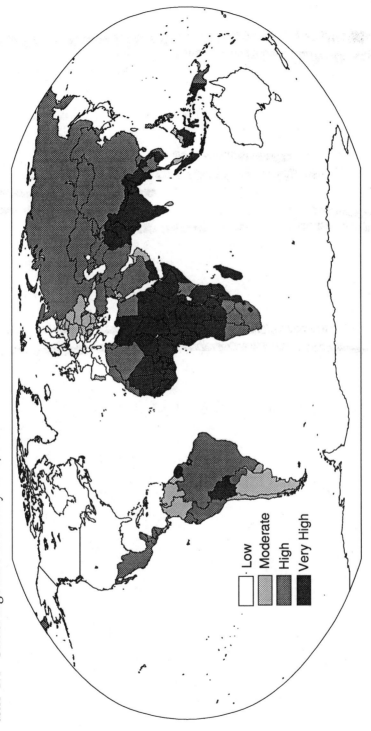

MAP 2.1 Under Age Five Mortality Rate, 1993

Child mortality is only one of several key indicators of global inequality that we will explore in this chapter. After looking at other types of inequality, we focus attention on six broad trends that are shaping the world.

Other Forms of Inequality

One of the most basic forms of inequality in the world today is clearly evident in the gross national product (GNP) per capita from country to country. This measure simply refers to the *average annual income* among a country's citizens. The richest countries include the United States, Japan, Australia, Canada, and several countries in Europe and Asia. With the exception of Australia, note that all of the wealthiest countries are in the Northern Hemisphere. Although it is a fairly crude classification, scholars often refer to rich countries as "the North" and poor countries as "the South." Figure 2.4 shows the average income in three different groups of countries in the world. The disparity between rich and poor nations is remarkable. Poor countries have an average annual income of only $308, whereas rich countries have an average annual income of almost $22,000.

FIGURE 2.4

GNP per Capita (Average Income) in U.S. Dollars, 1992

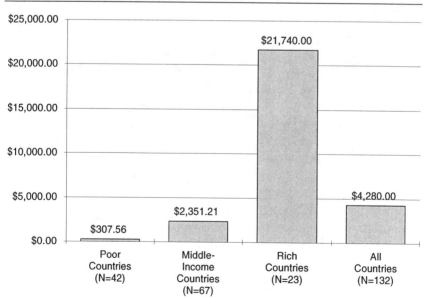

Source: World Bank 1994, 1995a, 1995b.

population expansion

A second form of inequality is found in *population expansion*. One graphic illustration of this point is to consider the fertility rates of different countries, the average number of children born to women of childbearing age. Not surprisingly, the poor countries of Africa, Asia, and Latin America tend to exhibit much higher fertility rates than rich countries do (see Figure 2.5). In many African countries, for instance, the total fertility rate exceeds six and even seven, whereas in developed countries the number averages less than two. It is also important to underscore that high fertility—and therefore rapid population growth—is occurring in those countries that already have substantial poverty, abundant disease, and few overall resources.

life expectancy

A third form of inequality is *life expectancy*, that is, how long people can expect to live on average. Life expectancy is a good measure of the overall quality of life in a country since it reflects a combination of good health care, good nutrition, good sanitation, and the absence of catastrophic, life-threatening events like wars and civil strife. Current life expectancies range from only thirty-nine in Guinea-Bissau (in West Africa) to seventy-nine in Japan. Again, the lowest life expectancies are in poor countries that are least able to promote a good quality of life for their citizens, whereas

FIGURE 2.5

Fertility Rate, 1992

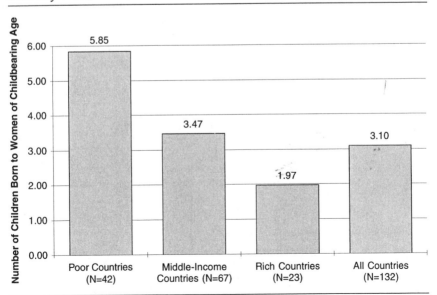

Source: World Bank 1994, 1995a.

the highest are in rich nations. Figure 2.6 shows average life expectancies for different types of countries.

A fourth form of inequality relates to *educational achievement*. Although many children throughout the world have the opportunity to attend primary school, few have a chance to attend secondary school (high school) or college in poor countries. As shown in Figure 2.7, for instance, relatively few secondary-age children (only about 21 percent) attend secondary school in poor countries, whereas nearly 90 percent do so in rich countries. Moreover, except for rich countries, fewer girls than boys attend secondary school throughout the world.

College enrollment rates are especially low in poor countries, where only about 3 percent of college-age youth have an opportunity to enroll in college or some type of vocational program (Figure 2.8; separate statistics are not available for women). By contrast, nearly 40 percent of college-age people in wealthy countries enroll in college or vocational school programs. Of course, not everyone obtains a degree. European countries have lower college enrollment rates than the United States and Canada, where more than 60 percent of college-age people enroll in college or other post–high school education programs. European countries begin selecting the very brightest students for college at a young age, meaning that only a select few have the opportunity to attend excellent universities and colleges.

FIGURE 2.6

Life Expectancy, 1992

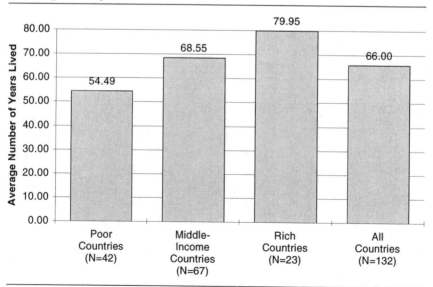

Source: World Bank 1994, 1995a.

FIGURE 2.7

Percent of Secondary-Age Youth Enrolled in Secondary School, 1992

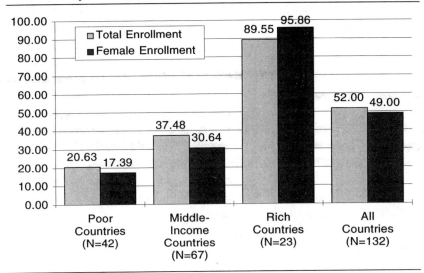

Source: World Bank 1994, 1995a.

FIGURE 2.8

Percent of College-Age Persons Enrolled in College, 1992

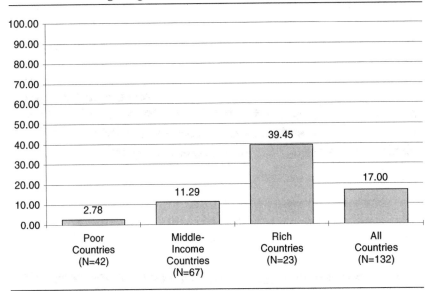

Source: World Bank 1994, 1995a.

The United States and Canada enable a larger percentage of students to attend higher education. The trade-off is that while many more students may attain a college degree, the value of that degree is diminished. Attaining a college degree is a bit like attaining a fishing license: It entitles you to look for many of the better jobs that require a college degree, but it does not ensure that you will land one of these jobs.

Beyond indicators related to education, health, and economics, it is also interesting to examine inequality of political opportunity and freedom around the world. Map 2.2 provides a "map of freedom" based on information published by the well-known Freedom House. "Free" countries, although not perfect, are democracies that have fair and competitive elections, freedom of the press, and individual and group freedoms such as being allowed to demonstrate against the government. "Partly free" countries are partial democracies that exhibit some of these freedoms, but not others. For instance, they might have competitive elections but not freedom to publish antigovernment newspapers. "Not free" countries lack democracy and most basic freedoms.

On balance, the most developed regions of the world are also free countries. Many developing countries in Latin America also fit into this category, as do several in Asia and Africa. There are far more free and partly free countries today than only twenty years ago (discussed later in the book). Consider two illustrative facts: Only ten years ago (1) Eastern Europe and the former Soviet Union were not free and (2) almost all of Africa was either not free or partly free. Democracy certainly does not exist everywhere in the world, but the overall global trend is toward greater democratization. However, we should also be cautious about idealizing the notions of "democracy" and "freedom," as many countries that fit into these categories also have significant problems.

Finally, it is difficult to quantify some types of inequality or present them concisely in a figure or map. For instance, let's consider international inequalities in the ability to cope with emergencies and "new" diseases. Some countries have more resources and technology to deal with disasters than other countries. Consider the fight against the disease AIDS. The World Bank (1993, 99) notes:

> Historians will look back on the latter half of this century as having one great medical triumph, the eradication of smallpox, and one great medical tragedy, AIDS. Unknown prior to 1981, AIDS now dominates public health programs and health services in several countries and may come to dominate many others.

More than 85 percent of current AIDS cases are in the poor countries of the world, a number that will increase to about 95 percent by the year 2000! But

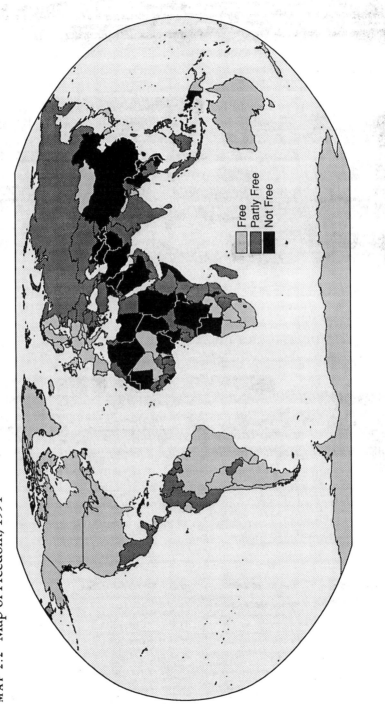

MAP 2.2 Map of Freedom, 1994

Free

Partly Free

Not Free

of the $2 billion a year that is spent on AIDS prevention and education around the world, only about 10 percent of that is spent in the poor countries where the problem is most severe (UNICEF 1995, 22).

Let's conclude this section by playing a game of prediction. What will the United States and world look like in the year 2040, about the time that today's typical 20-year-old college student nears retirement? Take a few minutes to ponder your future. What is the world going to look like economically, politically, and socially in the year 2040? Is social security going to support you (most experts say it will not)? How many wars will be fought before that time (could a nuclear war end it all)? What type of jobs will be available? How will different races, ethnic groups, and nationalities get along? Will there be a cure for AIDS? What type of health care system will be popular? Will women lead more countries, corporations, and organizations? How many children will starve? What new inventions will we see? Will crime continue to be a problem? What type of future do you see? Are you optimistic, pessimistic, confused?

Contemporary Global Trends: A World of Changes and Contradictions

To answer the questions posed at the end of the previous section with any degree of accuracy, consider these two things: First, we need to learn about *substantive changes* that are occurring (and have occurred) in the world. Stated another way, it is important that we really know what is going on in our country and the world. Second, we need a contemporary theoretical model to help explain these changes and to make sense of them. Chapter 3 will examine such a model. However, first, we should understand that, perhaps more than at any other time in history, the world is experiencing a number of fascinating trends that underscore its dynamic character. The following six are representative of major changes now occurring in the global village.

Trend 1: The global economy is becoming increasingly interconnected and consolidated.

This trend is discussed extensively by John Naisbitt in his book *Global Paradox* (1994). Despite numerous cultural differences throughout the world, many countries share a similar language, the language of money. Multinational corporations invest in and trade with countries around the world. National governments and international banks such as Citicorp, American

Express, and others loan money to countries and institutions abroad. Computers, fax machines, and electronic mail make it easy to communicate and transact business throughout the world in a matter of seconds. We do not mean to imply that Third World countries have economies that approximate the economically developed world; they do not. But even many poor countries do have a (small) modern economic sector that participates in the global economy. For example, if you travel in the Third World and need cash, you can almost always find a local bank that will give you a cash advance on your American- or European-issued credit card. If you are lucky, you will even discover an ATM machine ready to do business. (Beware of exorbitant service charges!)

One consequence of economic consolidation is that the world is developing several significant trading blocs (Naisbitt 1994). Consider three major ones: (1) *Asia* is without a doubt the strongest emerging bloc of countries, led by Japan, Taiwan, South Korea, Singapore, Hong Kong, Thailand, China, Malaysia, and Vietnam. These countries trade with each other, invest in each other, *and* maintain economic linkages outside of Asia. (2) *In Western Europe* a relatively new agreement calls for a unified European community, including a common currency and close political alliances. Some people doubt that such unity will ever occur, but others predict nothing short of a "single Europe" ready to compete against the rest of the world. Optimists also suggest that, following the path of German reunification, Eastern Europe will merge closer to a unified Western Europe. (3) *North and South America* include the United States, Canada, Mexico, and many other Latin American countries. In 1993, after a bitter debate, the U.S. Congress passed the North American Free Trade Agreement (NAFTA). The agreement eases trade barriers and other restrictions between the United States, Mexico, and Canada. Make no mistake about it—NAFTA is the wave of the future. In fact, many Latin American countries have their own versions of NAFTA that make regional trade attractive.

One of the most effective regional alliances in history occurred in the 1970s, when the Organization of Petroleum Exporting Countries (OPEC) literally dominated the world economy for six or seven years. In the early 1970s, this alliance of mainly Middle Eastern countries set limits on the amount of oil that each member could produce and set the price that each could charge. The alliance worked incredibly well and world oil prices went from $3 for a forty-two-gallon barrel of oil in 1973 to $39 per barrel in 1979. OPEC countries were rich, making a collective $8.7 billion a day at the peak of profits (Lamb 1988, 230)! Of course, oil and gas prices skyrocketed in many countries around the world, including the United States, which had to ration gasoline in some areas. The OPEC alliance broke up in the early 1980s, however, as some OPEC members became embroiled in pricing disagreements and even war (Iran versus Iraq). The developed countries of the world had also begun to produce more efficient automobiles and had implemented other energy-saving measures to lessen their dependence on foreign oil and gas. Although OPEC is little threat to the world today, it did teach the world something about the incredible power of economic alliances.

Trend 2: Formal political structures are becoming increasingly fragmented, despite the consolidation of the world economy.

Three main points help underscore this trend. First, there are more and more political structures (countries) in the world today, although many of them are very fragile. Countries are dividing up along ethnic, cultural, or religious lines, with different groups calling for "self-rule" based on one (or more) characteristics (Naisbitt 1994). Consider the following facts. There were 51 countries in the world when the United Nations was founded in 1945. This number increased to 100 in 1960, 159 in 1984, 172 in 1992, 192 in 1994, and, according to Naisbitt's projections, could grow to at least 300 by the turn of the century. Twenty-five countries were added to the globe between 1991 and 1993 alone, as the former Soviet Union and other parts of Eastern Europe disintegrated. Naisbitt foresees a world of perhaps 1,000 countries in the future as countries continue to divide up (Naisbitt 1994, 33–37). Is this realistic? Maybe. There are literally thousands of ethnic groups, cultures, and languages in the world. Moreover, with only a few exceptions, most countries have at least two ethnic, cultural, or religious groups within their borders. Many groups want independence.

This situation is just as true in North America as it is in other regions. In October 1995, Canadian voters in Quebec province very narrowly defeated a referendum to separate from Canada and establish their own country. (The "separatist" side received just under 50 percent of the vote.) French-speaking Quebec has a much different culture than English-speaking Canada. Quebec is also an economically vibrant province that contains a substantial portion of Canada's industrial and financial base. Thus, if Quebec had separated from the larger country, Canada would have faced very serious economic consequences. In fact, many Canadian companies (and citizens) transferred large sums of money out of Quebec in the final days leading up to the election. Moreover, other countries (especially the United States) were "campaigning against Quebec's separation because it would require the renegotiation of various trade and political agreements with the new country. The U.S. government breathed a giant sigh of relief after Quebec voted to stay in the union. But, and this is a safe bet, Quebec will vote again on its independence in the future and eventually will leave larger Canada. Quebec has voted before to remain part of Canada, but with each election, the margin becomes narrower (Farnsworth 1995).

Other independence movements in North America are also important to mention. In Mexico, the Zapatista National Liberation Army has engaged in an armed struggle with the Mexican government to separate the state of Chiapas from the country (Golden 1995). And, in the United States, there is a growing movement among the 140,000 native Hawaiians (13 percent of Hawaii) to separate from the U.S. mainland in order to create their own nation (*New York Times* 1994). Although neither of these movements will likely prevail in the near future, they could ultimately succeed and thereby increase the number of countries in North America.

A second piece of evidence regarding fragmentation of formal political structures is that most wars currently being fought around the world are over ethnic issues. The newspaper headlines only begin to tell the story: more than 200,000 killed in the former Yugoslavia as Serbs, Croats, and Muslims fight; up to 1,000,000 slaughtered in Rwanda during 1994 and 1995 as two ethnic groups (Hutus and Tutsis) fight each other; about 300,000 killed (or starved) in Somalia in 1991 and 1992 as rival clans fight each other for control of the country. But these three headlines, though serious, hardly tell the whole story of global ethnic conflict. More wars are now being fought around the world than ever before (nearly thirty-five), and the majority are over ethnic issues. Most of these conflicts are civil wars between ethnic minorities or between ethnic groups and a national government (Carter 1993). In addition, there are many other violent ethnic conflicts that have not yet devolved into full-scale wars in Europe, Asia, Africa, Latin America, and North America (remember the Los Angeles riots in 1992). Violent ethnic conflict will contribute to the increasing fragmentation of political structures around the world.

Another type of global warfare is terrorism, which normally refers to clandestine warfare waged by political "extremists" that often is directed at civilians. Terrorism normally is used by groups that feel aggrieved over some issue but lack the conventional military might to force a change. Thus, these groups "fight back" by taking hostages, bombing, killing, or otherwise harming people or property. Their justification is that they are merely fighting for independence from global domination. It has been said, "One person's terrorist is another person's freedom fighter." Interestingly, the number of terrorist incidents around the world have decreased over the last few years, from a peak of 666 in 1987 to 321 in 1994. The decline may be due to peace initiatives in the Middle East and elsewhere, along with strong antiterrorist policies put in place by many countries. However, despite the decline in attacks, the number of casualties has not declined. The highest casualty total occurred in 1993, when 109 people were killed and another 1,393 were injured in terrorist attacks (Center for National Security Studies 1995).

An *international terrorist incident* is defined by the FBI as "one committed by a group or individual that is foreign-based and/or directed by countries or groups outside the United States or whose activities transcend national boundaries" (Center for National Security Studies 1995, 1). Only two international terrorist incidents have taken place in the United States during the last eleven years. The worst occurred in 1993, when a fringe political group allegedly from the Middle East bombed the World Trade Center in the heart of the New York City financial district. The attack killed five people, injured nearly 1,000, and was effective in disrupting financial markets and attracting worldwide publicity (McFadden 1993).

Terrorist activities can also be directed at fellow citizens in the same country. This is termed *domestic terrorism*. For instance, a federal government office building in Oklahoma City was bombed in 1995, killing 169 people and injuring hundreds. Two Americans (perhaps with help from other Americans), who were upset with the U.S. government for supposedly trampling individual rights and freedoms, have been charged. And, in Japan, a Japanese cult known as the Supreme Truth is strongly suspected of a deadly nerve gas attack against civilians in a crowded Tokyo subway in 1995. Nerve gas was released during rush hour, killing eleven people and sickening thousands of others. The incident shocked Japan—a very safe country—and also frightened other nations. Imagine nerve gas being released into the subways of New York during rush hour! The Supreme Truth denies involvement in the Tokyo attack, but at the cult compound police have found tons of chemicals and equipment that could be used to make nerve gas.

The third indicator of formal political fragmentation is that *nongovernment organizations* (NGOs), such as relief agencies and development groups, are becoming increasingly influential because of government weakness in the developing world. Third World governments have little money, little capacity to borrow capital from abroad, and almost no legitimacy among their increasingly impoverished citizens (Bradshaw and Fuller 1996). Thus, NGOs are called upon to shoulder a greater burden in development and humanitarian efforts. Some NGOs are based entirely in developing countries and work to mobilize modest resources at the local level (for example, teaching farmers how to produce more food). Many other NGOs have local offices but are headquartered in developed countries. It is estimated that NGOs headquartered in wealthy countries distribute about $6.4 billion to developing countries (Livernash 1992). Although NGOs clearly have a beneficial effect on development, they cannot do it alone (Ndegwa 1996; Kaiser 1996).

The United States and other developed countries are also calling on more churches, private voluntary organizations, and other NGOs to assume a greater burden in providing services to people. One of George Bush's themes in his 1988 presidential campaign was to create "a thousand points of light," his metaphor for a world of more volunteers and philanthropists. There is now a major debate in the United States over the proper role of government in providing social services. Some Americans claim that the government should play a significant role in funding and coordinating social services, whereas others feel that private efforts should assume most of the burden.

One of President Clinton's proposals takes a middle ground, providing some federal money for a program that would combine government development efforts with community-based programs. His national service program, AmeriCorps, would function as a domestic Peace Corps. In exchange for a year of volunteer service on community projects, about 20,000 young people would receive higher education grants and a small stipend from the government. Clinton calls AmeriCorps "the program that I'm most proud of," but it faces opposition from conservative budget cutters in Washington, D.C.

Trend 3: Global population expansion is threatening the quality of life in many regions.

Consider the following facts: 275 humans are born around the world every minute, 16,482 each hour, 395,579 a day, and 144 million per year (Calhoun, Light, and Keller 1994, 498). Importantly, the vast majority of new people will be born in areas that are already overcrowded:

> Of the 3.2 billion people projected to join the human race over the next thirty-five years, 3 billion—95 percent—will be born in the less developed countries of the Southern Hemisphere, compared to fewer than 200 million in the developed countries of the Northern Hemisphere. . . . The population of Sweden will take about 350 years to double if current growth rates are maintained. At the other extreme, India's population is expected to double within twenty years, at which point India will be even more populous than China. (Calhoun, Light, and Keller 1994, 498)

Developing regions have high fertility rates that show little sign of slowing appreciably in the near future.

Most Westerners blame overpopulation on lack of education, absence of birth control, and lack of self-discipline. Although there is some truth to the first two factors, there are other reasons for population growth in poor countries. Consider several issues: (1) Many economically underdeveloped countries are based on agriculture. Thus, because families cannot afford to hire workers, they need numerous children to work the land. (2) Poor countries lack viable social security systems, which means that parents must rely on several children to care for them in their old age. (3) Third World countries still have high infant and child mortality rates, meaning that parents often produce "extra" children in order to ensure the survival of several children in the future. (4) Some countries clearly have cultural factors that stress the value of children, especially male children. Many men want to continue to have children, particularly if they do not have a boy. It is important to note that this trend is declining in some urban areas of the developing world, where parents realize the disincentives of large families such as the high cost of housing, education, and food.

Regardless of the causes of overpopulation, it is clear that it has several negative consequences in many regions of the world. First, the world will have difficulty feeding its growing population. In fact, we do not have to look far to see the ravages of famine and malnutrition across many areas of the world. At the present time, it is estimated that about one billion out of the world's five billion people are chronically hungry, with many dying from lack of food or suffering from diseases born of malnutrition. A famous agricultural economist, Lester Brown, estimates that the growing world population will require 28 million more tons of grain each year during the 1990s (Brown et al. 1990; Calhoun, Light, and Keller 1994, 504–505). This added output will not happen. It is very clear that the world's supply of food is shrinking relative to the rate of population expansion. Malnutrition, hunger, and starvation are bad now—and they will probably grow worse in the future.

Second, overpopulation leads to declining levels of health in many areas of the world. The presence of more people puts stress on finite natural resources, resulting in inadequate levels of food, sanitation, medication, and health facilities. The vast majority of Third World citizens do not enjoy good health, and overpopulation will make the situation worse.

Third, a growing population is also contributing to an urban population explosion around the world. "Overurbanization" occurs when cities have too many people relative to their capacity to provide food, housing, and services for their citizens (Timberlake and Kentor 1983; London 1987; Gugler 1988; Smith 1991). Overcrowded cities have more disease, pollution, squalid slums, violent crime, and drugs compared to rural areas. By the year 2000, it is estimated that twenty-one cities will have more than 10 million citizens, and seventeen will be in developing countries. São Paulo, Brazil, and Mexico City already have close to 20 million inhabitants (U.S. Bureau of the Census 1993). Growing urbanization is both a symptom of overpopulation and a cause of declining quality of life.

Trend 4: There is growing environmental awareness throughout the United States and the world.

When the first Earth Day was held in April 1970, the groups who organized the event were considered "radicals," "alarmists," and "freaks." What a difference twenty-five years makes! Today, three out of four Americans call themselves "environmentalists," and even conservative corporations expound upon the benefits of recycling, reforestation, and overall "environmental friendliness." Certainly environmental awareness has translated into some very positive developments: Recycling is the law in many communities; cars emit far less toxic gas than even ten years ago; almost all states have cleaner air compared to the late 1980s; some endangered species (like the bald eagle) are no longer considered in immediate danger of extinction; and, in just seven years, American manufacturers reduced their emission of toxic chemicals by 43 percent (Calhoun, Light, and Keller 1994, 506; Stevens 1995a). However, beneath the surface of these success stories lie a number of severe problems that should concern all citizens.

Let's consider one environmental problem that has economic, social, and political implications throughout the world. As we discuss in Chapter 7, large chunks of the world are being deforested every day, a process that will seriously disturb *every* major rain forest in the world by the turn of the century. The effects are devastating: Many medications come from plants in the rain forest (recall our earlier story about a possible cure for HIV); many animal species are destroyed; and droughts are intensified because rain forests "recharge" clouds through evaporation.

Although these are severe problems, there are a number of "logical" reasons for deforestation: (1) Because many people do not have electricity or natural gas in the Third World, they rely on firewood for cooking, warm bathing, and general warmth. Population growth increases demand for additional firewood, thereby threatening more and more forests. Population expansion also requires more land for agricultural production, encouraging farmers to clear-cut forests to produce additional crops. (2) Deforestation is profitable for some people. Ranchers cut forests to raise cattle for consumption in rich nations, and multinational corporations and local businesspeople cut forests for the export of wood and construction of wood products. This occurs in the United States too, where vast tracts of western forests are cut to provide wood for exports (especially to Japan), for homes, and for furniture. In fact, the United States is one of the most deforested countries in the world, a process that has occurred over many generations.

Some people are beginning to argue that forests have the capacity to fight back against human intrusion. The best-selling book *The Hot Zone* (Preston 1994) is so popular because, in part, it is an environmental parable. Preston describes a world where human greed for more timber, more highways, and more animals for medical research and zoos cannot go on without consequence. The rain forest is answering these attacks by infecting human intruders with its worst viruses, including HIV, which are carried out of the forest and spread deeper and deeper into the human population. Preston (1994, 290) makes the strong statement that "AIDS is the revenge of the rain forest. It is only the first act of the revenge." Some people disagree with Preston (Gladwell 1995). But whether he is correct or not, his ideas underscore the possibility that people can no longer harm the world's natural resources with impunity.

Trend 5: Life chances are becoming increasingly polarized.

Stated simply, the world is being divided increasingly into "haves" and "have-nots." Let's look at several factors. First, children are becoming an increasingly disadvantaged group in many societies. Although the United Nations, national governments, and other groups pass initiatives to help children, the rhetoric exceeds the reality. Around the world and in the United States, the number of children falling into poverty is growing, as are cases of child malnutrition, disease, and abuse. The most exploited group in Third World cities clearly is children, who work for little or no money and often turn to drug running or prostitution to survive (UNICEF 1995).

Children in the United States are also in trouble. Almost a quarter of all U.S. children under the age of six live below the poverty line! The numbers for African American children and Latino (Hispanic) children are astounding: 50 percent of all African American children and 40 percent of all Latino children under the age of six live below the poverty line. (About 14 percent of young white children live in poverty.) Part of the reason for high poverty rates is the growing number of single-parent households in America. In 1970, 12 percent of all households were headed by one parent (36 percent in African American households); in 1993, 30 percent of all households were headed by one parent (63 percent in African American households) (U.S. Bureau of the Census 1993).

Women also constitute a disadvantaged group in many societies across the world and their situation is improving only slowly, if at all. Women earn substantially less money than men, and they make up only 10 percent of all national-level legislators and 6 percent of cabinet-level positions worldwide (Reskin and Padavic 1994; UNICEF 1994b). Moreover, cultural traditions in some countries prevent them from taking high-wage jobs, voting, refusing sexual relations with husbands, and even driving a car. We have a long way to go in the United States as well. Although a growing number of young professional women are making more money than ever before, the vast majority of U.S. women make substantially less than men. And, despite discussions of political equality, women make up only 11 percent of Senate and House members in Washington, D.C. (UNICEF 1994b).

Women, children, and other disadvantaged groups have limited access to health care. An intense health care debate is taking place in America today, largely because about 37 million people have no health insurance at all and more than 50 million people are without health insurance for at least part of each year (usually because of temporary layoffs from work). This means that many people lack even basic health care such as regular checkups, prenatal care, and childhood immunizations. The United States has the most advanced medical technology in the world, but many citizens do not have access to very basic health procedures that require relatively little technology.

The health situation in the developing world is much bleaker. Basic diseases continue to kill and maim millions of people. Most of these diseases could be reduced greatly or even eliminated with a modest global effort. Consider an almost unbelievable statistic that few people know: The disease hepatitis B kills more people every *day* than AIDS kills in a year. This liver disease affects one out of every six people in the world. It is responsible for about 80 percent of all liver cancers and more cases of cirrhosis of the liver than alcohol. This killer could be eradicated from the face of the earth for about $100 million per year, about the amount spent by the world on military arms—every hour (UNICEF 1992, 54)! Hepatitis B is also a growing health concern in developed countries.

Trend 6: Ethnicity and multiculturalism are becoming even larger issues throughout the world today.

In fact, we cannot really think of a more dynamic, volatile, and potentially divisive issue than ethnicity and the multicultural dimensions that it fosters. Consider a few statistics from the United States. In 1990 (the year of the last census), 21.5 percent of the American workforce was composed of people of African, Hispanic, or Asian descent. Minority populations consitituted 24 percent of our society (U.S. Bureau of the Census 1993). By the year 2005, it is estimated that 27 percent of the American workforce will be composed of minority populations, and society as a whole will be close to 35 percent minority. This will lead to incredible changes in our workplaces and institutions. The United States truly stands at a crossroads: It can learn to live in an increasingly multicultural world or face the consequences of cultural clashes. Many Americans are not optimistic about this aspect of the future, even though many businesses, schools, and other organizations are beginning to educate their workers (and students) on the value of teamwork in situations of diversity. Forward-looking organizations are stressing the theme "excellence through diversity," reflecting their belief that diversity is a positive development.

The United States is doing better in ethnic and cultural assimilation than some areas of the world. As we have already noted, the global trend is clearly toward ethnic conflict and ethnic separation. Many of these conflicts have produced unprecedented waves of refugees, that is, people who flee their own region or country because of civil strife or other economic and political problems. The number of refugees worldwide is virtually impossible to measure but it clearly runs into the millions, with one estimate placing the total at more than 16 million (U.S. Committee for Refugees 1994).

History teaches us that ethnicity is an enduring issue, one that often is the source of conflict. Ethnic minorities historically have faced economic discrimination, political repression, and violence (Gurr 1993). Table 2.1 presents data on the number of minorities at risk around the world. To be included, a minority group must (1) be relatively large (usually exceeding

TABLE 2.1

Minority Populations at Risk, 1990

World Region	Total (millions)	Percent of Total Regional Population
Western Democracies and Japan	84.023	10.8%
Eastern Europe and former Soviet Union	153.658	35.0%
Asia	273.064	10.2%
North Africa and the Middle East	118.205	28.8%
Sub-Saharan Africa	237.023	42.3%
Latin America	49.371	11.0%
Total	915.344	17.3%

Source: Gurr 1993.

100,000) and (2) experience economic and/or political discrimination. Look carefully at the last column of the table. The percentage of the world population considered a minority at risk is about 17 percent, including 42 percent in sub-Saharan Africa, 35 percent in Eastern Europe and the former Soviet Union, and 29 percent in North Africa and the Middle East. It is not a coincidence that countries with a large population at risk also have substantial conflict, some violent and some not violent. Dominant ethnic groups often harm minority ethnic groups; sometimes the latter are in a position to fight back, and sometimes they are not.

Conclusions

This chapter has introduced you to some major forms of global inequality, from child mortality to rates of HIV infection. Many people in the developed world are unaware of the incredible differences between their quality of life and the life experienced by people in poorer countries. Moreover, it is important to remember that the vast majority of the world's population lives in such countries.

We have also reviewed six important trends in the United States and the world: The world economy is becoming more homogenous; global political structures are growing more fragmented; the global population is expanding; environmental awareness is gaining strength; life chances are becoming more polarized; and ethnicity and multiculturalism are becoming even more important issues. We certainly do not claim that these are the only global issues, and you might rank others ahead of them.

We now need a theoretical perspective to help us understand and explain the history and the future of global inequality. In Chapter 3, we examine two popular (and competing) theories. We also discuss how to rethink these perspectives in light of the rapid changes occurring in today's world.

3

Constructing a Model of Global Inequalities

Years ago a prominent social scientist came under verbal assault at a national academic meeting. He had spent years constructing a sweeping theory that explained how societies change around the world. But his theory did not impress everyone, including one scholar who argued vigorously that the theory was fanciful and totally divorced from the facts. The social scientist sat unfazed near the front of the room listening to the "sins" of his theory. Finally, the moderator of the meeting turned to him and asked for his response. He rose from his seat, smiled easily, shrugged his shoulders, and stated affably: "Damn the evidence, a good theory is hard to find."

Indeed, the word *theory* often suggests incredibly abstract and philosophical arguments bearing little relationship to reality. Although there is some truth to this view at times, it is our intention to show how theories can help explain past, current, and future trends of global inequality in a comprehensive and understandable fashion. We present two prominent post–World War II theories of inequality and social change, and then we suggest several themes that will help extend and improve our perspective on global inequality.

Two Traditional Explanations for Global Inequality

Why are some countries richer than others? Why do some countries have better life chances than others? Why do some countries present more opportunities for their citizens than others? These types of questions have been asked by countless students, teachers, and interested observers. One theoretical explanation focuses primarily on factors *within* countries and another focuses on factors *between* countries.

Modernization Theory: Blaming the Victim

Since the end of World War II, some scholars and government officials have argued that underdeveloped countries are poor simply because they lack modern economies, modern psychological traits, modern cultures, and modern institutions. According to these advocates of *modernization theory*, underdeveloped countries should "get modern" if they ever want to attain the status of being "developed." These theorists stress the virtues and promise of national modernity. In fact, proponents of modernization theory divide the world into two basic types of countries: modern and traditional. Let's look at these two dimensions in more detail. Keep in mind, however, that these arguments are not fact; they merely represent the perspective of modernization theory.

The Basic Argument

First, developed countries have *modern economies*, characterized by high levels of industrialization, a large middle class of consumers, food self-sufficiency, low unemployment, advanced technology, and an educated population. By contrast, underdeveloped countries have traditional economies, characterized by low levels of industrialization, a very small middle class, lack of food, high rates of unemployment and underemployment, little advanced technology, and a poorly educated population (Rostow 1960).

Second, developed countries have citizens with *modern psychological and cultural traits*, such as a desire to work hard, achieve goals, invest and save money, be on time, and engage in other practices valued by rich Western countries like the United States. By contrast, underdeveloped countries have citizens with traditional psychological and cultural traits, which place less value on achievement, hard work, investment, savings, and other such characteristics. Instead, these citizens emphasize subsistence living (for example, growing enough food to survive) and cultural values embraced by local communities and religions (Inkeles and Smith 1974). An ethnic group in East Africa known as the Masai, for example, has a lifestyle that revolves around raising cattle, which they consider sacred creatures. The Masai also equate cattle with wealth; thus, they trade cattle to settle debts, pay dowries, and complete other transactions.

Third, developed countries have *modern institutions* like a functioning judicial system, a good educational system, an elected parliament or legislature, regular and fair elections, and other features of multiparty democracy and mass political participation (Delacroix and Ragin 1978). Historically, most developed countries have a representative democracy that allows citizens the opportunity to vote in general elections (Rueschemeyer, Stephens, and Stephens 1992; Bollen and Jackman 1989). By contrast, many traditional societies are governed by alternative systems, such as dictatorships, one-party states, monarchies, military regimes, or religious governments (for example, Islamic regimes). Instead of placing power in the hands of the people, traditional societies stress the governing power of small groups, individuals, or traditional institutions that resist modernization.

After formulating their perspective in the late 1940s and 1950s, the original modernization theorists began to ask an important question: How can the United States and its allies help transform underdeveloped traditional societies into developed modern countries? During the naive and innocent days of the 1950s, many U.S. officials were very optimistic that developed countries could help "modernize" the Third World into mini-versions of themselves. After all, the United States had helped to rebuild Europe and Japan immediately following World War II. From 1946 through 1955, the United States poured $33 billion into Western Europe and another $3 billion into Japan (U.S. Bureau of the Census 1994, 813–814). Because these regions (especially Western Europe) were rebuilt with U.S. assistance, the assumption was that poor countries could be helped in the same way.

Accordingly, the United States and other rich countries would give substantial economic and military assistance to poor countries. *Economic* aid supposedly would stimulate industrialization, and *military* assistance supposedly would stop the spread of communism. Modernization theorists considered communism nothing short of a disease that could strangle a country's quest for modernity. Thus, since the mid-1950s, the United States has given more than $240 billion to developing countries around the world (U.S. Bureau of the Census 1994, 813). In addition, President John F. Kennedy started the Peace Corps in the early 1960s, a program that has sent thousands of dedicated young Americans around the world to work on grassroots development projects. Many other educational and cultural exchange programs were also initiated to promote Western-style development. Again, according to modernization theorists, the objective of all foreign aid was to spread modern economics, values, and ways of life to traditional regions.

Modernization theory is a theory of social change. With the assistance of Western countries, the underdeveloped world supposedly can develop into modern countries with modern institutions and modern people. Some scholars claim that societies evolve by creating and using new, modern forms of information and technology. Gerhard Lenski, for instance, argues that technological advances and innovation are crucial for economic and social development. Societies that undertake such advances become wealthier and more developed, whereas societies that fail to advance technologically will stagnate and possibly not survive. Many factors can limit a society's commitment to innovation and change, including its values, beliefs, amount of contact with other societies, and physical environment (Lenski, Lenski, and Nolan 1991).

At first glance, modernization theory makes a lot of sense to the citizens of developed countries. They have been raised to value hard work, thrift, democracy, and other characteristics advocated by this perspective. Beneath the surface, however, there are some problems with modernization theory that have eroded its popularity and validity over the last two decades.

Criticisms of the Theory

First, the theory has long been criticized for being *ethnocentric,* meaning that it is based on an assumption that Western culture, institutions, and ways of life are superior to what is found in non-Western societies. The underlying theme behind modernization theory is the adage "the West is best." This theory is also implicitly racist since the majority of citizens in the wealthy Western societies are white and the majority of citizens in the "backward," non-Western societies are nonwhite.

Second, modernization theory assumes that, in the words of Daniel Chirot (1977, 3), "the United States is a rich old uncle trying to teach his nephews the secret of success." Certainly, the United States has been involved in some very decent acts of humanitarian assistance to underdeveloped regions. Thousands of Peace Corps volunteers, for instance, have worked hard to advance the quality of life in poor countries by staffing schools, hospitals, and orphanages; working on agricultural projects; building modern sewage facilities; and teaching birth control and parenting techniques to indigenous populations. At the same time, however, it is also clear that U.S. foreign policy is based primarily on the interests of the United States. For example, since its military defeat in Vietnam in the mid-1970s, the United States has given the vast majority of its foreign assistance not to the poorest countries of the world, but to strategic military allies. Consider a couple of astounding statistics. From 1991 through 1992, 34 percent of all U.S. foreign aid for economic assistance and 65 percent of all U.S. foreign aid for military assistance went to just *two* trusted friends: Israel and Egypt. The poorest *continent* on earth, Africa, received only 12 percent of all U.S. economic aid and 2 percent of U.S. military assistance (U.S. Bureau of the Census 1994, 813–817). The U.S. position certainly is not unique. Like most rich countries, the United States chooses to give most of its aid not to those countries in the greatest need, but to those who will align themselves with U.S. interests in the world.

Third, modernization theory may greatly overestimate the capacity of poor countries to develop. Certainly, there are successful stories of development in some countries around the world. The so-called Four Little Dragons—South Korea, Taiwan, Hong Kong, and Singapore—have experienced rapid economic growth and other forms of development over the last several decades (Vogel 1991). Other countries experiencing significant development in recent years are Mexico, Brazil, Thailand, Malaysia, India, and China. Despite these examples, however, the vast majority of the world remains poor and the gap between rich and poor countries is growing. The problem is especially acute across Africa, where income and nutrition levels today are lower than two decades ago (World Bank 1994). Moreover, as alluded to earlier, the developed world has little interest in providing substantial aid or resources to very underdeveloped areas. Massive foreign aid is always unpopular, especially now, when developed countries have so many problems confronting them. The United States currently allocates a total of only $11.6 billion per year in economic assistance to foreign countries and another $4.8 billion in military aid (U.S. Bureau of the Census 1994, 813–817). Again, this is about half the amount that Americans spend on beer each year.

Fourth, modernization theory is based on the idea that countries can develop almost exclusively from *within* themselves, especially if they receive a little assistance from developed nations. If underdeveloped countries can just acquire and nurture modern characteristics, then they supposedly can join the family of developed countries. The problem with this logic is that it is overly simplistic. Countries can do some things to help themselves; but they will have a difficult time overcoming some external constraints like lack of money, lack of technology, lack of medicine, and lack of other resources. Many people in developed countries like to pretend that poor countries can develop themselves if they would just try hard enough, but this sentiment is unrealistic in many cases. How can a country develop its economy if it does not have sufficient resources to ward off the most routine diseases like measles, diarrhea, and whooping cough? Most poor countries do not have the technology to manufacture medication and are too poor to import it.

To summarize, modernization theory contains some useful ideas, but it is cloaked in an ethnocentric view that glorifies Western culture and denigrates worthwhile elements of the cultures of poor countries. It blames the victims—the poor countries—for their failure to develop without acknowledging power inequities between rich and poor countries. Most government leaders in rich countries still cling to this view of development and formulate policies that reflect its values, even though the theory has been heavily criticized by many people. The inadequacy of this perspective has sparked a lively debate about alternative theories of development, a debate that culminated with a very different perspective.

World-System Theory: Blaming Outside Actors

Starting in the late 1950s and intensifying in the 1960s, a group of scholars began to launch vigorous attacks against modernization theory. They claimed that it was inaccurate, ethnocentric, and simply naive. According to this view, there is inequality in the world not because poor countries lack modernization, but because rich countries historically have exploited poor countries. This perspective became very popular in 1974, when a sociology professor, Immanuel Wallerstein, published a book that introduced the theoretical model known as *world-system theory*. Although world-system theory has become almost as controversial as the modernization theory it challenged, it does a much better job of identifying external factors that restrict the development of poor countries. This theory holds that the economic realities of the world system help rich countries stay rich while poor countries stay poor. The theory has developed an enthusiastic following in academic circles over the years and, despite its limitations, must be taken seriously as a possible explanation for the inequality among nations.

The Basic Historical Argument

World-system theory rests on a historical view of development that stresses economic, political, and military events over the last 500 years (Wallerstein 1974; Chase-Dunn 1989). According to this model, the affluence of rich countries in the contemporary world results from the long-term economic exploitation of poor countries. These same exploitative relations perpetuate the poverty of poor countries and provide very little opportunity for them to lift themselves out of the bottom of the world system.

The world-system model divides the modern world into three parts: *core* countries, *peripheral* countries, and *semiperipheral* countries. These categories basically correspond to the rich, poor, and middle-income countries that are displayed graphically in Chapter 2. The core comprises highly industrialized wealthy countries—Western Europe, the United

States, Japan, and Australia—that exert both economic and political power in the world system. The core also enjoys a very high standard of living and good quality of life. The periphery comprises the poorest, weakest, and least industrialized countries of the world. Most peripheral countries are located in Africa, Asia, and Latin America, although none of these regions contains only peripheral countries. The semiperiphery comprises middle-income countries that have achieved at least a moderate level of industrialization and overall development. *Advanced* semiperipheral countries include the four Little Dragons—South Korea, Taiwan, Singapore, and Hong Kong—and other newly industrializing countries (NICs) like Brazil, Mexico, Malaysia, and others.

The heart of the world-system theory is its explanation of the *exploitative process* that has enabled core countries to retain their wealth and power at the expense of peripheral and semiperipheral nations. In the world-system model, this process has two major features. First, core nations historically have sought the raw materials that exist in relative abundance in noncore countries. Raw materials include a variety of minerals and metals that are required to produce industrial products, automobiles, weapons, and luxury items (for example, gold for jewelry) in the developed world. Without access to these raw materials, core nations simply would not be as wealthy as they are today. Raw materials also include agricultural products grown in the warm weather climates of the periphery that are manufactured into food and beverages for consumption in core countries. For instance, coffee, tea, sugar, cocoa, peanuts, and many other products are grown in peripheral and semiperipheral nations. They are exported and sold in the core.

Core countries have devised a number of ways to gain access to raw materials. European nations originally sailed to the far-off lands of Asia, Latin America, and Africa in search of raw materials (Chirot 1994a, 68–70). Europe created *colonies* out of these regions, forcing European economic, political, and cultural systems upon them. Spain occupied much of Latin America starting in the fifteenth and sixteenth centuries, and Portugal established a large number of trading posts throughout the Indian Ocean during the same period. England, France, and the Netherlands also became involved throughout the world, gradually expanding into new areas and also taking over territory previously belonging to the Spanish and Portuguese. During the seventeenth century, for instance, England, France, and the Netherlands took over many Caribbean islands and established sugar plantations on them. The English became an especially strong and aggressive global power, colonizing India in the eighteenth century and also expanding deeper into Asia, even forcing China to give up some trading ports. In the late nineteenth and early twentieth centuries, the Europeans expanded into Africa in search of more raw materials. Although England and France were the greatest colonizers in Africa, other Europeans were also involved including Portugal, Italy, Germany, Belgium, and Spain. By 1914, European colonial masters controlled a substantial portion of the earth's land. This is illustrated in Map 3.1.

Colonialism enabled Europeans to exploit their colonies for minerals and metals, food and beverages, and spices and fabrics, much of which was shipped back to Europe with little compensation to the colonies. These activities fueled the growing economies of Europe and satisfied the demand for luxury items by European elites. European development came at the expense of its colonies, however, which were left with fewer resources and greater underdevelopment. The people of colonial areas also became increasingly disenchanted with their colonial masters, who insisted on implementing European ways even where they were not welcome (Chirot 1994a, 68–70).

The second major exploitative component, according to world-system theory, is that core nations historically have sought cheap labor in colonial areas. Slavery is an extreme (but very real) illustration of this point. Caribbean sugar plantations needed labor, so Europeans traded products to buy slaves captured in the coastal areas of Africa. Over time, more than 12 million Africans were enslaved and sent around the world, including to the United States (Mazrui 1986, 231). Even though the United States was never a formal colonial power, it still benefited from colonial activities that harmed people in economically underdeveloped areas. Other Africans were actually enslaved in Africa. These slaves were forced to build railroads, work in mines, serve as domestic servants, and provide various other forms of labor for Europeans in Africa. This process facilitated further raw material extraction from colonial areas, and it also generated even more intense resentment against colonialists (Chirot 1994a, 68-70).

Slavery was an extremely humiliating experience for its victims. This emotion was captured by a famous African professor, Dr. Ali Mazrui, when he visited "slave caves" in West Africa as part of a highly acclaimed television documentary for U.S. public television. Slaves were forcibly held in these caves while waiting to be loaded onto ships for the torturous sail across the ocean. Many female slaves were held separately so that white masters could have sexual access to them. Reflecting on the entire slavery process for the television cameras, the normally composed Mazrui became emotional and said, "I am just beginning to understand what a Jew must feel like who visits Auschwitz or some other Nazi concentration camp and experiences these powerful emotions of bewilderment, of anger, and infinite sadness."

MAP 3.1 The World in the Early Twentieth Century at the Height of European Power

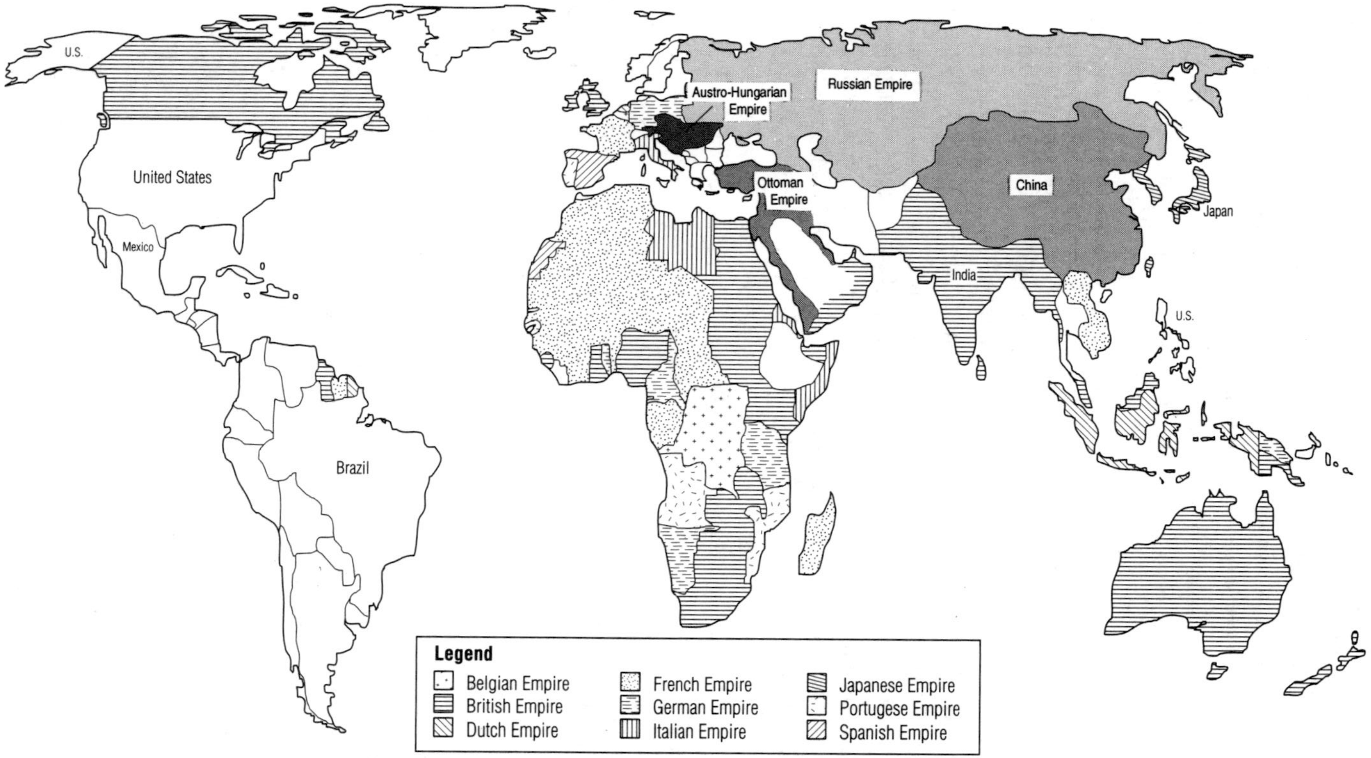
U.S.
United States
Mexico
Brazil
Austro-Hungarian Empire
Russian Empire
Ottoman Empire
China
Japan
India
U.S.
Legend
Belgian Empire
British Empire
Dutch Empire
French Empire
German Empire
Italian Empire
Japanese Empire
Portugese Empire
Spanish Empire

Slaves were captured and controlled with whips, balls and chains, and cages. They were then packed into ships with their legs and hands shackled. The captives were forced to lay next to and on top of each other during the journey. Chained humans sweated, urinated, and defecated on each other as white masters kept their distance above the hellish "cargo" chambers. It is little wonder that up to one-third of all slaves died from cholera and other diseases on the journey overseas. Slave traders often would try to calculate how tightly to pack the ship; a "normal" load of slaves would result in fewer deaths, whereas a "tight pack" would load more slaves onto the ship but result in more disease-related deaths along the way. Such considerations were important to slave traders, who were serious businessmen (Mazrui 1986, 231). Slaves were nothing more than commodities to them—a person's worth was not much different from that of a coffee plant.

The legacy of slavery, domination, and brutality created increasingly more resentment in poor countries. At the same time, colonialism became very expensive for the colonizers and therefore could not last forever. It was expensive to maintain political structures in far-off lands and to preserve European-style "law and order" as shown by the fact that most Spanish colonies in the Americas gained independence in the 1800s. This problem became even more acute as many European countries grew weaker during the twentieth century, partly as a result of World War I and World War II. Moreover, some colonies began to revolt against European powers, making the entire colonial process even more costly (Walton 1984). Small uprisings eventually turned into full-scale guerilla warfare in some regions of the world. Such instability, combined with a weakening Europe, led to the downfall of formal colonialism after World War II. In 1947, India became the first major colony to gain political independence from Britain. Over the next twenty years, most (but not all) colonies became independent from Britain, France, Germany, Portugal, and other European powers. Almost every African country gained political independence in the early 1960s, although a few did not achieve this goal until the 1980s. One of the last remaining colonies in the world is Hong Kong, scheduled to break free of British control in 1997.

The Basic Contemporary Argument

So, did the exploitative relationship between core and peripheral regions end with the close of the colonial era? No, claims world-system theory. This perspective argues that, since the 1960s, the original colonial period has been replaced by a newer form of colonialism, *neocolonialism*. Accordingly, core countries are still able to exploit noncore countries through the mechanism of the multinational corporations (MNCs), huge entities that are headquartered in core countries but do business in multiple nations, both rich and poor.

Before specifying exactly what MNCs do, let's look at their incredible size. As amazing as it may seem, the largest MNCs are bigger economic entities than most noncore *countries* of the world. Table 3.1 shows the largest fifty economic entities in the world, excluding core countries and the six strongest semiperipheral countries from consideration. This table compares the sales of the largest MNCs of the world to the total economic output of most semiperipheral and all peripheral countries, as measured by their gross domestic products (GDP). As you can see, of the fifty largest economic entities displayed in the table, thirty-three are MNCs (in capital

TABLE 3.1

The Fifty Richest Economic Entities in the World, Excluding Core and Strong Semiperipheral Countries

Entity	Millions of U.S. Dollars (1992)	Entity	Millions of U.S. Dollars (1992)
1. China	$506,075	26. PHILIP MORRIS	$50,621
2. Russian Federated Rep.	$387,476	27. IRI	$50,488
3. India	$214,598	28. SIEMENS	$50,381
4. GENERAL MOTORS	$133,622	29. Colombia	$48,583
5. Indonesia	$126,364	30. VOLKSWAGEN	$46,312
6. Thailand	$110,337	31. CHRYSLER	$43,600
7. Iran, Islamic Rep.	$110,258	32. Pakistan	$41,904
8. FORD MOTOR	$108,521	33. UNILEVER	$41,843
9. Turkey	$99,696	34. Chile	$41,203
10. EXXON	$97,825	35. NESTLE	$38,895
11. ROYAL DUTCH/SHELL GROUP	$95,134	36. Myanmar	$37,749
12. Ukraine	$94,831	37. ELF AQUITAINE	$37,016
13. TOYOTA MOTOR	$85,283	38. HONDA MOTOR	$35,798
14. Poland	$83,823	39. Algeria	$35,674
15. HITACHI	$68,581	40. ENI	$34,791
16. INTERNATIONAL BUSINESS MACHINES	$62,716	41. FIAT	$34,707
		42. SONY	$34,603
17. MATSUSHITA ELECTRIC IND.	$61,385	43. TEXACO	$34,359
18. GENERAL ELECTRIC	$60,823	44. Egypt, Arab Republic	$33,553
19. DAIMLER-BENZ	$59,102	45. NEC	$33,176
20. Malaysia	$57,568	46. E. I. DU PONT DE NEM	$32,621
21. MOBIL	$56,576	47. CHEVRON	$32,123
22. NISSAN MOTOR	$53,760	48. PHILLIPS ELECTRONICS	$31,666
23. BRITISH PETROLEUM	$52,485	49. DAEWOO	$30,893
24. Philippines	$52,462	50. PROCTOR & GAMBLE	$30,433
25. SAMSUNG	$51,345		

Sources: Multinational sales data from Haight 1994; GDP data from World Bank 1994.

letters) located in Asia (especially Japan), the United States, and Europe. These thirty-three companies are richer than the more than 100 semi-peripheral and peripheral nations around the world that were too poor to make it onto this list.

World-system theory claims that MNCs are still interested in exploiting the raw materials and cheap labor of noncore countries. Southern climates are still conducive to the production of food and other raw materials. Multinationals often produce such goods in these climates and then ship them back to the United States and the rest of the core, where they are sold for a substantial profit. For instance, if you are grocery shopping in the United States, you may well find that your coffee came from Colombia, your berries from Guatemala or Chile, your bananas from Honduras or Guatemala, and your soybeans from Brazil. If you are shopping for an expensive gold bracelet or diamond, there is a good chance that it came from southern Africa. If you are shopping for cars or heavy weapons, there is a good chance that many of the components came from raw materials found in poor countries. The majority of the world's cobalt, chrome, platinum, iron ore, and other metals and minerals come from poor countries (Griffiths 1993). Without access to these raw materials, the core would not enjoy nearly the comfortable lifestyle that it does today.

World-system theorists still believe that the core's development is achieved at the expense of peripheral and semiperipheral countries. Most important, noncore countries lack the ability to convert their raw materials into manufactured products. Thus, these countries allow MNCs to take raw materials (in exchange for money) and export them back to rich countries. Rich countries therefore become even stronger by transforming these raw materials into finished products, while poor countries are left with even fewer resources and less potential. Rich countries end up with fancy cars while poor countries are left with holes in the ground. Moreover, some noncore countries sell land to MNCs so that the latter can grow agricultural products for export. Some of this land is taken from peasants who produce food for the country.

Multinationals also rely on noncore regions for inexpensive labor. Take a minute right now to look at your shoes, your clothes, your computer, your television set, and your compact disc (CD) player. What do they have in common? There is a good chance that each product was at least partially assembled or manufactured in a noncore country, especially semiperipheral countries like Taiwan, Malaysia, South Korea, Singapore, Hong Kong, China, the Philippines, Indonesia, Brazil, or Mexico. To save money on labor costs, MNCs employ many young, uneducated women at low wages in these countries, enabling the companies to make a healthy profit.

(Remember the earlier story about Sadisah, the young Indonesian Nike employee.)

Many automobiles driven in the core are also produced in other countries. The four largest automakers in the world are U.S.-based General Motors, U.S.-based Ford, Japan-based Toyota, and German-based Volkswagen. The percentage of total automobiles produced outside the home country of each automaker is 41.8 percent, 58.7 percent, 8.3 percent, and 30.5 percent, respectively (Dicken 1992, 290). One reason that cars are assembled abroad is low labor costs. It makes perfect sense for core-based companies (in numerous fields) to move some of their production facilities to countries with lower wages, fewer requirements for health care, and fewer safety regulations in factories. Of course, this situation also means a loss of jobs in America and other core countries, a topic examined later in the book.

Cheap labor in foreign countries affects both core and noncore countries. In the former, many workers have lost their jobs through *deindustrialization*, a process whereby many industrial jobs are moving from developed to underdeveloped countries. In underdeveloped countries, by contrast, it is true that MNC investment has created a few industrial jobs. World-system theorists are still critical of such jobs, however, because they pay low wages, offer few health benefits, and provide a relatively unsafe working environment.

Many social scientists acknowledge the contributions of world-system theory. It offers a historical explanation of underdevelopment; it explains how some countries have exploited other countries; and it offers a strong dose of reality to go along with an academic perspective. Many recent academic studies support *some* aspects of world-system theory, especially that MNC investment (1) slows economic development in poor countries (Bornschier and Chase-Dunn 1985); (2) harms their quality of life (Wimberley 1990; London and Williams 1990); (3) exploits women in poor countries (Nash and Fernandez-Kelly 1983; Ward 1990); and (4) increases political instability in some developing regions (Boswell and Dixon 1990). Despite this support, world-system arguments have received substantial criticism over the last few years. We briefly summarize these criticisms next.

Criticisms of the Theory

First, just as modernization theory places too much blame on poor countries for their own underdevelopment, world-system theory errs at the other extreme: It places almost total blame for Third World poverty on core countries. Modernization theory sees the United States as a kindly uncle, but world-system theory views the United States as Darth Vader overseeing an evil empire of capitalist greed. It is true that core countries have been guilty of exploitation, but poor countries must also share part of the blame for their own underdevelopment. As we will discuss later in the book, some poor countries have squandered their resources, suffered from abysmal leadership, and been drained by corrupt governments and businesses. Students and scholars typically become much less supportive of world-system theory after they conduct research and live in poor countries for a period of time. They begin to realize that, in addition to the harmful influence of some outside actors, there are also many other factors that contribute to Third World poverty and underdevelopment.

Second, some scholars argue that world-system theory has exaggerated the harmful effects of MNCs (Firebaugh 1992, Firebaugh and Beck 1994). According to this perspective, countries that have a lot of MNC investment are, on balance, better off than countries without such investment. In fact, these critics argue that foreign investment is one of the only sources of money in developing societies. Multinationals do provide some money, jobs, and technology for poor countries, even if such resources do not "trickle down" to the mass population.

Third, world-system theory is becoming dated and out of touch with current realities in the world (Bradshaw, Noonan, Gash, and Buchmann 1993). Let's focus on just three facts that world-system theory is poorly equipped to explain: (1) An incredible international debt crisis is influencing the world today. Peripheral and semiperipheral countries now owe more than $1.5 trillion to banks, governments, and other organizations in rich countries (World Bank 1994). This problem is creating tremendous problems for all sides. Lenders want their money but poor countries are too poor to repay, restricting their ability to borrow additional money for development projects. Instead of examining this debt crisis, world-system theory continues to focus primarily on the effects of foreign investment. (2) Wars, especially ethnic wars, are tearing the world apart. Instead of recognizing the historical importance of ethnicity, world-system theory tends to attribute all conflict to economic exploitation. (3) Environmental issues are beginning to influence global economic and political actions, more so than has been acknowledged by world-system theory. One example is that international environmental groups are proposing "debt for nature swaps" with poor countries. Environmental groups agree to pay off part of a country's foreign debt in exchange for the country's guarantee that it will protect part of a forest or other nature preserve.

To overcome some of the problems associated with world-system theory and modernization theory, we discuss how to combine and elaborate the theories to provide a more comprehensive explanation of global inequality.

Combining External and Internal Explanations of Global Inequality

Strong advocates of one theoretical position seldom want to endorse other positions. In this case, followers of modernization theory normally disagree with those who follow world-system theory, and vice versa. Part of the problem is ideological and political. Modernization theorists gravitate toward the conservative end of the political spectrum, believing that countries should help themselves and stop blaming others for their problems. World-system theorists generally occupy the opposite end of the political spectrum, blaming the world capitalist system for Third World poverty and overall global inequality.

We propose a theoretical orientation that puts aside ideology and combines the best features of world-system and modernization arguments. This is not a new theory by any means, just an attempt to broaden conventional explanations of global inequality. Moreover, we present several ideas that are lacking in both perspectives. We present our model in a fairly brief fashion here, and then apply it to different regions of the world in the next four chapters. Our approach in this book will emphasize six basic themes.

Theme 1: *External and internal factors influence the world.*

Clearly, global inequality is influenced by a variety of internal and external factors, which affect each other. Consider two simple examples. First, as previously discussed, MNCs extract raw materials from the periphery and also build factories there to manufacture products cheaply. But MNCs can be influenced, to some extent, by factors within countries; governments of poor countries can place environmental restrictions on MNCs or tax them more heavily when operating factories. This is a situation where internal factors would influence external factors. Of course, if developing countries place too many restrictions on MNCs or tax them too heavily, MNCs will leave such countries and look for greener pastures. Second, because some developing countries are so heavily indebted to international banks and foreign governments, they often cannot borrow additional money for development projects unless they follow very strict conditions imposed upon them by lenders. One condition requires developing countries' governments to cut spending on social services, thereby saving money, which can then be used to repay national debts. Although this sounds logical, these spending cuts clearly harm very poor citizens who rely on government services for the most basic necessities of life (Walton and Ragin 1990). This is a situation where external factors (pressure from lenders) influence internal conditions (spending cuts on social programs).

Theme 2: Move beyond external and internal characteristics to also include regional and community factors.

Some forward-thinking scholars have realized the importance of examining the interaction between internal and external factors (London 1987; Chirot 1994a; Bollen and Jackman 1989). We now need to go one step further and discuss the interaction among factors at the global, regional, national, and community levels (Bradshaw, Kaiser, and Ndegwa 1995). For example, let's consider how these levels operate to influence the consolidation of the global economy, one of the trends we discussed in Chapter 2. Many people consider this trend a *global-level* phenomenon. Importantly, though, *regional* blocs and *national* governments must make a decision to consolidate at the global level. Moreover, *local* communities can also pressure their national government to undertake action that may facilitate or inhibit this consolidation. For example, some local communities in the United States strongly opposed passage of the NAFTA trade agreement with Canada and Mexico. They pressured their government representatives to vote against the treaty on the grounds that it would encourage local companies (and jobs) to move to Mexico. Many congressional representatives did vote against the treaty and, in the end, the agreement barely passed despite very strong support from President Clinton. Local communities and their representatives came very close to stopping an agreement that led to a trade merger throughout North America, an excellent example of regional economic consolidation.

Theme 3: Ethnicity is very important at every level.

Many social science theories, including the world-system and modernization perspectives, tend to ignore ethnicity as a major determinant of inequality. As we discussed earlier, however, ethnic factors are forcing us to redraw global and national maps. They are also forcing regional actors to become involved in ethnic disputes; for example, Europe is negotiating for peace in the former Yugoslavia. Ethnic cleavages often begin at the subnational level when particular ethnic groups are dissatisfied with the government and want to break away from the nation. Contemporary theories must place a greater emphasis on such considerations, and we do so in this book.

Ethnicity is a particularly difficult issue for both of the major theories examined in this chapter. World-system theory stresses the economic and political power of the core, with ethnicity and other factors assuming a much less prominent position. Modernization theory is so Western-oriented that it does not appreciate the importance and power of various ethnic groups and cultures. Ethnicity, along with economics, politics, and other characteristics, is an important determinant of inequality and change.

Theme 4: *Demonstrate more respect for non-Western cultures.*

One of the major themes of this book is that we need to appreciate the unique features of other cultures. Most social science theories are developed in the core countries of the West and therefore explain the world primarily from a Western perspective. This is natural to some extent: We see the world through our own eyes and experiences (remember the map exercise in Chapter 1). For example, modernization theory generally assumes that, in order to develop fully, countries need to adopt values that come from the Judeo-Christian heritage (Judaism and Christianity). But how do we explain the rapid development of Japan and other Asian countries, which have relatively few followers of either Judaism or Christianity? To answer these types of questions, we need to expand our view (and knowledge) of the world in order to understand different cultures. Starting in Chapter 4, we provide numerous stories and examples that illustrate the necessity of looking at events from new perspectives.

Theme 5: *Place greater emphasis on women, children, refugees, and other "vulnerable" groups in society.*

Broad theories of inequality and change often lose sight of what they are really studying, namely, human conditions. And, when discussing human conditions, we need a sharper focus on those groups faced with the greatest hardship. When economies decline, children and women are affected most; when wars break out, the majority of casualties are children and women; when ethnic cleansing begins, refugees become the most oppressed and vulnerable citizens on earth. Theories should pay attention to various groups within society. It is fine to study economics, politics, and culture, but we need to come out of the abstract world and really focus on people when studying inequality.

Theme 6: Move beyond disciplinary boundaries to examine social, economic, cultural, political, historical, and other characteristics.

Unfortunately, academic disciplines have become so territorial that they give little serious attention to other disciplines. Economists usually dwell on the economy, political scientists on politics, sociologists on society, anthropologists on culture, and historians on history. The dimensions studied by each discipline often influence one another, however. For example, economic development in today's world is difficult without some level of political strength and viability; and economic and political vitality provide resources for social development and even cultural advancement. Historical events, such as colonialism, leave behind a legacy that can profoundly influence a country's (or region's) economic, political, and cultural dimensions. Although some of these points may seem logical and simple, they often are overlooked in theoretical models, partly because such models are wedded to one disciplinary orientation or another. Although we are sociologists by training, we attempt to transcend disciplinary boundaries when conducting our analysis.

Application to World Regions

We have not proposed a new theory in this chapter. To the contrary, we have discussed two major theories of inequality and social change, outlining their major arguments and presenting criticisms of each view. We have also suggested six basic themes that would improve these (and many other) theories. Two points should be remembered as we apply this model to the real world. First, there are many other theories of global inequality and social change. We have selected modernization theory and world-system theory because they are important and broad perspectives that have influenced social science. They also reflect the external and internal divide that plagues many other theories. Second, although we feel that the six themes discussed are important for any theory of global inequality, they are not necessarily the only ones available. You might well discover others that you consider even more important.

The remainder of the book will look at issues of inequality and development in four world regions. We do not have a magic formula for investigating issues in these areas. Instead, we have selected interesting and important substantive events that have occurred within the regions. At the end of each chapter, we use our theoretical models to try to analyze and interpret some of the major issues discussed in the chapters. Theoretical interpretation separates social scientists from other observers of society, for example, journalists. Both social scientists and journalists collect information (data), organize it, analyze it, and report it. But social scientists also use theoretical models to interpret events and place them in a larger context. Theoretical models are most useful when they provide a framework to understand the causes of events in more than one society and at more than one point in time. For example, a theoretical model might attempt to explain the causes of war not just in a place like Bosnia during 1995, but in other countries and regions as well. A good theory, therefore, helps us to explain past events and predict future ones.

We start our investigation with Africa. This may seem an unusual place to start our journey. Many books barely discuss Africa or put it off to the very end. We depart from this practice and begin with a continent that receives little attention.

MAP 4.1

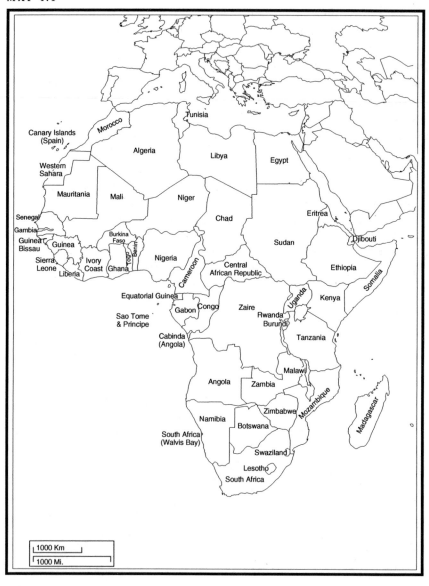

4

Africa: A Continued Decline?

A Land of Contradictions

The world's second largest continent is a land of incredible—almost incomprehensible—contradictions and contrasts. Westerners are somewhat familiar with one side of the story. Africa is a land of famines, civil wars, coups d'état (government overthrows), an AIDS epidemic, orphans, and ethnic divisions. It is a land of growing indebtedness and financial ineptitude that plagues its capacity to do business in the global marketplace. It is also a land that has a pathetic infrastructure: dilapidated schools, health clinics, roads, and communications facilities. An African joke states that a drunken driver is someone who drives straight, instead of swerving all over the road to avoid the omnipresent potholes. Western visitors often are shocked at African countries' inability to function relative to Western standards. Telephone calls are difficult to make, fax messages often fail, E-mail is hard to find, hotel bookings may be ignored, scheduled air flights may not run on any given day, appointments at many offices are nearly impossible to schedule, and corruption is a way of life in some countries. Asked why this is so, an African will likely respond that it is because of a lack of money and other resources; a Westerner, conversely, may respond that it is due to poor organization or just sheer incompetence or laziness. Neither side is totally correct.

What is true is that many Westerners lack familiarity with the positive historical, cultural, and social features of the continent. Consider three examples. First, Africa is known as the "cradle of civilization," primarily because the skeleton of the oldest known human was found in Kenya by Richard Leakey and Kamoya Kimeu. This suggests that the earliest human societies were located on the continent that is stereotyped as having little notable history. As Ali Mazrui notes (1986, 42), "If there was a Garden of Eden where the first man and woman lived, the garden was in Africa." Second, Africa is also the "genesis of civilization" (42). One of the most advanced civilizations of ancient times—the Pharaonic period of early

Egypt—illustrates one of Africa's most profound contributions to history. The pyramids of this time period, marvels of architectural technology, are still studied by experts from around the world. Third, contemporary Africa has a family and social structure that is a model for other regions around the world. Divorce is rare; retirement homes are virtually nonexistent as old people live with their relatives; and families and villages take care of each other. Many African languages do not even have a word for "niece" or "nephew" because people regard the children of a brother or sister as practically their own children.

Africa's strong tradition of family is illustrated by a true story about a Zambian friend of ours named Joseph Taguma. Several years ago he was living in a "hired" (rented) room in a nice London home. The home owner was a middle-aged woman whose mother lived alone across the city. One day the mother continued to call her daughter and, since the daughter was out of the house, Joseph continued to answer the phone. On the fifth call in under two hours, our friend finally asked, "Madam, is there something I can help you with?" The elderly woman replied, "No, I'm just so lonely." Having just arrived in London after living in Africa his entire life, our friend could not understand how any elderly person could feel this way. He inquired, "Madam, you are a very old woman, how could you possibly be lonely?" He interpreted the situation from his own culture, where elderly people are (1) deeply respected and (2) never without the company of other family members. His remarks may have sounded harsh to a Westerner, but they reflected genuine confusion and concern on his part. Africans see Westerners as too quick to dispose of an older and wiser generation.

Despite these positive aspects of Africa, it is undeniable that much of the continent is in bad shape, even on the brink of disaster. Across the continent, the 1980s and early 1990s were a near catastrophe. Economies decreased in size; population expanded faster than the continent's ability to care for new lives; democracies emerged in some countries but were rejected in others; wars erupted and intensified; quality of life worsened; and, perhaps most important, the world started to forget about Africa. Foreign aid was increasingly channeled to more economically viable countries in Eastern Europe, and international businesses curtailed investment in the sagging African economies. The world is writing off large portions of Africa, and the continent seems unable or unwilling to help reverse the trend. If the worst feeling in the world is to be ignored, then Africa will experience constant depression as we approach the twenty-first century.

Is the situation in Africa hopeless? This is one of the major questions we will examine. We look at the continent's economic, political, social, and cultural situation. Although its prospects look dim from a distance, a closer look at Africa reveals glimmers of hope, a spirit of resilience and re-sourcefulness, and the possibility of positive changes. We will look at all of these aspects.

Africa's History: A Brief Look

Here is a strange concept to ponder: Africans did not consider themselves "Africans" until a century or so ago, when Europeans began using the term. Prior to the late 1800s, most Africans lived not in countries as we know them today, but in ethnic groups and villages across the continent. In fact, a map of Africa before 1880 would not even be recognizable today, as there were few defined countries or territories. The emphasis was on subsistence living, not on nationhood, industrialization, or foreign policy. Most Africans did not travel far from home. Moreover, the outside world knew relatively little about the continent during this time period. Al-though Europeans and others extracted some raw materials and then slaves from Africa, the continent was not respected or treated as a region worth knowing.

This situation began to change in 1884, when European powers met in Germany at the famous Berlin Conference. The purpose of the meeting was to divide up Africa, to decide which European countries would con-trol what sections of the resource-rich continent. European countries needed a cheap supply of resources and labor to fuel their growing econo-mies back home. Suddenly, the continent began to look entirely different: Europeans forced Africans to observe boundaries and borders that later would form the basis for countries. These territories were colonies of Eu-ropean powers, with Europeans trying to create regions in their own im-age economically, politically, socially, and culturally. But the borders often made no sense at all from an African perspective. Ethnic groups and "natural groupings" were divided up because they did not fit the Euro-pean conception of how the continent should look. The world wars of the twentieth century further changed the boundaries of Africa, as European powers shifted and some retreated from Africa because the cost of main-taining colonies was too great. In 1950, at the height of the colonial era, Africa was divided as it is in Map 4.2, which denotes the colonial master of each country. Compare this to Map 4.3, depicting Africa in 1878, before Europe's major involvement in the continent.

By 1964, most African countries had gained formal independence from their European colonial powers. Political independence was supposed to

MAP 4.2 European Control of Africa, 1950

usher in a new period of development and prosperity for Africa. The new countries designed their own flags, mobilized their own armies, elected their own officials, and began a whole new era. But these new symbols and institutions did not ensure prosperity. As colonial powers left Africa, the continent had few educated citizens, little money, little advanced technology, and an unrealistic vision of what development would entail.

The tragedy of Africa is that it has grown progressively *less* developed since independence. Why? Here we see the clash between modernization

MAP 4.3 European Control of Africa, 1878

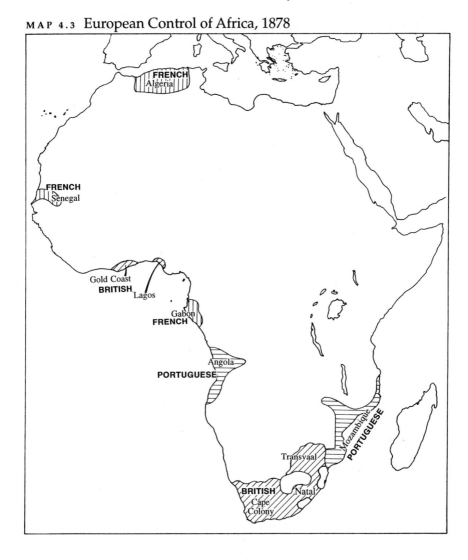

and world-system perspectives. If you ask old white colonialists who opposed political independence, they will tell you that Africa is unable to govern itself and run modern economies. By contrast, if you ask African leaders, they will tell you that the colonial era doomed Africa to a long period of underdevelopment. Perhaps a more balanced view is given by journalist David Lamb, who wrote a controversial book on his experiences in Africa. Lamb (1985, xv) wrote, "The colonialists designed the scenario for disaster and the Africans seem to be trying their best to fulfill it." Colonial powers did leave Africa, as they should have, but few African countries have formulated development plans that actually enhance modernization. In many cases, white colonialists were replaced by African leaders who have exploited fellow Africans just as the colonialists did before them. The rest of this chapter looks at contemporary Africa.

Contemporary Life in Africa

Imagine trying to describe life in America in a few pages. It would be difficult if not impossible, and the same is true of Africa, only more so. First and foremost, Africa is a land of incredible contrasts. Take the geography and climate. Northern Africa is hot, arid, and dominated by the Sahara Desert, producing a climate that is much like the "Middle East." The situation south of the Sahara differs greatly. Some areas are hot and humid tropical rain forests, some are flat and arid (much like North Africa), some are simply savannas and grasslands, some are fertile farmlands, and some are high mountains that even have snow. Ernest Hemingway's famous short story "The Snows of Kilimanjaro" takes its name from Mount Kilimanjaro, Africa's tallest mountain. In contrast to the typical image, parts of Africa are very cold.

The continent also displays great diversity in lifestyles and jobs. About 75 percent of Africans south of the Sahara work in agriculture. Food is produced for domestic consumption, and coffee, tea, peanuts, and other crops are exported for money. Less than one-third of African citizens reside in cities, and only 10 to 20 percent of urban citizens have "modern" wage-earning jobs as professionals, secretaries, laborers, and office workers. Many urban jobs are in the "informal sector" and often are held by migrants from rural areas. Informal-sector jobs include a variety of activities that do not pay a steady and formal wage—activities like shoe shining, basket weaving, auto repair, street sweeping, trading, prostitution, and many others. Some informal workers make a very good living (and do not pay taxes); others barely make enough money to keep from starving. Still other urban citizens are unemployed and resort to begging, stealing, and similar activities. Almost all large African cities are populated with beggars, and, as discussed later, an increasing number of them are children (Griffiths 1993).

Table 4.1 compares a few characteristics of Africa with those of the United States. For Africa, note the low average annual incomes, the high under-five mortality rates (the number of children who die before age five out of every one thousand children born), the low urbanization rates, and the small proportion of workers in nonagricultural jobs.

TABLE 4.1

Development Indicators for Selected African Countries
and the United States, 1992–1993

Country	GNP per Capita (average income)	Under-Five Mortality	Percent of Total Population Living in Urban Areas	Percent of Workers in Nonagricultural Jobs
Botswana	$2,590	56	26%	approx. 50%
Ghana	$430	170	35%	45%
Kenya	$270	105	26%	20–25%
Namibia	$1,660	79	35%	40%
Nigeria	$310	191	38%	46%
Rwanda	$200	141	6%	7%
South Africa	$2,900	69	50%	70%
Tanzania	$100	167	23%	10%
Uganda	$190	185	12%	under 20%
Zaire	$230	187	29%	25%
Zambia	$370	203	42%	15%*
United States	$24,750	10	76%	97.1%

*Why does Zambia have a relatively large urban population and a relatively small non-agricultural workforce? It is because many urban areas are in the "copper belt," where cities grow up around copper mines. Only men work in the mines (a nonagricultural job), but their entire families live with them in the city. Copper mining is a capital-intensive job, however, meaning that relatively few men are needed for this type of enterprise. Thus, most of the nation's jobs are still in the agricultural sector.
Sources: World Bank 1995a; UNICEF 1995; Government of Kenya and UNICEF 1992; CIA 1995.

Jobs, activities, and lifestyles are segregated sharply by gender, especially in rural areas. Let's look briefly at four groups: (1) *Rural women* across Africa are responsible for taking care of children (the average woman bears at least six children), working in the fields to produce food for the family, fetching water from rivers (many villages have no running water), and cooking. It is estimated that African women contribute three-quarters of the labor required to produce food for the continent (Lele 1991). (2) *Rural men* work in commercial agriculture, often in the export sector (for example, growing coffee), and many eventually migrate to cities for temporary work. These men return home periodically and are expected to bring money with them. (3) *Urban women* are responsible for child care and cooking. And, although some work in "modern" urban jobs, they hold very few high-level positions in business, government, or academics. Many urban women are also very poor, trying to make a living in the informal sector. (4) *Urban men* work in a wide variety of activities, from top government and financial positions to poor-paying informal activities. Again, a substantial number of urban laborers help support families back in the countryside.

African societies are also sharply divided by ethnicity. One of the biggest misconceptions among Westerners is that Africans make up a single racial, ethnic, or tribal group. This could not be more wrong. It is estimated that the continent has about 1,000 ethnic groups, which have dramatically different beliefs, customs, and ways of life. Later, we will examine some of the effects of ethnic diversity.

Another factor that influences contemporary Africa is religion. The majority of North Africans have been Muslims for centuries. (A Muslim is a follower of Islam.) Christianity and other religions have a relatively small influence in this region, although, ironically, northeast Africa is not far from the birthplace of Christianity more than 2,000 years ago. The situation is quite different south of the Sahara Desert, however. In this region, about one-third of the people follow Islam, one-third follow Christianity, and one-third follow indigenous (traditional) religions. Islam and traditional religions have been around for centuries, but Christianity is a relative newcomer to the continent. Christian missionaries started traveling to Africa (on a large scale) only about one hundred years ago, trying to impose a new morality at the same time that colonial governments tried to impose new economic and political systems. Although some missionaries were arrogant and condescending toward African cultures, they were remarkably successful at converting local citizens and in building many schools, health clinics, and, of course, churches. (A classic and very readable novel on the topic of missionaries in Africa is called *The River Between*, by Ngugi wa Thiong'o [1965].)

Missionaries certainly have not converted all Africans, many of whom still practice some type of traditional religion. Although these religions vary widely, typically they are *pantheistic*. Pantheism makes little distinction between humans, nature, and divine spirits. God is present in nature: The sunset may be God's smile, a windstorm may be God's anger, a waterfall may reflect God's goodness, and so on. The Langi ethnic group in Uganda worship a spirit known as Jok:

> Jok, like the wind or air, omnipresent, and like the wind, though its presence may be heard and appreciated, Jok has never been seen by anyone. . . . His dwelling is everywhere: in trees it may be, or in rocks and hills, in some springs and pools . . . or vaguely in the air. (Mazrui 1986, 50)

This holistic view of life explains why nature and animals are highly valued in traditional African culture. The practice of poaching and trapping is a Western influence, reducing animals to commodities that are killed for horns, tusks, and skins or captured for Western zoos.

African religions also regulate daily life through a series of customs, rituals, and practices that promote community spirit, not individualism. Missionaries disliked African religions because such religions do not accept the idea of a single deity (God the Father) and also reject some moral teachings of Christianity. It is certainly incorrect, however, to assume that Africans who do not practice Christianity or Islam are "godless."

Strong Societies and Weak States

Although Africa has many unhappy features, it also exhibits several positive aspects. Most of these occur in Africa's *societies*, that is, in its villages, communities, churches, and local-level institutions. Joel Migdal (1988) argues that many developing countries (including those in Africa) have strong societies but weak states. (*State* is just another term for government.) More specifically, many developing countries are essentially governed not by the state, but by the regulations, values, and norms of society. The state does not have the resources, power, or legitimacy to influence people to any appreciable degree. Instead, people listen to and are influenced by their societies.

This is possible in Africa because of strong societal institutions. In addition to strong families, African *communities* exhibit collective resilience by undertaking many development projects without much assistance from the government. They build schools, health clinics, dams, and other projects. In Kenya, there is a decades-long tradition known as *harambee*, a Swahili word meaning "Let us all pull together." Communities have pooled their limited resources and built hundreds of schools across the country. Despite this incredible effort, local communities are poor and do not have enough resources to purchase the necessary books, materials, and teachers to operate high-quality educational institutions. Moreover, weak governments (or states) are unable to provide sufficient resources to help schools (Bradshaw 1993).

Not surprisingly, a substantial number of nongovernment organizations (NGOs) have provided resources to communities in order to assist their efforts in self-reliance. These NGOs include churches, international relief agencies, charities, and other organizations. Kenya has the largest number of NGOs in Africa: More than 500 of them provide about

40 percent of all social services throughout the country (Bratton 1989; Ndegwa 1996). Although they give substantial resources, it still is not nearly enough to provide all the medicine, books, and other resources required for development. Ideally, there would be a stronger partnership between communities, NGOs, and the national government to create more comprehensive and effective development efforts.

One particularly effective NGO is the Green Belt Movement, a grassroots environmental group in Kenya that fights deforestation by planting trees (Ndegwa 1996). Since its start in 1977, the Green Belt Movement has accumulated 50,000 members in 2,000 communities across the country. Most members are rural women, who have now planted 10 million trees throughout Kenya. The Green Belt Movement and its dynamic leader, Wangari Maathi, have attracted international attention and substantial funding from abroad. In fact, the movement is almost totally dependent on outside funds for financial support. The Kenyan government does not support the movement because Maathi is a vocal critic of its policies. In particular, she has organized protests against government plans to build on large public parks. She has also advocated greater democracy in Kenya and started the Movement for Free and Fair Elections, which provides educational seminars on the value of democracy. Maathi and her organizations have made a real difference in the struggles for a better environment and more democracy in Kenya, struggles that have occurred at the grassroots level.

To summarize, the best aspects of Africa occur at the local level among families, communities, and grassroots organizations. These local-level actors make up part of *civil society*, the part of society that is influenced not by the state, but by communities and civic organizations (for example, the church and other NGOs) operating outside the state. Despite a vibrant civil society, however, Africa is still a very underdeveloped continent that has many problems, perhaps the most important of which is poverty.

The Persistence of Grinding Poverty

Colonialism has come and gone but Africa remains mired in poverty— grinding poverty. African countries consistently are among the poorest in the world. Each year the World Bank ranks all countries in the world from the poorest to the richest. The Bank places all countries into one of four categories—low-income economies, lower-middle-income economies, upper-middle-income economies, and high-income economies. Not surprisingly, the majority of African countries are in the lowest category. In fact, twenty-seven of the poorest forty countries in the world are in Africa. The four poorest countries in the world have an annual per capita income of $80 (Mozambique), $100 (Tanzania), $120 (Ethiopia), and Uganda ($170), respectively (World Bank 1993, 238). How much do you spend *each week?*

Poverty leads to other negative consequences: population growth, bad health, lack of education, poor nutrition, and other factors that result in a poor quality of life. Let's examine these issues by focusing on the quality of life of African children. In June 1993, Kenya's most influential paper ran an urgent editorial describing children's situation as "horrendous" and "extremely bleak." It further noted:

> Today, the continent commemorates Day of the African Child, and honest observers can only say that unless local governments and the international community take deliberate, practical steps to curb poverty and the deterioration of the health and educational infrastructure, the children are truly and firmly candidates for "endangered species." (*Daily Nation* 1993, 6)

After twenty or thirty years of experiencing improved health, African children are now less healthy and dying in larger numbers than just a few years ago. Years of development have been reversed by economic decline, HIV/AIDS, a crumbling infrastructure, government incompetence, and corruption. Children are among the primary victims of this deterioration.

To illustrate this issue, we present the findings of recent research that we conducted in Kenya (Bradshaw, Buchmann, and Mbatia 1994). Although we could write a book specifically on the topic of children's quality of life, we will focus on two issues. First, children are sicker than ever before. For 1989, out of every 1,000 children born in the country, 105 were expected to die before the age of five. And the situation is getting worse. By the end of the 1990s, it is estimated that the figure will rise to 189 children. What is so tragic is that between 1960 and 1989 the under-five mortality rate had been cut in half (Figure 4.1). Thus, nearly three decades of progress is expected to be wiped out in the 1990s (Government of Kenya and UNICEF 1992, 43, 57). Why this reversal of fortunes?

A major cause of this increase is AIDS, which is prevalent in Kenya and other African countries. A newly published report states unequivocally that "AIDS alone threatens to eliminate 30 years of steady progress in reducing child death rates in Kenya" (Government of Kenya and UNICEF 1992, 43). Kenya is not alone, of course. The *World Development Report* shows that other African countries with high levels of HIV infections are also experiencing growing child mortality rates (World Bank 1993). HIV infection makes it easier for Africa's many tropical diseases to attack the

FIGURE 4.1

Number of Kenyan Children Dying Before Age Five per 1,000
Births, 1960, 1989, and 1999

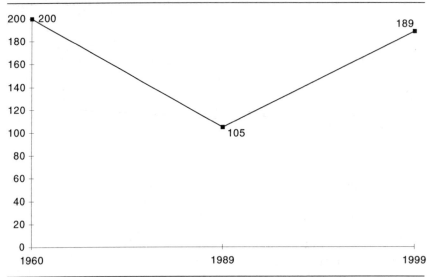

Source: Government of Kenya and UNICEF 1992.

body. The vast majority of child deaths in Kenya are ultimately caused by
one of the following diseases: malaria, acute respiratory infections, diar-
rheal diseases, measles, polio, and tuberculosis. Of course, not every child
who dies from these diseases is infected with HIV. These diseases have
long killed African children, but their toll is heightened when HIV is in the
population.

The second area we want to examine is the incredible growth of home-
lessness and "street children," one of the most tragic events unfolding in
Africa and other underdeveloped regions. In Kenya alone, more than
500,000 children live primarily on the street (Government of Kenya and
UNICEF 1992, 14). Poverty and high birth rates force increasingly more
children onto the street to earn money for their families and themselves.
Moreover, AIDS, war, and other catastrophes have orphaned a growing
number of children, making them responsible for their own survival.
Many children beg for money, steal, or work difficult jobs for very low
wages—or just for a place to live. For example, a growing number of
young boys are "parking boys," who wait on crowded urban streets for
cars to approach. The child (or children) "assists" the driver in pulling into
a parking place and then cleans and guards the car while the driver is

away. He hopes the driver will pay him a tip for his efforts. Young girls often are recruited as "housegirls" (maids), where they work very long hours doing housework and caring for young children. Housegirls seldom have the opportunity to attend school and are paid little or nothing for their labor; they often are given room and food only (Government of Kenya and UNICEF 1992, 112).

One of the most alarming increases in child labor is in prostitution. The Government of Kenya and UNICEF (1992, 132) state candidly:

> Recent surveys reveal that child prostitution is the leading form of child exploitation in Kenya today, particularly in urban centers. The majority of girls are from poor families—abandoned, neglected or orphaned children are exposed to this lifestyle during their problematic young lives.

Although good estimates concerning the number of children engaged in prostitution are not available, there is a consensus that the numbers are growing for at least two reasons: (1) Poverty is a breeding ground for sexual and other forms of exploitation as desperate children and teens sell themselves; and (2) the alarming increase in AIDS has caused men to look for ever-younger sex partners in the belief that they will escape the disease.

It is clear that poverty is one feature that harms quality of life in Africa. Another is ethnic divisions. In the next section, we tell you an amazing story about the incredible effects of ethnicity on society.

Battles for the Body

Five days before Christmas in 1986, a very modern, successful, wealthy trial lawyer, S. M. Otieno, died suddenly of heart failure in Nairobi, Kenya. Although he lived in a poor country, Otieno's lifestyle resembled that of many upper-middle class Westerners: He had a high-paying job, a nice home, televisions, a VCR, and other amenities. He sent his children to school in the United States, an enormously expensive undertaking. No outsider would ever know that Otieno had grown up among the very traditional Luo ethnic group that lives 200 miles from Nairobi. Rural Luos shun modern lifestyles, embrace traditional marriages (with dowries), believe that improper burials will encourage evil spirits to haunt the group, and think that circumcision is disgusting.

But Otieno had long since renounced Luo ways. He refused to follow their customs and rituals, rarely spoke their language, and refused to visit "home" for more than short periods of time. He further infuriated his relatives by marrying across ethnic lines, to a member of the rival Kikuyu group that lives near Nairobi. Some relatives had not spoken to him for more than twenty years because of this action. Otieno considered himself an *individual* (a very Western concept), not a member of an ethnic group. While living, he had declared that he wanted to be buried on his own land according to his own beliefs. After Otieno's death, his wife Wambui honored his request and scheduled his funeral and burial.

This sad but very ordinary event suddenly turned extraordinary, even slightly bizarre. Immediately after Otieno's death, his estranged relatives showed up in Nairobi and declared their intentions to return his body to Luo country for a proper Luo burial. The Luos believed that "once a Luo always a Luo"; moreover, Otieno's spirit might haunt Luo villages and communities if he were not buried in a proper Luo ceremony. Like Otieno's widow, the Luos also scheduled a funeral and dug a grave for him back "home." As Blaine Harden (1990, 95) describes, the "battle for the body" was underway, as both sides filed court injunctions for the corpse. The court canceled both funerals and the body was transferred to a Nairobi morgue and held under twenty-four-hour police guard. Over the next several weeks, Otieno's body became "the twice-embalmed star of a morbid soap opera that seized the imagination of Kenya and much of Africa. The dead lawyer made millions of Africans reexamine just how modern they and their continent had become: Should an African be compelled, in death, to comply with tribal customs he had renounced when he was alive" (96)?

Court proceedings over Otieno's body lasted for three weeks, as witness after witness was called: a Luo spokesperson, Wambui, a philosopher, a traditional healer, a gravedigger, and many others. The courtroom was electric with hatred as both sides sought to discredit, demean, and humiliate the other side. Otieno's son testified that his father considered Luos "lazy" and their customs "primitive" and "uncivilized" (117). A Luo witness used especially sexist language when discounting the "right" of Otieno's widow to select the burial site: "I told you that it is only men who decide on burial sites. Women are told what to do" (119).

In the end, the court was more persuaded by Luo arguments; it ruled that the body should be returned to Luo country because tribal customs are more important than the wishes of an individual. Upon hearing the verdict, thousands of Luos raced to the city morgue to retrieve their newly won prize. Riot police turned away the crowd, but the atmosphere remained virtually uncontrollable.

The case was not yet settled. Otieno's body remained in the morgue while his widow appealed the case. Several months later the court ruled against her and the body was then turned over to the Luos. Five months after he died, Otieno's decaying corpse was buried in Luo territory. But before burial, his corpse was placed on public display, as stipulated by Luo custom. Witnesses reported that the body "did not look good. His face needed a shave and his lips had shrunken away from his teeth. His tongue was hanging out" (127). The battle was over, but nothing lasting was settled. (The story of Otieno is taken from Harden 1990, 95–129; Ojwang and Mugambi 1989; and leading Kenyan newspapers.)

Taken further, Otieno's decaying body symbolizes what is occurring on a larger scale throughout parts of Africa. Consider Rwanda, located in Central Africa. Rwanda is dying, literally. Since April 1994, about half of the country's 7.5 million citizens have either been killed or fled the country. The numbers are almost meaningless at this point: 500,000 to 1 million have been butchered in ethnic fighting within the country and more than 2 million Rwandan refugees have fled to Tanzania, Zaire, Uganda, and Kenya. At least 100,000 of these refugees have died of cholera, dysentery, hunger, or some other disease born of unsanitary conditions or poverty. Up to 100,000 children have lost parents and relatives (either killed or fled), relegating them to the status of orphans on a continent that has few orphanages. The destruction and suffering have been almost indescribable. A missionary in Rwanda lamented, "There are no devils left in Hell. They are all in Rwanda" (Gibbs 1994a, 57). A resident of a refugee camp in neighboring Zaire declared, "This is the beginning of the final days. This is the apocalypse" (Gibbs 1994b, 30). Some Western journalists sent to cover the story were seen weeping openly and asking to be reassigned to a less hellish region. If anyone is looking for a holocaust, they need look no farther than Central Africa.

What caused this incredible disaster? It has a long history dating back to the colonial era. In the nineteenth century, before colonialism, Rwanda and neighboring Burundi had two ethnic groups that coexisted within a feudal structure. The minority *Tutsis* (about 15 percent of the population) were an aristocratic class that provided cattle and protection to the *Hutus* (about 85 percent of the population) in exchange for their services. The relationship between the groups, though unequal, was not openly antagonistic until Belgian colonizers interfered with the situation. The Belgians strongly favored the Tutsi aristocracy and enabled Tutsis to accumulate more power, more services, and more resources at the expense of the Hutus. Ethnic differences gradually developed into ethnic hatreds. In 1959, just before independence, Hutus overthrew the Tutsi monarchy, killing many people (probably thousands) and driving tens of thousands of others into neighboring countries, especially Uganda. The Tutsis tried to regain control in 1963, but the Hutus put down the attempt after more fighting and killing (Ungar 1985). Hutus have remained in control of

Rwanda since independence. They still compose between 85 to 90 percent of the population.

The latest fighting between the two ethnic groups erupted in April 1994, when an airplane carrying Rwanda's Hutu president was mysteriously shot down while he was returning home from a peace mission in Tanzania. Hutus blamed a group of Tutsi rebels, the Rwandan Patriotic Front (RPF), for the assassination. Within minutes, Rwanda became a killing field. The Hutu army and its supporters went on an orgy of killing, directing their hatred primarily at Tutsi civilians. The killing spread, becoming increasingly brutal. People were murdered on the street, in homes, in churches, in hospitals, everywhere. Babies were sliced in half; mothers were knifed, bayoneted, and raped; and men were killed in a similarly brutal fashion. No Tutsi seemed to be immune from the slaughter. Some Hutus were also killed, both by Tutsis and by extreme Hutu factions that resisted all moderation from members of their own ethnic group.

Tutsi rebels continued to fight, amassing substantial strength by the summer. By July 1994, they had chased the Hutu government out of power and then installed two moderate *Hutus* as president and prime minister. The Hutu puppets were supposed to signify a spirit of healing and compromise to Hutus who had fled the country and to the increasingly concerned international community. But, few people, especially Hutus, trusted the new regime. After the Tutsis had taken control of the government, Hutu refugees fled to Zaire because they feared Tutsi reprisals.

In response to the increasingly tense situation, the French sent peacekeeping forces to Rwanda and Zaire to try to ensure peace. They stayed for several months and then left. U.S. military forces were dispatched to distribute clean water and other forms of aid in both Zaire and Rwanda, but they specifically resisted becoming involved in the use of force. They also left after several weeks. The rest of the world, including other African nations, stood by and watched the genocide, doing nothing. African leaders do not want to use scarce resources to settle other people's wars, and they dread entanglement in ethnic conflicts that are all too common across the continent. But Africans' inaction has prompted some in the West to ask, "If Africa won't do anything, why should we?"

Although Rwanda represents an extreme example of conflict in Africa, it is not totally unique. In October 1993, about 100,000 Burundians died in ethnic fighting between (again) the Tutsis and Hutus. The fighting has continued; no one knows how many have died. Hundreds of thousands of other citizens were killed during the 1980s and 1990s in the Sudan, Angola, Mozambique, Liberia, Sierra Leone, South Africa, and other countries. Some of the worst killing occurred in Uganda during the 1970s, when Idi Amin and his army killed 250,000 people (including children), often after horrendous torture (Chirot 1994b).

Beyond mass killing, instability has also reached the highest ranks of African governments. Since achieving independence, African countries have suffered eighty successful coups d'état. Of the thirty-one countries that have experienced successful coups, twenty-two have had more than one coup and six countries have experienced at least five (Griffiths 1993, 80–81, 215). Many of Africa's leaders were trained not in the halls of parliament, but in various military academies across the continent and world. Guns and bullets have dominated the political picture across much of the African continent (Jenkins and Kposowa 1990).

"Presidents for Life," Sort Of

African leaders view political term limits differently than Americans do. With very few exceptions, African heads of state have left office in one of two ways: by natural death (usually at an old age) or by military coup (usually by their own army or a rebel army). The fate of forced-out leaders has varied: Some have been killed, some have been tortured and then killed, some have fled the country, some have been imprisoned, and some have returned to power again—with the help of an army. African presidents have seldom lost elections because they have seldom held real elections. In more than thirty years, only two incumbent presidents have lost competitive elections in independent Africa—Kenneth Kaunda in Zambia and Hastings Banda in Malawi. (Banda, who believed he was appointed by God to rule, called himself "President for Life." Many other leaders have also used the term. Most have been overthrown.) Only two long-standing African leaders have voluntarily retired from office—Julius Nyerere in Tanzania and Leopold Senghor in Senegal.

Africa has had its share of long-term leaders. If the continent had a "decade in power" club, it would be an interesting collection of people. The chairperson would be Mobutu Sese Seko, who has ruled Zaire for three decades. He has stolen billions of dollars from his country, depositing this fortune in European bank accounts. (It is estimated that Mobutu is worth $5 billion.) Moreover, he has systematically cut telephone lines and other communications facilities throughout his desperately poor country to prevent people from mobilizing against him (French 1995a). The vice chairperson would be Daniel arap Moi, Kenya's leader for nearly twenty years. Moi also is one of Africa's biggest kleptomaniacs, stealing his country's money and enriching himself. He has billions of dollars of real estate in Kenya and in foreign bank accounts. Two other members of the club would be Lt. Jerry Rawlings of Ghana and Robert Mugabe of Zimbabwe, both of whom have now governed for about fifteen years. Although neither has championed democracy, neither has been nearly as destructive as Mobutu and Moi.

Honorary members of the "decade in power" club would be Kenneth Kaunda and Hastings Banda, both of whom ruled for nearly thirty years before their defeat, and Julius Nyerere and Leopold Senghor, both of whom ruled more than twenty years before retiring. None of these men would be popular members of the club. Two were "foolish" enough to hold free and fair elections, and two set a historic example by retiring from office. Current presidents would rather follow the example of Felix Houphouet-Boigny of the Côte d'Ivoire (Ivory Coast). He led his country for more than thirty years before dying recently at about age 90 (no one is really sure of his age).

It is hard to describe a long-term African leader. Blaine Harden (1990, 217) humorously attempts such a description:

> His face is on the money. His photograph hangs in every office in his realm. His ministers wear gold pins with tiny photographs of Him on the lapels of their tailored pin-striped suits. He names streets, football stadiums, hospitals, and universities after himself. He carries a silver-inlaid ivory mace or an ornately carved walking stick or a fly whisk or a chiefly stool. He insists on being called "doctor" or "conqueror" or "teacher" or "the big elephant" or "the number-one peasant" or the "wise old man" or the "national miracle" or "the most popular leader in the world." . . . He bans all political parties except the one he controls. He rigs elections. He emasculates the courts. He cows the press. He stifles academia. He goes to church.

This description may seem harsh, even derogatory. But it underscores how incompetent and horribly destructive some African leaders have been through the years. They have slowed development, repressed democracy, and tortured and killed opponents. Importantly, though, our comments about long-term leaders should be qualified in three ways. First, the leaders of Africa are not representative of the *people* of Africa. The African people deserve far better than their leaders. Many African *societies* (not governments) have a strong history of democracy. Traditional African villages are models of democracy, with village elders sitting around and talking about each issue until a consensus is reached. Communities, churches, and other nongovernment organizations in Africa are putting great pressure on African governments for democracy (Ndegwa 1996). They are assisted by outside organizations and governments, which also put political and economic pressure on African states for democracy. For instance, some organizations and governments are withholding foreign aid from governments that do not consent to democratic elections.

Second, the West is partly to blame for long-term African leaders. Colonial powers introduced new political systems that were foreign to African countries. When the colonialists left, power-hungry African leaders took advantage of the political vacuum and assumed power, often through the use of force. Moreover, Western governments have continued to provide foreign aid to some corrupt African governments. For instance, the United States and France have consistently given aid to Zaire and then "looked the other way" because Mobutu is a strong military ally. Moreover, the United States has also given substantial foreign aid to Kenya because Moi allows the United States to use strategic military bases along the Indian Ocean. These bases might be important if the United States became involved in a conflict in the "Middle East."

Third, despite the destructive leadership in many African countries, there are some hopeful trends on the continent. Today, more multiparty democracies exist across Africa than ever before, primarily because several countries have held elections in the last six years. Eleven African nations now have democratic governments—fifteen if you count four island countries off the continent (*Africa Demos* 1994). Although a few democracies were created by the defeat or retirement of long-standing leaders (discussed earlier), others emerged when entire systems were changed to allow competitive democratic elections. If the new democratic systems are sustained, it means that more African leaders will win and lose elections in the near future. Several other countries are making the transition to democracy, but it is unclear whether they will succeed.

A very positive development is in the Republic of South Africa, which held historic presidential elections in 1994. Nelson Mandela, the winner, was the first black person allowed to run for president of the country, despite the fact that 74 percent of its population is black. South Africa's system of apartheid (separateness) had excluded black citizens from voting or otherwise participating in the nation's government. Moreover, the black majority population was forced to live in horrible slums (called townships) that have poor schools, deplorable health facilities, and extensive unemployment and hopelessness. Although South Africa still has sprawling townships and a black unemployment rate of 45 percent, it also has new hope in Mandela's government. Mandela is considered a true hero in South Africa and beyond, partly because he spent twenty-seven years in a South African prison for opposing apartheid. Released in 1990, he immediately moved to transform South Africa into a democratic system where *all* citizens can vote. Despite spending almost three decades in prison, Mandela has remained extremely conciliatory and gracious toward all people, assuring whites that they are needed and welcome in the new South Africa.

Experts are divided over the prospects for sustained democracy in South Africa. On the one hand, South Africa has the most developed economic infrastructure on the continent: good roads, modern cities, substantial natural resources (including much of the world's gold supply), and extensive foreign investment. It also has a modern police force, a well-armed military (with nuclear technology), and a disciplined government. On the other hand, South African democracy is new and fragile, and it faces a daunting task: creating development for the majority black population. This means finding resources to create jobs and to build schools, houses, sanitation facilities, health clinics, and hope in depressed townships. It also means dealing with a small, but radical, white extremist group that wants an armed war with blacks. And it means soothing nervous foreign investors, who are concerned about the country's growing crime rate and the relatively high taxes levied on corporations (Wells 1995). But one thing is for sure: If South Africa can make a successful transition to democracy and development, it will be a historical moment that would set an example for the continent.

Two other bright spots on the continent are also in southern Africa: Botswana and Namibia. Both have democratic governments, small populations, abundant natural resources (especially diamonds), and growing economies. Moreover, neither faces the challenge of overcoming an apartheid regime. To lure more foreign investment, Botswana and Namibia have recently lowered their tax rates and offered other incentives to multinational corporations. Such incentives may encourage a few foreign investors to put their money in Botswana and Namibia, instead of in the much larger South Africa (Wells 1995). World-system theorists claim that this emphasis on attracting foreign investment will make southern Africa increasingly dependent on the West. However, until African countries develop more *domestic businesses,* they will have to rely on foreign investment and aid or have little money for development.

Many African countries are much worse off than Botswana, Namibia, and South Africa. Such countries do not have the infrastructure and capital base to even begin to launch full-scale development efforts. This fact does not auger well for the future of African democracy because virtually no country on earth has ever sustained a democratic regime in times of extreme economic crisis (Rueschemeyer 1991). Democratic governments must establish legitimacy among their citizens; that is, citizens must believe that their government is really helping them. When economies are as bad as those in Africa today, governments are unable to distribute resources for education, health, agricultural development, road construction, food programs, and other programs that help people. Democracy is a great idea, but it may not be possible until the continent experiences economic growth.

Extreme ethnic diversity also makes democracy difficult in Africa, as it does elsewhere. People tend to vote along ethnic lines, and ethnic conflict has produced some of the most brutal incidents in Africa, as well as in other areas of the world. However, not all African countries (even those with ethnic diversity) are racked by ethnic tension. For instance, Zambia has little ethnic conflict and a high rate of marriage across ethnic groups, something that is rare in many African countries. But there is a reason for this situation. Outside of South Africa, Zambia is the most urbanized country in Africa (Table 4.1), primarily because the country's economy has been based largely on the mining of copper. The "copper belt" consists of many towns and small cities that recruit workers from all over the country. Thus, different ethnic groups have lived and worked together for years, enhancing relations between such groups. It is no wonder that Zambia is now considered one of the most democratic countries on the African continent, even though its economy is in terrible shape and may make democracy difficult to sustain.

Becoming Irrelevant to Others

It hurts when others consider you irrelevant. The West has considered Africa irrelevant for most of recorded history. Only a few African countries receive much private foreign investment, and one reason is that the continent is hopelessly in debt. African countries have borrowed billions of dollars over the last twenty years. African governments, foreign governments, and international financial institutions were once relatively optimistic about the future of African development. Thus, foreign governments and institutions loaned money to Africa, and African governments happily accepted the new capital.

But things fell apart in the 1980s when a global recession, more wars, continued population growth, and government ineptitude all combined to slow economic growth in Africa. The result was the beginning of an economic disaster for Africa: growing foreign debts and less ability to pay them off. Think of it this way: You graduate from college and get a well-paying job. Like many successful college graduates, you are so optimistic about the future that you take out a thirty-year mortgage (loan) for $100,000 to buy a house. You can handle the *monthly* payments to the bank of about $800, but it requires some sacrifices. Suddenly, however, the national economy turns sour and your company lays you off with little notice. You have to accept a job that pays you half your current salary. The problem, of course, is that you still owe that bank a lot of money, and now you don't earn enough to make even your monthly payments. You have a serious debt problem.

Africa's debt problem is extremely serious. Figure 4.2 shows the increasing debt in Africa compared to other world regions. Incredibly, Africa's collective foreign debt is now larger than the total economic output of the continent, measured by GNP. (Economic output and foreign debt are equivalent when foreign debt is 100 percent of GNP.) Mozambique's debt is almost four times its GNP; Tanzania's, Somalia's, and Zambia's debts are almost three times their respective GNPs; and numerous other countries have debts that are one or two times their GNPs (World Bank 1994). Let's go back to our analogy. If you were in Mozambique's position, you might have a debt of nearly $100,000 even though your combined assets are $30,000. You would not even be able to pay the

FIGURE 4.2

Debt Burden: Total Debt as Percentage of GNP, 1980–1992

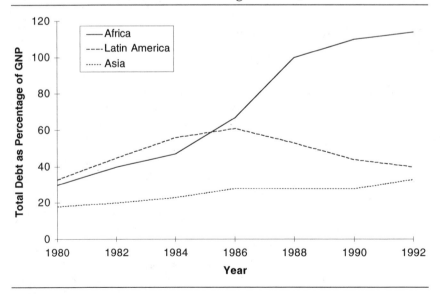

Source: UNICEF 1994a.

interest on your debt, just like most African countries. International lenders simply cannot take Africa seriously from an economic standpoint when it has such large debts, such economic deterioration, and such poor prospects for the future. Africa is being increasingly written off by private investors and even by Western governments and other financial institutions. There is no way that Africa will repay even a portion of its debt in the near future, and probably not ever.

Foreign debt is especially harmful to the poorest citizens of Africa when their governments implement structural adjustment policies (SAPs). These policies cut government spending on food, health services, social services, and education, thereby saving money that is allocated to debt repayment (Buchmann 1996). But SAPs also exact a heavy toll on the poorest citizens of Africa, who depend on government services for some of the most basic necessities of life. UNICEF has bitterly opposed SAPs, asserting that "hundreds of thousands of the developing world's children have given their lives to pay their countries' debts, and many millions more are still paying the interest with their malnourished bodies" (UNICEF 1990, 30). UNICEF and others have called for "adjustment with a human face," meaning that any adjustments should be done gradually and without eliminating programs for the most needy citizens (Cornia, Jolly, and Stewart 1987).

This call has been largely ignored, however, because international banks and foreign governments strongly favor SAPs in an effort to recover some of their loan money. When African governments implement a strict package of SAPs, banks and foreign governments are sometimes willing to loan them additional money or forgive some outstanding debts. According to world-system theorists, international pressure to continue SAPs is another form of exploitation. Poor countries can gain access to more money only when they comply with the wishes of global banks and core governments. To be fair, however, international banks point out that they are not charitable institutions. Accordingly, banks make loans only to good credit risks, and African countries will not fit into this category until they implement SAPs to get their houses in order. (What do you think?)

The economic news in Africa is not all bad, however. A positive sign concerning private investment comes from inside Africa. South Africa, with a strong infrastructure and new democracy, is becoming the economic leader of the continent. South African companies are investing all over Africa: digging mines, building hotels, constructing railways, setting up telecommunications facilities, and selling airplanes. Imports and exports between South Africa and the rest of Africa are booming. From 1993 to 1995, South Africa's exports to the rest of Africa rose 50 percent to $2.5 billion, and imports from other African countries rose 300 percent to $664 million (French 1995b). As investors from Europe and the United States pull out of Africa, South Africa moves in. If the continent had four or five South Africas, then Africa might be able to stimulate its own growth, as in Asia (next chapter).

Beyond economic problems, political problems also make Africa increasingly irrelevant to outsiders. Wars, slow democratization, and other obstacles discourage international interest in Africa. Still, there are times when the international community has become involved in the continent, if only briefly. In 1992, the international community (led by the United Nations and United States) dispatched soldiers to Somalia to stop a civil war so that food could be distributed to starving citizens. The mission was very successful at first: People were fed and armed factions stopped their fighting. After several months, however, conflicts between foreign soldiers and Somali fighters led to the deaths of Somali civilians and soldiers on all sides. One dead American soldier was dragged naked through the streets of Somalia in full view of television cameras. This horrendous scene had its impact on viewers in the West. The United States subsequently pulled out of Somalia and, since then, American citizens and the American government have shied away from intervention in Africa and other parts of the world. As we noted earlier, the United States and other countries did send troops to slow the holocaust in Rwanda, but they did not stay long because, in part, they feared "another Somalia." Unfortunately, the only hope for stopping some brutal internal conflicts lies with the international community.

Political fragmentation, especially when accompanied by ethnic conflict and economic underdevelopment, leads to a terrible dilemma. On the one hand, the conflict-ridden areas of Africa lack the resources, stability, and legitimacy to prevent the bloodshed that threatens the region. There currently is no government in Somalia and the governments of Rwanda and Burundi are shaky, at best. Certainly, not all African governments are unstable, but there are several hotspots that could erupt and endanger the lives of many people. If the international community does not become involved in stopping some of these conflicts, thousands of people will die. On the other hand, becoming involved is a no-win situation. Involvement reminds Africans of the colonial era, when white Europeans invaded the continent. Most Africans *do* favor outside intervention when the political situation becomes desperate, but they want outsiders to just keep the peace and not try to establish governments. It is a tall order to ask outsiders to become involved at all, however, since much of Africa is not considered a region of strategic importance to the West.

Reduced to Symbols

One of the saddest aspects of contemporary Africa is that it is being reduced to a symbolic presence on the world stage. Let's consider two areas: government and education. We can examine governments from several levels. On the global level, African governments are not taken seriously by most international bodies. They lack resources and are perceived as ineffective, corrupt, and undemocratic. Importantly, though, African governments do retain the international symbols accorded to any government in the world: They have seats at the United Nations, they have embassies around the world, and they visit other world leaders. But symbols of power and leadership are not necessarily translated into reality.

At the regional level, African governments seldom cooperate with each other in an effort to mobilize scarce resources. Statesmanship is largely absent in Africa. The Organization of African Unity (OAU) comprises every African country. It meets once a year to discuss how the continent can better cooperate on critical issues. But the OAU is merely a symbol of the unity that is desired, not realized. Each member country is supposed to pay dues to the OAU, but the organization is owed millions of dollars by delinquent countries. Moreover, OAU meetings are characterized by squabbles, long-winded speeches, and not much else.

At the national and local levels, African governments are still largely symbolic. Yes, they have military forces, police forces, expensive cars, palaces, and parliaments; but they are unable to mobilize development to any appreciable degree. As we discussed earlier, African states are weak precisely because they are unable (or unwilling) to lead their countries toward development. A government cannot achieve legitimacy unless its citizens believe that it is effectively working for their interests. Many African governments are merely ineffective symbols of what should be, not what is.

Another area in which Africa has been reduced to symbols is education. Almost all studies show that education raises incomes and improves quality of life (Buchmann 1996). Not surprisingly, therefore, virtually every country in the world officially endorses the value of education. In an excellent book, Bruce Fuller (1991) argues that African citizens and governments consider education a true symbol of modernity and Westernization. Many African families have sacrificed greatly to enable their children to attend primary and then secondary schools, which are not free in many countries. But something has gone terribly wrong. Despite the desire for education across the continent, governments and other organizations are unable to maintain schools, buy books, and train teachers for a quality educational system. One of the most disturbing facts across Africa is the deplorable state of most schools. They often lack even the most basic materials such as chalk, desks, and adequate space, not to mention books. Although education still symbolizes progress, this symbol is beginning to lose its power as many parents realize that an education does not guarantee their child a better way of life.

The situation is even worse at the university level. During the 1960s and part of the 1970s, Africa had a number of extremely good universities: nice buildings, excellent students and faculty, and adequate books and materials. These universities were more than just symbols of progress and development; they were true institutions of higher learning. But the situation changed during the 1970s in two important ways. First, the continent's foreign debt started increasing and its economic decline grew more serious, resulting in fewer resources for educational purposes. Second, African universities became increasingly political. The president of the *country* became the chancellor of each university within a country. Universities became simply extensions of the political system, not institutions of higher learning. Today, faculty and students dare not offend the government. Moreover, some governments pay students to act as informants of antigovernment behavior on the part of fellow students and faculty.

African presidents are far more interested in keeping universities quiet than they are in creating an environment conducive to teaching and learning. But the universities often are not quiet. Students (and sympathetic nonstudents) often demonstrate and riot on university grounds over government policy. The government usually responds by dispatching riot police to the university to "restore order" and beat up a few students. If things do not quiet down quickly, the universities are closed for substantial periods of time. Some universities have been closed for months and even years at a time, totally disrupting higher education. This type of climate has caused many excellent professors to leave the university and take jobs outside of academia and in other countries. It has also destroyed African universities. Yes, the universities have all the symbols of higher education: buildings, libraries, and students. Unfortunately, however, the buildings are falling apart, the libraries have few books, and the students are taught by largely unqualified faculty. Moreover, the university climate is not enjoyable, comfortable, and conducive to learning, as everyone seeks to avoid offending paranoid governments. It is a very disturbing situation.

Let us tell you a story that illustrates many of these points. One author of this book, York Bradshaw, has taught at several African universities since the 1980s. Two years ago while teaching at a once-prominent east African university, he had an appointment to meet with the vice chancellor of the university over several issues. (The vice chancellor is the acting head of the university; the chancellor, remember, is the president of the country.) The visitor waited outside the vice chancellor's office in a room that displayed a wall-sized photograph of the president of the country presiding over graduation at the university. Entering the vice chancellor's office, the visitor couldn't help noticing the five telephones on his desk. Remembering the dead telephone lines that adorned most other university offices, the visitor chuckled to himself, "Even the boss can't find a working phone." But one thing is no laughing matter: Rest assured that one of those phones was working and carried a direct line to the president. The president could expel a student, fire a faculty member, shut down a department, close the university, or change any aspect of university policy with a phone call. Leaving the vice chancellor's office thirty minutes later, the visitor walked passed the vice chancellor's government-supplied Mercedes-Benz and a student elevator that had not worked since the 1970s, much like the university itself.

Classes were canceled the very next day. Students were rioting over an increase in educational costs. They demanded to see the vice chancellor and, much to everyone's surprise, he appeared in an open courtyard to address the students. The visiting faculty member watched the proceedings from his office with several graduate students, who looked out the window and then back at their foreign professor: "You know professor, that is a very nervous man down there. He only has one chance to calm those students." If he could not calm them, they would carry their riots outside the university into the city center. This would draw national and perhaps international news coverage, symbolizing the breakdown of African universities and society. Such coverage might also cause one of those five telephones to ring. Vice chancellors are not exempt from the chancellor's wrath; they too can lose their jobs on a moment's notice. Maintaining symbols is a high-stakes business, and certainly a full-time job.

In conclusion, symbols can be powerful. Think of the power of symbols in your own life: the flag, the Cross, the Star of David, the Crescent, a ring, and numerous rituals. Symbols are deeply meaningful when they represent something real, moving, and dynamic. Governments without legitimacy and educational institutions that are ineffective constitute empty symbols, and are not worth much to most citizens.

Africa in Theoretical Perspective

Contemporary Africa is a difficult region to explain. World-system theory is a good place to start. The colonial era exploited the raw materials and cheap labor of Africa, helping to underdevelop the continent. As we saw in Rwanda, colonizers also interfered with African forms of governance and exacerbated ethnic differences that later erupted into horrific violence. After independence, multinational corporations in a few countries continued to extract raw materials from the continent and to employ cheap labor on plantations, in mines, and in factories. And now international banks and foreign governments insist on the implementation of SAPs, which worsen the quality of life for many Africans. But world-system theory has a difficult time explaining many of the internal dynamics of Africa, including its resilient civil society, fledgling democracies, deteriorating institutions, and other issues. World-system theory attributes everything to external factors, but this explanation is too simplistic for Africa.

Modernization theory can help us understand some of the internal dynamics of African countries, but not all of them. On balance, these countries lack functioning schools, political institutions, and health services. They also lag far behind the rest of the world in scientific knowledge, computer technology, and overall technological innovation, all of which are crucial factors to modernization theory. But modernization theory does not capture some of the traditional internal dynamics that have facilitated development in many African societies. Civil society and nongovernment organizations have built schools, health clinics, and dams; they have also planted food, immunized villages against disease, and employed street children. Civil society and NGOs, which may not be considered modern institutions by modernization theorists, are the backbone of African development.

Analyzing Africa theoretically requires us to look at the interaction among external and internal factors. You can take many issues discussed in the chapter and think about how external *and* internal factors affect them. For example, African institutions are pressuring their governments for greater democracy. They are joined by international aid agencies and Western governments, some of which have withdrawn aid (or threatened to withdraw aid) if democracy is stifled. It is doubtful that only internal pressure or only external pressure would be sufficient to encourage democracy in Africa. Pressure for democracy also demonstrates the importance of interaction among actors at different levels of analysis: Global actors (international organizations) and local actors (communities, churches, and NGOs) place pressure on national actors (African governments) to democratize.

Theoretical treatments of Africa should also consider the omnipresent issue of ethnicity, especially as it interacts with other factors. Ethnicity is at the root of much of Africa's misery (for example, civil wars) and becomes especially prominent under conditions of extreme poverty. People tend to fight over scarce resources in any society and, in African societies, the fight often is between ethnic groups. The situation is exacerbated by politics. Politicians usually favor their own ethnic groups, giving them additional money for more social services, roads, and other infrastructure. In Kenya, for instance, a visitor might wonder why roads leading from Nairobi to western Kenya are outstanding, whereas roads heading north out of the city are not so good. A major reason is because President Moi's home area is in western Kenya and the region north of Nairobi opposes Moi every chance it gets.

If African societies had broader economic development and less poverty, it is possible that ethnicity would become a less significant force. One scholar of Africa, for instance, argues that African development will occur only after internal market forces are strong enough to overcome the continent's "economy of affection" (Hyden 1983; Hyden and Peters, 1991). The *economy of affection* is his term for the fact that ethnicity and other forms of kinship drive African economies and society. One does not get a job or succeed because of his or her talents, but because of whom he or she knows in particular ethnic groups. However, with more money and more businesses throughout the continent, people might become more independent and therefore less tied to their ethnic identity.

In concluding, we can also draw on theory to help think about possible solutions to African underdevelopment. We certainly don't have any definite answers to the continent's problems. But we can introduce some ideas that you might consider when developing your own ideas on this issue. First, many experts continue to argue that development must come from within the continent, especially from local-level actors in villages, churches, and other NGOs. African citizens have worked incredibly hard to develop their societies. Importantly, though, they do not have enough money, resources, or technology to finish some projects, such as supplying hospitals with medicine. This means that local-level actors must do without these resources or attempt to find other actors to assist them.

Assistance might come from the international community. Many people are now calling for the international community to bypass African governments and give money directly to development programs at the local level. For instance, Wangari Maathi's Green Belt Movement has received substantial funding from foreign donors. This situation is unusual, however, because women's groups normally receive little funding from foreign or domestic sources, despite the fact that women grow much of Africa's food and are actively involved in many development projects. Most international aid to Africa currently goes to African *governments*, which then use or misuse aid as they deem appropriate. Billions of dollars have been wasted in this manner. Of course, you can also imagine why

African governments would object if foreign aid bypassed them and went directly to local actors. Governments would lose the power to reward, punish, or manipulate their citizens under this arrangement. Moreover, many Western governments like to give money directly to Third World governments for the same reason—to reward, punish, or manipulate them. Politics and assistance often are connected, a relationship that seldom maximizes development opportunities for ordinary citizens in Africa.

Beyond local-level dynamics, regional factors are also important to consider. Shortly after independence, idealistic leaders across Africa started talking about regional solutions to underdevelopment. African countries would pool their resources, share technology, trade with each other, and resist exploitation by the developed world. These plans sounded good, but they disintegrated because of poverty, wars, coups d'état, and general disagreements. Moreover, the Organization of African Unity embodies these negative features and seems unable to bind the continent together in a successful regional effort.

Africa is now revisiting the possibility of a regional solution to its underdevelopment. The international community is turning its attention toward the booming markets of Asia and Latin America and the potential markets of Eastern Europe. Foreign investment and aid from the West are increasingly channeled to other regions, not that Africa ever received that much in the first place. However, without regional solutions, most of Africa will have even fewer resources than before. Thus, South Africa's new business alliances with African countries might represent the start of several regional economic efforts across the continent. The problem, of course, is that there are few African economies as strong as that of South Africa, meaning that regional efforts may go only so far. Nonetheless, these alliances are a start and, with time, may result in more development and less dependence on the West.

Finally, international banks and governments may need to consider assisting Africa in reducing its incredible debt. Why, you might ask? Africa borrowed a lot of money and it should repay in full! This is true at one level, but it may be shortsighted from a global perspective. Because it must allocate some of its money for debt repayment, an indebted continent cannot invest in itself and it cannot buy as many products on the world market. Thus, it is in every region's interest to reduce debt in Africa. One proposal calls for debt forgiveness, of either part or all of the debt, in exchange for political and economic reforms in Africa. For instance, a government requesting debt forgiveness might be forced to make some economic reforms or to call democratic elections or to reduce deforestation. The logic is: Africa can't pay all of its debt anyway, so why not cancel some of the debt and create positive changes in the process. President Clinton has called for partial debt forgiveness of Africa and several Scandinavian countries have called for total debt forgiveness. (What do you think?)

In our frequent travels around Africa, we are often told by Africans, "Development will take time." It is a very reasonable statement. Many of these countries are only thirty years old—less than a decade older than many readers of this book. It takes time to build democracy and construct development plans. Still, the first thirty years have produced meager results—there may not be time for more false starts.

MAP 5.1

5

Asia: An Emerging Giant

Bats, Balls, and Whips

Baseball was invented in America and is considered a uniquely American game. But baseball is also popular in some other countries, including Japan, where large crowds enthusiastically follow the Hiroshima Carp, the Yomiuri Giants, the Yakult Swallows, the Taiyo Whales, the Nippon Ham Fighters (owned by a pork producer), and other teams. A handful of American players have joined Japanese teams in recent years, expecting to find the familiar rules and rhythms that guide American baseball. Yes, there are nine players on a team, nine innings to a game, and a Japan Series in October to crown a national baseball champion. At the same time, however, there are profound differences between American baseball and Japanese *besuboru*, differences that transcend sports and reflect deep cultural differences between the two societies (Whiting 1990).

Let's look at two differences. First, Japanese baseball is most concerned with group harmony, or *wa*, a characteristic that permeates every aspect of Japanese society. For example, few Japanese players demand exorbitant contracts because it would show that the player is placing his own interests above those of the team. Few players throw temper tantrums, fire "beanballs" at opponents, fight, complain, pout, or do anything else that draws attention to themselves or upsets team wa. One Japanese player who did violate this code of behavior was Takashi Nishimoto, who openly ignored his coach's instructions one day, a gross violation of the discipline and respect for authority that accompany harmony. It was unacceptable and called for drastic action on the part of the coach, who promptly punched Nishimoto between the eyes. Nishimoto was then forced to apologize and pay a substantial fine for insubordination (Whiting 1990, 71–72). The cultural lesson was learned well: The errant individual was returned to the group and wa was restored.

By contrast, American baseball players are not shy about holding out for more money, even if it creates tremendous salary inequality on the team. Moreover, American baseball fans have seen their share of arguments, fights, whining, and complaining on (and sometimes off) the field of play. Yes, American players are a team, but they also are individuals who look out for their own interests. One of the biggest authorities on Japanese baseball, Robert Whiting (1990, 70), notes the essential societal differences that are reflected in the two nations' games: "While 'Let It All Hang Out' and 'Do Your Own Thing' are mottoes of contemporary American society, the Japanese have their own credo in the well-worn proverb, 'The Nail That Sticks Up Shall Be Hammered Down.' It is practically a national slogan."

A second major difference between Japanese and American baseball is that the former allows ties. No extra innings are allowed after four hours or twelve innings of play (fifteen innings in a second Japanese league). The game is officially declared a tie at this point. Several American players in Japan have complained that their teams occasionally play for ties when approaching the time limit. American Rick Lancelotti, who played for the Hiroshima Carp, was frustrated when he described the following situation for the PBS television documentary "American Game, Japanese Rules": The game was tied and approaching the time limit; the bases were loaded, and his team allowed one of its worst hitters to bat instead of substituting a better hitter for him. The player struck out, the game ended, and everybody went home happy!

Happy with a tie? Yes, because above all else the Japanese value harmony, conformity, and teamwork. If the teams play hard and the game ends in a tie (or is a close game), then both teams can go home without "losing face." The key is that each team must put forth its absolute best effort, or *doryoku*, in every game (Whiting 1990, 60–61). Teams do try to win, but a hard-fought tie is also fine because it combines two of the most important elements of Japanese society: doryoku and wa, effort and harmony. By contrast, the American emphasis is on winning, with little appreciation for ties. When American baseball players are interviewed, they might well mention the words *win* and *effort*, but seldom the word *harmony*.

Japan's emphasis on harmony is not unique in Asia. Consider an example from Singapore. In October 1993, an 18-year-old American named Michael Fay was arrested in that country for vandalism. He confessed to being part of a group that spray-painted eighteen cars and threw eggs at other cars. It was his first brush with the law. Fay later recanted his confession and claimed that it was coerced during nine days of brutal interrogation. Singaporean officials rejected his recantation and sentenced him to four months in prison, a $2,230 fine, and, most severe of all, six lashes with a half-inch-thick rattan cane moistened in water. The lashes are delivered across the bare buttocks and leave permanent scars. Many people report that the pain is so excruciating that the offender can lose consciousness after just a few strokes. If this occurs, the punishment is suspended briefly so that the offender can be revived to receive the full benefit of *his* punishment (it is illegal to cane women or older men in Singapore).

Fay was lucky in one sense. Because President Clinton appealed on behalf of this American, Fay was lashed only four times before being expelled from the country forever. Clinton argued that caning is a barbaric form of punishment and asked that the discipline be suspended. (Many international human rights organizations agree with Clinton and consider caning an act of torture.) The government of Singapore refused to back down completely, however, arguing that tough laws keep the country orderly and relatively crime free. Indeed, Singapore does have a very low crime rate.

The case of Michael Fay can be used to draw three simple contrasts between Asian societies and American society. First, Asian societies stress the collective good over individual rights and pursuits. Severe punishment, few opportunities for appeals, and limited discussion of the *individual* clearly place an emphasis on collective responsibility. In 1994, an estimated 1,000 people were caned in Singapore and 76 were hanged, double the number of executions relative to the United States, which has a population eighty times larger than Singapore (Kamm 1995). The basic message from Singapore is this: So what if guilty people are caned, executed swiftly, or locked up for long sentences in tough prisons? It sends a strong message to the greater society and produces one of the safest countries on earth. By contrast, American society emphasizes the individual over the collective society. In the American legal system, an individual is presumed innocent until proven guilty by society. In Asian legal systems, an individual must "prove" her or his innocence upon being charged with a crime by society. (Interestingly, polls taken in the United States during the Fay incident showed that a majority of people supported his caning. This reflects the deep frustration that many Americans feel over crime in their own country.)

Second, Asian societies stress self-discipline and control. Again, in order for the collective good to be emphasized, people must subjugate their personal wishes and desires to those of the larger society. This emphasis begins early in life. In Japanese schools, students are taught to follow rules, obey elders, and avoid situations that can lead to "trouble." School officials keep close track of students. For example, they scrutinize junior high "romances" and often inform parents so they can monitor the couple. And, graffiti and vandalism are seldom problems because students, not janitors, clean the schools. Why make a mess when you are going to have to clean it up (Kristof 1995a)?

Third, Asian societies transfer individual values and beliefs to their economic systems, which also embody strong discipline and a collective spirit. Teamwork, savings, and long work hours, combined with a changing global economy (see later), have helped to produce some remarkable economic achievements throughout Asia. In fact, the rate of economic growth in many Asian countries has been two to three times greater than in the United States over the last decade (World Bank 1995a, b). Asian countries are major world exporters in electronics, computers, clothes, and many other products. Let's think about Singapore again. This tiny country is about $3\frac{1}{2}$ times the size of the District of Columbia and contains only 3 million people (the same population as Oregon), yet it is the world's leading exporter of disc drives, has the world's biggest container port, and is the world's third largest oil-refining center (Naisbitt 1994, 252).

Overall, Asia is a booming economic region, in contrast to some other regions of the world such as Africa and Europe. Asia's economic growth will lead the world into the next century. Of course, the region will also face significant challenges that are not solved by economic development alone.

Magic Dragons?

The dragon has long been a symbol of power in East Asia. Ezra Vogel (1991, 1) writes:

> Traditionally Asia's dragon throne was in China, but in the first part of the twentieth century Japan, by developing a superior industrial base, replaced China as Asia's leading power. In the first decade after its defeat in World War II, Japan resumed its industrialization, progressing at a pace the world had never seen. Over the next three decades, four nearby little dragons— Taiwan, South Korea, Hong Kong, and Singapore—modernized even more quickly.

Indeed, the word *miracle* has been used repeatedly to explain the economic growth of Japan and the four little dragons. And, although miracle may be too strong to describe the recent economic expansion of China, Vietnam, and other Asian countries, it is clear that Asia is on the move. The approaching twenty-first century may well be the Asian century.

But how should we go about studying Asia? It is the largest continent in the world and a land of many countries, cultures, languages, religions, and economic and political systems. In addition to the countries already mentioned, Asia includes part of the former Soviet Union, as well as Mongolia, Indonesia, Thailand, Malaysia, India, Pakistan, the Philippines, Cambodia, Afghanistan, Iran, and several other countries (Map 5.1). In this chapter, we focus primarily on seven countries: Japan, South Korea, Singapore, Taiwan, Hong Kong, China, and Vietnam. Japan is the quintessential Asian success story, the next four are the booming "four little dragons," and the last two are awakening economic giants. Despite the differences shown in Table 5.1, the countries have two common features: market-driven economies and a group-oriented approach to economics and society.

Asia used to be considered a poor region that could only make cheap products of inferior quality for the lower end of the market in the United States and other developed countries. Many middle-aged Americans remember the slogan "Made in Japan" as a sign of poor quality. Not any more. Today, Japan and other Asian countries are world leaders in producing high-quality products such as automobiles, electronics, and clothing. And, although the Japanese like Western products, they are now sometimes wary of goods "Made in America" because these goods are thought to be of inferior quality.

It is no coincidence that Asia's economic success coincides with a trend in regional cooperation. Although there are some formal trade agreements—such as the Asia-Pacific Economic Cooperation (APEC) forum—a real key to Asian development concerns unofficial cooperative practices that encourage trade and economic investment among Asian countries. A few decades ago, Asian countries did not have the wealth or technology

TABLE 5.1

Descriptive Data for Selected Asian Countries, 1992–1993

Country	Population	GNP per Capita	Under-Five Mortality	Dominant Ethnic Group	
Japan	124.5 million	$31,450	6	Japanese	(99%)
Singapore	2.8 million	$19,310	7	Chinese	(76%)
Hong Kong	5.8 million	$17,860	7	Chinese	(98%)
Taiwan	20.7 million	$10,566	6	Taiwanese	(84%)
South Korea	43.7 million	$7,670	9	Korean	(99%)
China	1,162.2 million	$490	43	Chinese	(93%)
Vietnam	69.3 million	$170	49	Vietnamese	(87%)

Sources: World Bank 1994, 1995a, b; UNICEF 1995; Wright 1995.

to buy and sell to each other, which would have helped to develop the region. Times have changed. Although the United States is still Asia's largest export market (by far), the trend is clearly for Asian countries to trade and invest in Asia. For instance, the four little dragons now account for 35 percent of all foreign investment in the next tier of dragons: Malaysia, Thailand, Indonesia, and the Philippines (Naisbitt 1994, 257). Japan's foreign investment in Asian countries is soaring, expected to move from about 18 percent of Japan's total investment in 1992 to nearly 30 percent by 2002 (Neff 1995). And China's trade with other Asian countries has more than doubled since the late 1980s (Brauchli 1995).

This does not mean that Asia is isolating itself from other regions. To the contrary, Asia clearly is a major global player (Engardio 1993). Japan and Taiwan are the largest holders of foreign currency in the entire world. And, not surprisingly, Japan and the four little dragons have invested heavily in North America and Europe, far more than North America or Europe have invested in East Asia. If none of these facts surprises you, consider a few other items that underscore Asia's growing presence in the global economy: Japan and South Korea are the two largest shipbuilders in the world; steel consumption in Asia (even excluding Japan) is greater than in the United States or Europe; container and air freight traffic is greater in Asia than in either the United States or Europe; and Asian companies already control 25 percent of the entire personal computer market (Vogel 1991, 1–2; Naisbitt 1994, 257).

Asia is a world leader partly because it is consolidating its regional economy. Increasingly, Asian countries have sufficient amounts of money to invest in their own countries, in neighboring Asian countries, and in other regions of the world. This pattern contrasts with that found in Africa, where countries have little capital to invest in themselves or in their African neighbors. Thus, Africa is far from achieving the level of economic independence found in Asia. In Asia, the combination of capital investment and cooperation have led to explosive economic growth, despite some profound political differences. Importantly, though, these dragons are more interested in economics than politics.

Late Industrialization

Have you ever seen the long-running television game show *Jeopardy*? The host gives the players an *answer*, and then the first player to *ask* the correct question is awarded points. Let's play. Today's category is "world societies." Ready? Here's the first answer: "These five countries account for less than 1 percent of the world's land mass, less than 4 percent of the world's population, but for about 21 percent of the world's industrial output—despite starting their industrialization centuries after Europe and the United States." For $1,000, the correct question is: "What are Japan and the four little dragons?" Japan began to industrialize in the early twentieth century and accelerated its industrialization after World War II, and the four little dragons started to industrialize only in the 1950s.

What is so amazing is that most "experts" once considered industrialization strictly a Western phenomenon, reserved for Europe (which industrialized in the eighteenth century) and the United States (which industrialized in the nineteenth century). Following the tenets of modernization theory, the path to industrialization was supposedly reserved for societies with a Judeo-Christian heritage and other earmarks of Western culture.

How, then, can we explain the emergence of Japan and the four little dragons as world players in the industrialized world? It is not easy, because no single explanation accounts for this remarkable development. We will examine six important factors (Vogel 1991).

First, the United States gave substantial foreign aid to East Asia. Between 1946 and 1955 (following World War II), Japan was the largest recipient of U.S. nonmilitary foreign aid after France, the United Kingdom, Italy, and Germany (U.S. Bureau of the Census 1994). The United States wanted to rebuild Japan to prevent the spread of communism in Asia and to open up markets for U.S. products. After World War II, the occupying U.S. forces wrote the Japanese constitution, which exists to this day without amendment. The constitution severely limits the role of the Japanese military, a stipulation that has helped Japan by allowing the country to allocate more of its resources to economic development than to military expenditures. As a result, Japan typically spends more on business entertainment than on national defense.

The four little dragons, especially Taiwan and South Korea, also received generous U.S. economic and military aid between 1956 and 1985. The primary motivation was to fight communism, which was sponsored in the region by China and the Soviet Union. Taiwan and South Korea are strong Western allies, despite bordering the communist countries of China and North Korea, respectively. U.S. policy makers poured billions of dollars into these countries because of their strategic importance to the United States. And, during the Vietnam War in the 1960s and early 1970s, the largest single recipient of U.S. foreign aid (both military and nonmilitary) was South Vietnam, which was fighting communist North Vietnam. After the Vietnam War, Israel and Egypt began receiving the lion's share of U.S. foreign aid as the "Middle East" became a flash point for world tension (U.S. Bureau of the Census 1994).

Second, colonial powers lost their influence over the four little drag-ons. During the nineteenth and early twentieth centuries, Britain colo-nized Hong Kong and Singapore while Japan colonized Taiwan and Ko-rea. Japan later invaded Hong Kong and Singapore and took them away from the British. But Japan was crushed in World War II and lost its colo-nies as a result. Britain regained its colonial power over Hong Kong and Singapore after the war, but the relationship was much weaker than be-fore. In fact, the colonial era was effectively over at this point. Officially, Hong Kong is still a colony of Britain until 1997, but, since World War II, it has been virtually free of colonial control. In fact, Hong Kong (the colony) currently invests more money in Britain (the colonizer) than Britain in-vests in Hong Kong!

Third, the *governments* of Japan and the four other countries have ex-erted their muscle in several areas. They have formed strong industrial and trade policies, encouraged domestic savings, undertaken land reform to increase agricultural production, limited foreign products that might compete with domestic goods (for example, many U.S. products are not allowed into Japan), maintained low wages, and exercised heavy-handed tactics to keep order at home. Although Japan has been a democracy for decades, the four little dragons are considered authoritarian regimes and are just now experimenting with some form of democracy. Authoritarian states can produce economic dynamism and national discipline, but at a cost to civil liberties. Many U.S. citizens would not tolerate the harsh pun-ishments and restrictions on civil liberties (for example, press censorship) implemented by some Asian countries (Bradshaw, Kim, and London 1993). On the other hand, Asian leaders might respond by pointing out the economic successes experienced by the continent, successes partly attrib-utable to strong government policies.

Even big Asian companies can feel the wrath of their governments. In 1993, South Korea elected its first nonmilitary government in three de-cades. As a result, the country is undergoing some aspects of democrati-zation: a freer press, more active unions, and greater freedom to criticize the government. But President Kim's administration has clear limits. One of South Korea's largest companies is the huge Samsung Group, a multi-national corporation involved in activities ranging from automobile pro-duction to aerospace. The company is so powerful that some people refer to the Republic of Korea (South Korea) as "the republic of Samsung." The chairman of Samsung got carried away with his country's new democracy, or simply wanted to test it, while he was visiting China in early 1995. In Beijing, he publicly commented that President Kim's administration was "second class" and Korean politics were "fourth class." Upon returning home, the chairman found his business fortunes diminished. The government suddenly restricted his company's access to loans, interfered with Samsung's bid to buy a large share in a California computer maker, and delayed approving other Samsung business deals (Glain 1995). New democracies sometimes adopt old means of control.

A fourth reason for the industrial success of Japan and the four little dragons is the Confucian heritage that has influenced their cultures. Confucius (551–479 B.C.) was a Chinese philosopher who placed great value on parents, humanity, ancestor worship, and harmony in thought and deed. Confucianism alone is certainly not responsible for economic growth, because many Confucianist societies have not realized such expansion. But, combined with the other characteristics mentioned above, Confucianism has its role. Specifically, this philosophy promotes three factors that shape development, Asian style: (1) Confucianism instills tremendous respect for elders and authority figures. So the hierarchical organization of business enterprises is consistent with this principle of Confucian societies. (2) Confucianism emphasizes the group over the individual. Originally, this meant emphasis on the family, community, and other primary groups. Over time, however, this group emphasis has been extended to the work group, the company, and other economic groups. (3) Confucianism leads to a desire for "self-cultivation," that is, "a desire for more perfect control over one's emotions and required study and reflection" (Vogel 1991, 101). The drive for self-discipline fosters an orderliness in society that nurtures economic development.

Modernization theory has had a difficult time with the Confucian influence on East Asia. This philosophy is uniquely Eastern in origin, a contrast to the Western religions and philosophies that, according to modernization theory, are supposed to facilitate modernization. The outstanding performances by Japan, Hong Kong, Singapore, South Korea, and Taiwan are clear evidence that "West is not necessarily best" when it comes to rapid industrialization and development.

Fifth, as shown in Table 5.1, Japan and the four little dragons have a high level of ethnic homogeneity within each country. This reduces violent ethnic conflicts and also promotes solidarity, both inside and outside the workplace. Ethnically diverse societies (such as in Africa or the United States) are interesting in their own right, but they have to work harder to communicate, cooperate in the workplace, and develop a sense of collective solidarity.

Sixth, Asian companies—especially those in Japan—promote loyalty, productivity, and teamwork. Some large companies provide guaranteed lifetime employment and feature *company unions*—as opposed to labor unions—which include both white- and blue-collar workers. Moreover, the pay differential between the highest and lowest paid workers in Japan is much smaller than in the United States. Recent statistics show that on average, the highest-paid company officers in Japan make about 17 times more than the average factory worker (Byrne 1991, 93). In large U.S. companies, by contrast, chief executive officers make 149 times more, on average, than factory workers (Byrne 1994, 55). The Japanese emphasis on relative equality and company loyalty encourages worker morale, teamwork, and intense loyalty. Many Japanese workers begin the day with team calisthenics, a way to boost the morale, physical conditioning, and camaraderie of the group. (Imagine a group of U.S. factory workers doing jumping jacks before heading to the assembly line.) Japanese workers (especially men) also spend long hours together outside of the workplace, usually drinking and socializing in the evening.

It is often difficult for American businesspeople to adapt to the cultural expectations of Japanese society. We can illustrate this point with a story. An eager young American salesperson working for a large multinational corporation wanted to make an appointment with a potential Japanese client in Tokyo. Speaking fluent Japanese, he reached his client's secretary by telephone and politely gave his name, the city from which he was calling (New York), and his company's name. He then asked whether he could speak with the potential client. Several moments of awkward silence followed, and it soon became clear that his request was not being honored. What was the problem?

The problem is that the American had just violated a business (and cultural) norm in Japan. In Japan, a person's company, department, and title are far more important than his name. You are *not* James Smith from New York or even James Smith from Company X. Instead, you are representing Company X as an account manager in the computer software division. Only after providing this information will anyone be interested in your name. The Japanese emphasis is on the team and group (company and department), not on the individual. Although the concept of *team* is growing in American business, the primary emphasis is still on the value of the individual, who ultimately has the freedom to move around from company to company.

The six reasons examined here, representing a combination of internal and external factors, explain the rapid (and late) industrialization of Japan and the four little dragons. It was a uniquely Asian path to success. Although modernization theory points to Asia as evidence that countries can develop, it does not often discuss the non-Western features exhibited by this path to industrialization.

Economic Growth *and* a High Level of Equality? The Japanese Case

Japan and the four little dragons have experienced rapid economic growth and, by many accounts, maintained a relatively egalitarian society. But how much equality does exist? A country's level of equality is normally measured by looking at the percentage of national wealth held by the richest and poorest segments of society. If a small group of rich citizens hold a substantial amount of the country's wealth, then the society clearly exhibits income inequality.

Let's look first at Japan. Statistics reported in Table 5.2 show that this country is one of the most equal societies on earth. The richest 20 percent of the population hold only 37.5 percent of the national income, a lower percentage than most countries, including the United States, where the richest 20 percent of the population hold 41.9 percent of the national income. Moreover, the poorest 40 percent in Japan hold more of the national income (21.9 percent) than in most other countries, including the United States, where the poorest 40 percent hold only 15.7 percent of the national income (World Bank 1995a). Overall, the Japanese figures are comparable to those for Sweden, considered a welfare state and often cited as the most egalitarian society in the world (discussed in Chapter 6).

Japan's equality is due largely to two factors. First, as noted earlier, the salary structure is much more equal than in the United States. Because of the country's emphasis on teamwork and the group, exorbitant salaries are generally frowned upon. One reason for this relative salary equity is because Japan features company unions, not labor unions. The former are concerned with the overall salary structure in the company, while the latter emphasize better pay and benefits for workers only. Company unions would be considered "cop-outs" by many American trade unionists, who believe that workers must have a strong voice *against* management. But

TABLE 5.2

Percent of National Income Held by Poorest 40% and Richest 20% of the Population, 1992

Country	Poorest 40%	Richest 20%
Japan	21.9	37.5
United States	15.7	41.9

Source: World Bank 1995a.

company unions are in line with cultural norms in Japanese society, which stress teamwork and harmony. As noted by Chirot (1986, 246):

> Japan, then, much more than the United States, and perhaps even more than some of the small, social democratic welfare states of Scandinavia, has become a mass middle-class society in which the old class conflicts, status differences, and political disharmony of classical Western industrial societies have become things of the past.

Although this situation is changing slightly, it is clear that Japan remains a relatively egalitarian society. Second, Japan has much less mass poverty than other developed (and developing) countries. Economic growth, cultural homogeneity, and low unemployment have contributed to a very strong middle-class society.

Despite these figures, one should not conclude that Japan is utopian with respect to equality. In particular, women face substantial inequalities in the workplace and larger society. Although Japanese women participate in the workforce at comparable rates to women in industrialized Western societies, there are differences in the type of work performed. Compared to industrial Western societies, Japanese women (1) tend to work in nonsalary positions, where they are paid only for each item made, or (2) work for family businesses with low pay. Moreover, women seldom work in white-collar jobs, and they face a substantial female-male wage gap. Women are also expected to leave the workforce on getting married, although some return later (Brinton 1993). Overall, executive and high-level management positions are the domain of males in Japan, more so than in the United States and many other countries where women are beginning to make progress.

Japan is also facing other problems that could affect the overall health of the economy and, eventually, income equality. The country's huge banking sector, home to twenty of the thirty largest banks in the world (Sassen 1994, 13), is facing a crisis. These banks had a lot of extra money during the 1980s and therefore made more than $500 billion in loans to real-estate developers who wanted to buy land throughout Japanese cities. Unfortunately, however, the economy turned sour and many developers could not repay their loans, leaving banks with little hope of recovering their money (Williams and Sapsford 1995; WuDunn 1995). There is an old saying that is appropriate here: "If you owe the bank $500 and cannot repay, you have a problem; if you owe the bank $500 *billion* and cannot repay, the bank has a problem." Japanese banks have a problem. The problem is compounded by the fact that Japanese citizens, who traditionally place a higher percentage of their income in savings than any other country in the world, have begun withdrawing their money from the most troubled Japanese banks. Moreover, the banking problem, combined with lower corporate profits in the country, has contributed to a plunging Japanese stock market. It fell 27 percent during the first half of 1995 alone, at a time when the U.S. stock market was breaking all-time growth records. All of these economic problems have forced the Japanese government to begin discussions of whether to use taxpayer money to bail out the banking sector. This idea is exceedingly unpopular in Japan. Many citizens feel that the banking sector violates the societal emphasis on equality and harmony. Citizens blame the banks for driving up the price of all real estate in the late 1980s, increasing housing costs for many people. They also feel that bankers make far too much money for a society that values relative equality between its richest and poorest members (Williams and Sapsford 1995).

Lower corporate profits are forcing Japanese companies to respond in a way that is familiar to Americans, but not to Japanese citizens: The companies are moving industries to countries with cheaper labor. Japanese-made products such as electronics, computers, televisions, and automobiles are increasingly made in other nations, particularly in Asia. This means that Japanese companies are investing more and more money in Asian economies. Through 1994, Japan's cumulative investment in East Asia alone totaled $64 billion, compared to the $26 billion and $7 billion invested in the region by the United States and Germany, respectively (Neff 1995).

But this trend has three negative effects on Japanese equality. First, it may threaten the lifetime employment that some large Japanese companies provide to their employees. Although the Japanese are very hesitant to lay off workers, an uncertain economy and the export of some jobs may well result in fewer guarantees in the future. Second, young people are facing a very difficult job market due to downsized workforces and the hesitancy to lay off older workers (Andrews 1995). Hiring of new college graduates fell 33 percent in 1994 and was down 22 percent through the first half of 1995. While the unemployment rate for people ages 45 to 54 was only 2 percent (reflecting the stability of lifetime employment), the rate for people ages 15 to 24 was nearly 6 percent (Updike 1995). Third, female college graduates seem to be the main victims in this process. Of the few college graduates obtaining good jobs, the majority were male, again showing the preference for men when filling good jobs (Williams and Sapsford 1995).

Inequality in South Korea, Hong Kong, Taiwan, and Singapore

Every summer, thousands of Korean-American families send their thoroughly Westernized children (especially those of college age) to summer school in Korea. The parents hope that the children will learn the Korean language better, appreciate Korean customs and values more, and perhaps meet someone special. The children normally experience mixed emotions during the summer in Korea, emotions born out of a clash of cultures. They enjoy many aspects of Korean culture, including close families, strong support networks among friends and family, and the emphasis on education. At the same time, some feelings about the "new" country split along gender lines, with Korean-American men feeling more comfortable in the new culture than Korean-American women. Jennifer Kim, a 21-year-old from Laguna Beach, California, loves her Korean grandfather dearly, but she was dismayed to discover why he often knocked on the table during dinner: He was "asking" his granddaughter to get something for him in the kitchen. The gesture is not unusual in traditional Korean homes. But it clashed with Jennifer's Western outlook and made her feel uncomfortable, even though she was trying to appreciate local customs and lifestyles. Janet Hong of Seattle felt the same way. She liked her summer in Korea, but she too was frustrated over her lower status there compared to in the United States. She reported the highlights of her visit to Korea, but reflected, "Huh, guys are kings here" (Kristof 1995b).

Before looking at gender inequalities, we need to look at the popular view of Korea and the other little dragons with respect to overall societal inequality. In one respect, they have a high degree of equality—although that requires some explanation. Countries undergoing very recent industrialization often have more inequality than other countries, primarily because only a relatively small portion of the population has experienced the benefits of new growth. Thus, we would expect the richest 20 percent of the population in newly industrializing countries to have relatively more income than in a developed society. At one extreme, for example, in the South American country Brazil, the richest 20 percent of the population hold an astounding 67.5 percent of the national income, compared to only 7.0 percent held by the poorest 40 percent. By contrast, the four little dragons of Asia have roughly the same income distribution as in the United States. The richest 20 percent hold between 41.8 and 48.9 percent of the national income, and the poorest 40 percent hold between 15.0 and 19.7 percent of the national income (Table 5.3). These numbers suggest a high level of equality for countries that are not yet fully developed.

As in Japan, however, equality is not a reality for everyone. Rapid economic growth has been possible partly—perhaps largely—because of the hard work of young, poorly paid female factory workers. Factories that specialize in electronics, textiles, shoes, and other products tend to hire women for very low wages, something that is commonly accepted in these male-oriented societies (recall the story of Sadisah in Chapter 1). One

TABLE 5.3

Percent of National Income Held by Poorest 40% and Richest 20% of the Population, 1992

Country	Poorest 40%	Richest 20%
Hong Kong	16.2	47.0
Singapore	15.0	48.9
South Korea	19.7	42.7
Taiwan	17.4	41.8
Brazil	7.0	67.5
United States	15.7	41.9

Source: World Bank 1994.

study in Taiwan indicates that female factory workers' salaries are systematically fixed at a rate that is 10 to 20 percent below male factory workers' salaries (Bello and Rosenfeld 1990, 216). Some argue that female salaries are even lower than this level.

In addition to paying low wages, many Asian factories (some with substantial foreign investment) believe that women are better workers for other reasons. As noted by Bello and Rosenfeld (216):

> Among other reasons cited by employers were that women were more temperamentally suited to tedious, repetitive work than men; that women had the manual dexterity or nimble fingers required for textile work and electronics assembly; and that women were less likely than men to rebel. As one personnel manager at an electronics-assembly plant in the Kaohsiung [Taiwan] Export Processing Zone commented, "This job was done by boys two or three years ago. But we found that girls do the job as well and don't make trouble like the boys. They're obedient and pay attention to orders. So our policy is to hire all girls."

An "obedient" labor force is important, because labor unions are nonexistent (or weak), the workday is long, and factories do not often meet the safety standards found in the West. Moreover, these young female workers, who are poorly paid and lack power, are sometimes forced to exchange sexual favors for continued employment (218).

Aside from the very serious problem of sexual exploitation, are female Asian factory workers worse off than Asian women who have more traditional jobs? This is a debatable point. On the one hand, factory owners argue that these women receive a steady wage and, occasionally, other benefits such as cheap housing and medical care. They also point out that these workers are young, largely uneducated, and therefore could not expect similar wages outside of factories. Finally, they argue (often correctly) that safety and other working conditions are improving in Asian factories. On the other hand, critics argue that these reasons do not excuse the economic and social exploitation that does occur. They argue that Asian and foreign companies make exorbitant profits because of the cheap labor of young women. Accordingly, rich companies should pay more, invest in the women's education, and assure the best working conditions possible. These critics contend that rather than asking, "Are women better off in factories compared to another line of work?" we should be asking, "Are women being treated fairly relative to the abundant resources of their companies?" Which side do you take? Why?

China: From Mao Jackets to Calvin Klein Jeans

Back to our game of *Jeopardy*. The next category is "world languages." Here's the answer: "This Asian language is spoken by more than one billion people, more than any other language in the world." The question: "What is Chinese?" There are actually several dialects of the Chinese language, but even the most common one, Mandarin, is spoken by as many as 825 million people, far more than the next most common language, English, which is spoken by about 450 million people throughout the world (Wright 1995). The sheer numbers of people speaking Chinese, most of them in China of course, attests to China's importance in the world and the size of potential markets for foreign investors in China and other parts of southeast Asia.

What do you think of when the word *China* is mentioned? If you are like many Americans, you think about a highly populated country, the Great Wall, bicycles, colorless clothing, poverty, old leaders, and communism. This perception is partly correct, as China is the most populated country on earth (more than 1.2 billion people) and has an average annual income of only $490 (World Bank 1995a, b). Moreover, since 1949, when Mao Zedong declared that the People's Republic of China would be strongly communist and anti-Western, the country has remained one of the most closed societies in the world. Western influences were declared corrupt, exploitative, and evil, and therefore everything from colorful clothing to democracy was banned. The gray Mao suit was a symbol of anti-Western sentiment as well as a tribute to Mao and the Communist Party.

But wait a minute! The China of the 1990s is undergoing many changes that may surprise you. Consider a few facts: China will soon be the world's largest total economy (despite low average incomes); *communist* China now has 18 million entrepreneurs, one million millionaires, and two stock exchanges (Naisbitt 1994); in a recent Gallup Poll in China, 68 percent of those surveyed reported their main goal is to "work hard and get rich" and only 4 percent placed "service to society" above self-interest (World Trade 1995, 12); and some Chinese citizens watch soap operas (from Taiwan), listen to talk radio, and watch CNN (Barnathan 1994). This hardly sounds like a communist country.

Moreover, foreign investors are lining up to make significant investments in China. Some of the investors (and future investors) include AT&T, American Express, Coca-Cola, Procter & Gamble, 7-Eleven, Motorola, Eastman Kodak, Heinz, General Motors, Ford, Chrysler, R. J. Reynolds (China consumes more cigarettes than any country on earth), and many fashion designers such as Giorgio Armani, Chanel, Donna Karan, Calvin Klein, and others. Incredibly, foreign investment in China increased sixfold between 1989 and 1993 to almost $60 billion, the majority coming from Asian companies (Barnathan 1993, 56). Chairman Mao would spin in his grave at this thought: Chinese youth dressed in Calvin Klein jeans heading to 7-Eleven to buy a Coca-Cola.

You could observe a microcosm of China's rapid changes if you climbed into a car in Hong Kong and drove one hour north into China. You might run into a "village" known as Changan, which, only a decade ago, was so poor that many residents used to emigrate to Hong Kong in order to find work and live a better life. No longer. The village is now home to almost 700 factories that employ 100,000 workers from other regions of China. Changan will earn $40 million a year renting the factories to foreign investors who have established joint ventures with Chinese businesses. The businesses make Barbie dolls, tools, and a wide assortment of other products. A whole town has grown up around the new enterprises in Changan, including new homes, new roads, and new recreation facilities (Barnathan 1993).

What is responsible for these profound changes in China? We need to review some recent history to begin to find an answer. The country's isolationist status began to change in 1978, when Deng Xiaoping (chairman of the Communist Party) announced that China would begin to create markets and open its doors to the world. China would remain communist from a political standpoint, but it would start to open up its economy. Step 1 in this process entailed creating market economies for agriculture, something that was important because about 80 percent of the population lived in rural areas (about 75 percent today). Agricultural prices were raised and communist-style communes were abolished. These changes increased agricultural production and resulted in more family farms and more money for poor farmers. By generating more money in rural areas, China increased entrepreneurship and enabled citizens to buy other products throughout the country (Bradshaw and Fraser 1989).

Step 2 involved actively soliciting foreign investment. In 1984, the Chinese government designated fourteen coastal cities as centers for foreign investment, a policy that attracted investors from Asia and the West (China International Economic Consultants 1985; Bradshaw and Fraser 1989). The government further opened the country's economy by establishing several "special economic zones" to encourage foreign investment in the interior of the country. Foreign companies became increasingly interested in China because of its huge potential markets (1.2 billion people), its elimination of much government interference in the marketplace, and its rapidly expanding national economy. In 1992 alone, 47,000 new enterprises involving foreign capital were approved in China, and they agreed to invest $57.5 billion in the country (Naisbitt 1994, 189).

Agricultural reform and foreign investment have produced incredible economic growth in China since 1978. The economy has grown at an annual rate of more than 10 percent, among the highest in the world during that time period. In 1992 and 1993, the economy experienced annual growth rates of 13 percent, well above that in the United States, which managed only about 3 percent (Barnathan 1994). And, importantly, the level of foreign investment will not stop any time soon, as companies continue to line up to invest in the (soon to be) world's largest economy. This does not mean that China is the wealthiest country in the world; it certainly is not. Many people are poor and have not been touched by the country's rapid modernization. Still, the scope and pace of changes have altered many lives and communities in the country. Moreover, these changes are also solidifying China's role as a key player in the leading economic bloc in the world. Japan is still the largest economy in Asia, but China may well overtake it early in the next century (Brauchli 1995).

A Land of Paradox

China's economic strength has produced one of the greatest paradoxes in the world today: The fastest-emerging capitalist economy is evolving inside the cocoon of one of the last remaining communist countries. The Chinese government, still led by the aging Deng Xiaoping, is a brutal dictatorship: It murders students and other dissenters (remember the massacre in China's Tiananmen Square described in Chapter 1), it imprisons and tortures political "agitators," it has an abysmal human rights record, and it defies the global trend toward democracy. Unlike other communist leaders, however, Deng Xiaoping realized long ago that his country needed to open its economy in order to move forward. The resulting economic freedom will continue to produce stronger movements toward democracy, especially after he dies. China's paradox (capitalist economy, communist government) underscores one of the most perplexing trends in the world today: Almost in spite of the political organization of society, economies are consolidating as countries pursue the international language of money.

Advocates of democracy in China are not calling for a Western-style multiparty system, something that the country clearly is not ready for at this time. But many Chinese are calling for a more open political system that allows greater freedom of expression and a guarantee of basic human rights. A freer society, combined with solid economic growth, would set the stage for some form of democracy in the near future (probably voting for a limited number of candidates) and a broader system of democracy over time. The current Chinese government is resisting even the most basic forms of democracy, however, as it continues to violate basic human rights despite the opening economy.

The economic liberalization of China has made the United States and other foreign countries hesitant to take action against the country's abuse of human rights. Presidents Bush and Clinton have talked tough concerning the political abuses of China. The talk usually revolves around removing China from a list of countries that receive "most favored nation" economic status. If a country is removed from this list, it is much more difficult for American companies to do business with the country. Such action would hurt American companies investing in China, particularly if other Western investors did not follow suit. Thus, U.S. politicians are very hesitant to take tough political action against a country that is so vital to American business interests. By contrast, U.S. politicians are not shy about punishing repressive governments with weak economies. For instance, the U.S. government severely restricts American companies from doing business with communist Cuba (an economic basket case), even though Cuban leader Fidel Castro is clearly no worse than Chinese leaders from a human rights perspective.

Another paradox is that, although China has low average incomes, it does not exhibit many of the negative characteristics of other poor countries, such as those in Africa. For instance, China's under-five mortality rate is relatively low, food shortages are rare, and the birth rate is remarkably low. The average woman of childbearing age in China has only 2.5

children, a low rate for a country as poor as this one. (India—with its fertility rate of more than four children per woman—will likely pass China as the most populated country in the world within twenty years; World Bank 1993.) A major reason for low fertility in China is the country's "one-child policy," which mandates that people have only one child. Although many people obviously have more than one child (especially in rural areas), the policy has clearly helped to reduce fertility rates. Let's take a quick look at some of the stipulations associated with this policy.

To decrease births, the Chinese government has increased the minimum marrying age (twenty-two for men, twenty for women); distributes free contraceptives and strongly encourages abortions for a second pregnancy; pays couples who become sterilized, assuming they have fewer than two children; and provides one-child families with health and education subsidies, priority for some jobs, and extra land for housing (Whyte and Parish 1984; Banister 1987; Shaoyu 1988). In addition, each *urban* factory and other work organization is *collectively* allowed to have a limited number of children each year. The government rewards organizations with extra wages when they bear fewer children than their quota permits. This incentive means that work organizations closely monitor workers' menstrual cycles and contraceptive practices, encouraging abortions when women become pregnant out of turn (Whyte and Parish 1984, 160–161). Monitors often visit women at home to enquire about contraceptive practices and to further encourage compliance with the one-child policy.

Although China's one-child policy has been instrumental in slowing the rate of population growth, it has also produced several troubling consequences from a human rights perspective. First, because there is a strong desire among Chinese families to have at least one son, and since only one child is permitted, some infant girls are killed by families that desperately want a boy. Speaking at the Fourth World Conference on Women, held in China for the first time, Hillary Rodham Clinton spoke out forcefully on the topic of infanticide: "It is a violation of human rights when babies are denied food, or drowned, or suffocated, or their spines are broken, simply because they are girls." (By order of the Chinese government, her speech was not allowed on Chinese television or radio. But it was carried by CNN and shown around the world.)

The extent of infanticide may well be exaggerated by Westerners, however. Although the practice does exist in China, some people believe that it is not nearly as widespread as reported by the Western press. Because official data show that there are substantially more male Chinese babies than female Chinese babies, Westerners often draw the inference that many young girls are killed. An equally plausible explanation comes from the fact that all Chinese children must be registered with the government.

To get around the one-child policy, however, some rural parents simply do not register their girl babies with the government, thereby leaving open the possibility (probability) of having another child—hopefully a boy. It is more difficult to avoid registration procedures in urban areas, where work units track pregnancies and births are more likely to occur in hospitals.

Second, China's orphanages are full of young girls, almost exclusively girls in some regions of the country. Some families leave infant girls on the doorsteps of orphanages, as if the children never existed, "permitting" the families to try again for a boy. In response, China is opening the door to foreigners who want to adopt Chinese children, and foreigners are responding. In 1989, China issued just eleven visas to children who wanted to leave the country. In 1994, the number increased to more than 1,500, many of them for adopted children.

Third, abortions are performed more frequently when a woman knows that she is carrying a girl. The one-child policy, combined with the traditional preference for boys, has caused an unknown number of parents to use prenatal tests to determine the sex of the child and to opt for an abortion if it is female. This practice, which is increasingly common throughout the overpopulated developing world, has long-term implications for family structure and other societal institutions as these children mature into adulthood.

Although the closed nature of Chinese society makes it difficult to document differential treatment by gender, it is well known that women continue to face hardships as they become adults. They receive lower-paying jobs, are excluded from many high-level political positions, and must endure intrusion into the most personal aspects of their lives. At the same time, however, the Chinese communist government provides free health coverage for all citizens, which helps women enormously especially when they are pregnant. The government also provides several months of paid maternity leave after the birth of a child, something that the United States does not do. As capitalism spreads in the country, it will be interesting to see whether some positive aspects of communism are eroded. If so, yet another paradox may appear in the country: Greater economic freedom could be accompanied by a loss of various social services that provide some security (and sense of freedom) for women and other citizens.

Moving Beyond the Graveyard of Vietnam

Now for our final *Jeopardy* answer: "This country's bloody civil war resulted in the death of more than 58,000 U.S. troops who fought for the losing side." The question? Of course: "What is Vietnam?" U.S. involvement in Vietnam ended more than twenty years ago, when communist North Vietnam defeated U.S.-backed South Vietnam. Most Americans now acknowledge that the United States was soundly defeated in the war, and almost no American is happy about the entire experience. Conservatives think we should have made a stronger effort to win the war. Liberals think we had no business acting as a global anticommunist police force in the first place. Moderates supported the war at first and then turned against it in the end. And isolationists think the lesson of Vietnam is that we should avoid all foreign entanglements.

Regardless of your point of view, several ghastly facts continue to haunt the United States and Vietnam: 58,000 Americans and 3 million Vietnamese (many civilians) were killed in more than a decade of fighting; countless Vietnamese and Americans were maimed, disfigured, and psychologically disabled by the war; and Vietnam remains a desperately poor country twenty years after the war. Movies like *Apocalypse Now, The Killing Fields,* and *Born on the Fourth of July* attest to the enduring images of this terrible war on the American psyche.

If you visit the Vietnam Veterans Memorial Wall in Washington, D.C., you will quickly see that the war is not over for all Americans. The wall carries the engraved name of every American that was killed in the war or is still missing. Some of the scenes at the wall are heart-wrenching. Many veterans—some wearing worn-out battle fatigues—kneel beside the name of fallen comrades. Families and friends touch the names of loved ones and weep. Some trace a name from the wall onto a piece of paper. Others leave flowers, poems, love letters, and other remembrances that were never said. And many young adults come to the wall in search of the fathers they never knew. For most, it is the most vivid gravestone that they will ever see. One young pregnant woman left two sonograms and a framed note beneath her father's name:

> Happy Father's Day—Dad! Here are the first two images of your first grandchild. I don't know if it's a boy or a girl—if the baby is a boy—he'll be named after you. Dad—this child will know you. Just how I have grown to know and love you—even though the last time I saw you I was only 4 mo. old. I love you daddy. (Allen 1995, 17)

Other people visit the wall to exorcise the inevitable demons that possess the human soul following war. A tattered picture of a North Vietnamese soldier and a young girl (probably his daughter) was left at the wall. A letter lay next to it:

> Dear Sir, For twenty-two years I have carried your picture in my wallet. I was only eighteen years old that day that we faced one another on that trail in

Chu Lai, Vietnam. Why you didn't take my life I'll never know. You stared at me for so long, armed with your AK-47, and yet you did not fire. Forgive me for taking your life, I was reacting just the way I was trained, to kill. . . . So many times over the years I have stared at your picture and your daughter, I suspect. Each time my heart and guts would burn with the pain of guilt. I have two daughters myself now. . . . I perceive you as a brave soldier defending his homeland. Above all else, I can now respect the importance that life held for you. I suppose that is why I am able to be here today. . . . It is time for me to continue the life process and release my pain and guilt. Forgive me, Sir. (Allen 1995, 52–53)

Some formerly warring countries never forgive each other. Others forgive in a relatively short period of time, although they never forget the experience. For instance, Germany was welcomed as an ally of Britain, France, and the United States soon after World War II, even though Germany had killed many people from each of these countries. Japan and the United States also enjoy close ties (despite occasional tensions over foreign trade), even though Japan bombed Pearl Harbor and the United States dropped two atomic bombs on Japanese cities. Forgiveness often is the result of shared interests that compel the countries to put aside their differences, no matter how bitter. The United States gave substantial foreign aid to both Japan and Germany for two very selfish reasons: It wanted to reduce the threat of communism spreading into Western Europe or the Pacific Rim, and it wanted to develop new markets in these war-devastated regions. Shared economic and political interests have forged close ties between former enemies.

More than twenty years after the war in Vietnam, the United States and Vietnam are now ready to forgive each other. Vietnam is still a communist country and, like China, resists the global trend toward greater democracy. Nonetheless, Vietnam and the United States share a common interest: economics. Following the Chinese example, Vietnam is opening its economy to foreign investment, and American companies are ready to do business in this country of more than 70 million people. But, it was not until 1994 that the U.S. government lifted its trade embargo against Vietnam, allowing American companies to do business with the Vietnamese. The day after the embargo was lifted, several American companies, led by Coca-Cola and Pepsi, set up shop in Ho Chi Minh City (the capital). In 1995 the United States restored full diplomatic relations with Vietnam, a move that will make it even easier for American companies to do business in Vietnam. As with China, American businesses strongly pressured the government into opening formal ties with Vietnam, showing again that economic interests speed the forgiveness process.

American companies have joined the thousands of others now doing business in the economically revitalized Vietnam, the communist country that is adopting free markets (Engardio 1994). In 1986, the Vietnamese government adopted a policy of *doi moi*, or economic reform (rejuvenation). This radical policy was adopted for two reasons: (1) The Vietnamese economy was in desperate straits, with an annual inflation rate of 700 percent and a shortage of food and other products, and (2) the ailing Soviet Union could no longer afford to provide the $4 million per day in foreign assistance that it had been giving to Vietnam. Soviet aid was drying up as that country sought to save resources for its own development.

Vietnam's leaders enacted *doi moi* in an attempt to breathe some life into their fragile country. Out of desperation, the country enacted the most generous foreign investment policy in Asia (perhaps the world). Foreign companies can own 100 percent of their facilities in Vietnam. This is unusual. Host countries usually require foreign investors to enter into *joint ventures* in their countries, enabling domestic companies (or host governments) to own part of the business. Vietnam's foreign investment policy also allows foreign companies to send a high proportion of their profits out of the country, with few taxes. By contrast, most host governments restrict the amount of profits that can be sent out of the country and may enact steep taxes on the profits. Finally, Vietnamese investment policy allows foreign companies to hire and fire at will, something that is unusual for foreign investors in other countries, who normally retain only partial control over such matters. Overall, therefore, foreign companies find Vietnam a hospitable business environment: They can control their own facilities, pay low taxes, send money home, and retain absolute control over personnel matters (Butler 1995).

The new policies are comparable to a giant neon sign proclaiming, "Vietnam is open for business." Since 1988, the top five investors (by country) in Vietnam have been Taiwan ($1.9 billion), Hong Kong ($1.6 billion), South Korea ($855 million), Australia ($639 million), and Singapore ($621 million). By the end of 1994, a total of $11 billion had been committed for investment in Vietnam (Butler 1995, 60). Note again that most investors were from Asia. But the United States is also joining the act, with Chrysler, Ford, Pepsi, Coca-Cola, and many others ready to jump into the investment frenzy. And, importantly, foreign investment has helped to produce some positive economic developments. The national economy is growing at almost 9 percent a year, double its rate just three years ago; inflation has dropped to 14 percent, down from 68 percent a few years ago and 700 percent ten years ago; and a once-huge trade deficit has nearly been erased (Butler 1995, 60).

Along with opening up its economy to foreign investment, the Vietnamese government also reformed the agricultural sector. It distributed government land to private farmers, raised agricultural prices, and generally stressed private markets. As a result, food production has increased nearly 50 percent and rice exports have increased dramatically. In 1988, Vietnam did not export any rice, a crop it is well-suited to grow because of climate and terrain. Today, the country is the third leading rice exporter in the world, behind Thailand and the United States (Butler 1995, 60).

In conclusion, Vietnam currently resembles a "mini China" in some respects. Both have encouraged foreign investment and undertaken internal economic reforms. Both have experienced economic growth. And both have serious contradictions: open economies and closed political systems. And both will also face growing inequalities as some people benefit more than others from the positive changes that have occurred. Vietnam and China are grand experiments in social change and they will be fascinating to watch.

Asia in Theoretical Perspective

Modernization theorists point to Asia as basic confirmation of their arguments. Capitalist economies prevail, industrialization is stressed, technological innovation is spreading, education is a priority, and Western foreign aid (and now investment) is contributing to economic growth. According to these theorists, Asia has not sat idly by and played "victim" in the global economy. To the contrary, many of its countries have devised policies that improve economic development within their borders and within the region as a whole. Moreover, argue modernization theorists, economic dynamism will eventually produce greater democracy throughout the region.

Despite these points, it is clear that modernization theory cannot explain all developments in the region. Consider three issues. First, Asian countries are not dominated by Western religions, values, and cultures, although the discipline and self-cultivation stressed by Asian religions are similar to features stressed by Western religions. Second, Asian countries run the spectrum of political structures, from multiparty democracies (for example, Japan) to authoritarian systems in transition (for example, South Korea and Singapore) to communist regimes (for example, China and Vietnam). Ironically, diverse political structures have fostered quite similar economic policies, indicating the power of economics to cut across ideology. Third, the rise of Asia is much more complex than what is explained by modernization theory. Internal policies are important, but they must be explained within the context of regional efforts and the international economy.

World-system theory has also tried to explain Asia's changing fortunes, but the seven Asian countries discussed in this chapter defy simple explanations. Most world-system theorists classify Japan as a core country, the four little dragons as semiperipheral countries, and Vietnam and China as part of the periphery. But the awakening forces of economic change in these societies make such categorization appear obsolete.

It is true that in an earlier colonial era, Asian countries were exploited for their cheap labor and raw materials. But now, a number of Asian countries have companies—often in joint ventures with MNCs—that pay low wages for the production of manufactured goods. Many of these products are then exported to other Asian countries or to the West, where they are sold for a profit. World-system theory argues with some justification that noncore Asian countries are allowing MNCs from abroad to exploit their workers and, consequently, these countries will not achieve the independence needed to graduate to core status.

But world-system theory has difficulty explaining the national- and regional-level factors that are transforming Asia into an economic giant. Careful national planning, disciplined populations, and regional solidarity are creating an Asia that is becoming less dependent on outside regions. The United States and Europe are still important to Asia, but, as stated earlier, Asian countries are increasingly investing in and trading with each other. This trend will probably continue, although Japan and other Asian countries cannot afford to cut off their ties to the West in the near future. However, some Asians would like even more independence from the West. An influential maverick Japanese politician, Shintaro Ishihara, has long called on Japan to withdraw from the West. He argues, "This is a nation of Asian people with Asian blood. It seems natural that we recognize that we exist for Asia" (Neff 1995, 110).

In closing, we want to mention some challenges that confront contemporary Asia. First, although Asia has relatively low levels of internal inequality, this could change if economic growth continues and the money does not reach the majority of citizens, something that has occurred in Brazil and many other Latin American countries. Women may be particularly vulnerable because they are working in larger numbers, in lower-paying jobs, and within a cultural system that does not grant them first-class status in the labor force. Poverty is still a severe problem in most Asian societies and this problem will not be eradicated simply with economic expansion.

Second, economic changes are out of step with political realities in some countries, especially Vietnam and China. People throughout the world are demanding some type of democracy, including in China, where the government continues to crack down on leaders of the democracy movement. Such actions clash with the open markets and independence that many citizens are beginning to experience. However, just as in Africa, the road to democracy will not be easy. Governments first need to guarantee basic human rights, then worry about the possibility of elections and other profound societal changes. For instance, think for a moment about the need to develop legal systems that are appropriate for market economies. The current legal systems in China and Vietnam are not ready to negotiate contracts, arbitrate economic disputes, collect taxes in a responsible manner, and so forth. Moreover, the courts are not independent of the centralized government, something that must also change as markets and society become freer and increasingly separate from the government. Democratic societies need independent legal systems that are not dominated by their central governments.

Third, Asia is facing a number of health and environmental problems. For instance, AIDS arrived late in Asia but is now spreading rapidly in Thailand and other countries that are increasingly open to the outside world. AIDS is increasing faster in Asia than other areas, although the overall level of infection is still higher in other regions, especially Africa. Asia will have to spend additional resources on AIDS in the near future. Moreover, it needs to expend resources to deal with environmental destruction occurring in its rapidly industrializing countries. China has long had problems with air and water pollution, especially near large cities and other industrial areas. This problem has worsened in recent years as industrial growth continues to expand, often with the assistance of foreign capital. Likewise, Vietnam's situation will become very serious in the near future. The government's generous investment policies contain virtually no environmental safeguards, meaning that new industries can pollute the air and water almost at will. Heavy foreign investment and rapid economic growth almost always carry costs, and one of these costs is environmental damage.

Despite these problems, Asia will continue to grow and influence the world. It is the opposite of Africa in many respects. Asia has economic growth, regional strength, and few armed conflicts. Although there is substantial ethnic diversity *across* Asian countries, there is ethnic homogeneity *within* most of them. This reduces the probability of divisive internal ethnic conflicts, like those currently being witnessed in Africa. But conflict is possible, especially between countries. For example, there are always tensions between communist North Korea and "free" South Korea, tensions heightened because the former is thought to have nuclear technology; there is always the possibility of conflict between two old enemies, namely, communist China and Western-backed Taiwan; and wildly capitalistic Hong Kong is worried about relations with China after 1997, when Hong Kong will gain its independence from Britain and become part of China. There are also several internal conflicts around the continent that could flare up in future years (Brauchli and Hamilton 1995).

Still, Asia is so involved in economic progress that warfare seems remote in most cases. In fact, most analysts are planning for the twenty-first century, the Dragon Century, when an economic giant may engage in economic warfare against the former economic leaders in the Americas and Europe.

MAP 6.1

6

Europe: United or Divided?

Crumbling Walls

In August 1961, the citizens of Berlin awoke to a surprise: Their city had been divided in half by a barbed wire partition, which would later become a concrete wall. The wall was erected to prevent East German citizens from fleeing to freedom in West Germany. Despite the efforts of East German authorities, almost 3 million East Germans had fled their country since the end of World War II. This new barrier was designed to stop future escapes to the West.

The Berlin Wall was brutally effective in enforcing the separation between East and West. It was guarded day and night by soldiers, dogs, and roving spotlights; soldiers were instructed to shoot anyone trying to climb the concrete barrier. An estimated seventy-five East German citizens were killed trying to climb over the wall. One of the most horrifying scenes occurred in 1962, when Peter Fechter scurried up the wall before being hit by machine gun fire from East German guards. Fechter did not die immediately. He fell down and bled to death for an hour in plain view of guards and Western reporters and photographers. The 18-year-old Fechter was trying to join his family in West Germany.

Two years after the partition of Berlin, President John F. Kennedy traveled to the city and delivered one of his most eloquent speeches. He told listeners:

> Freedom is indivisible, and when one man is enslaved, all are not free. When all are free, then we can look forward to that day when this city will be joined as one. . . . When that day comes, as it will, the people of West Berlin can take sober satisfaction in the fact that they were in the front lines for almost two decades [since the end of World War II]. All free men, wherever they may live, are citizens of Berlin, and, therefore, as a free man, I take pride in the words "Ich bin ein Berliner." (I am a Berliner.) (U.S. Government Printing Office 1964, 525)

Despite Kennedy's uplifting tone, the wall would stand for another quarter of a century.

During this time, West Germany became an industrial powerhouse, with a high average income, an excellent quality of life, a good educational system, and technological sophistication exemplified by German companies like Mercedes, BMW, Volkswagen, and other leading industries. By contrast, East Germany and other East European countries became part of a failed communist experiment that ended in economic and social crisis. If Mercedes symbolizes West German successes, then the East German-produced Trabant might symbolize communism's failure. Charitably speaking, the Trabant is an exhaust-spewing contraption that . . . well, it's not a Mercedes! There are many unkind jokes about the Trabant, one ridiculing it as the product of a bad high-school science project. Although Eastern Europe is much more developed than the Third World, it is much less developed than Western Europe (Table 6.1). On balance, Western Europe has higher life expectancies, lower child mortality rates, higher average incomes, and lower inflation rates. Some analysts have referred to Eastern Europe as the Second World, existing somewhere between the most and least developed regions of the world.

The disparity between East and West provided a perfect symbol for Western leaders who wanted to denounce communist countries. Before 1989, many Western leaders traveled to the Berlin Wall, decried it, and called for its destruction along with the system it represented. Twenty-four years after President Kennedy's speech, President Ronald Reagan stood at the wall (for the second time) and angrily admonished the premier of the Soviet Union, "Mr. Gorbachev, open this gate! Mr. Gorbachev, tear down this wall!" (U.S. Government Printing Office 1989, 635).

Although he did not heed Reagan's call immediately, Gorbachev had already set in motion the process that would help bring down East European communism. Gorbachev called for openness, reforms, and restructuring (*perestroika*) throughout the communist empire; he cut aid to Soviet friends (colonies); and he refused to bail out embattled communist leaders in other countries. These facts, combined with economic crises in the Soviet Union and other East European countries, produced a revolution that literally changed the face of the world. In 1989, one of the most revolutionary years in history, millions of citizens began taking back their countries. The Chinese revolution failed during this year (recall Tiananmen Square), but the European one succeeded on a grand scale. Moreover, the revolutions of 1989 took almost everyone by surprise.

Here is a brief synopsis of that historic year. Poland had its first free elections in forty years and the communists lost almost every seat in government. Hungary cut its electrified barbed-wire fences along the Austrian border, allowing many East Europeans to emigrate to the West. Encouraged by events in Poland and Hungary, East German citizens began

TABLE 6.1 Descriptive Data for European Countries, 1993–1994

Country	Total Population	Life Expectancy at Birth	Under-Five Mortality Rate	GNP per Capita	Annual Economic Growth Rate	Inflation Rate on Consumer Prices	Unemployment Rate
Eastern Europe							
Bulgaria	8,832,000	73.0	19	$3,830	0.2%	122.0%	16.0%
Czech Republic	10,389,000	73.0	10	$7,350	2.2%	10.2%	3.2%
Hungary	10,324,000	71.0	15	$5,700	3.0%	21.0%	10.4%
Poland	38,520,000	72.5	15	$4,920	5.5%	30.0%	16.1%
Romania	23,172,000	71.0	29	$2,790	3.4%	62.0%	10.9%
Slovakia	5,376,000	72.5	18	$6,070	4.3%	12.0%	14.6%
Western Europe							
Austria	7,195,000	76.5	8	$23,120	2.5%	3.0%	4.3%
Belgium	10,041,000	76.5	10	$21,210	2.3%	2.5%	14.1%
Denmark	5,176,000	76.0	7	$26,510	4.5%	2.0%	12.3%
Finland	5,051,000	76.0	5	$18,970	3.5%	2.1%	22.0%
France	57,567,000	78.0	9	$22,360	2.4%	1.6%	12.6%
Germany	80,768,000	76.0	7	$23,560	2.9%	6.6%	11.8%
Greece	10,470,500	77.5	10	$7,390	0.4%	10.9%	10.1%
Ireland	3,530,000	75.5	7	$12,580	5.5%	2.7%	16.0%
Italy	58,109,000	77.5	9	$19,620	2.2%	3.9%	12.2%
Luxembourg	398,000	76.5	10	$35,850	2.6%	3.6%	2.4%
Netherlands	15,275,000	77.5	8	$20,710	2.0%	2.5%	8.8%
Norway	4,298,000	77.5	8	$26,340	5.5%	1.3%	8.4%
Portugal	10,486,000	75.0	11	$7,890	1.4%	6.1%	6.7%
Spain	39,207,000	77.5	9	$13,650	1.8%	4.9%	24.5%
Sweden	8,730,000	78.0	6	$24,830	2.4%	2.5%	8.8%
Switzerland	6,987,000	78.5	8	$36,410	1.8%	0.9%	4.7%
United Kingdom	57,970,000	76.0	8	$17,970	4.2%	2.4%	9.3%

Sources: UNICEF 1995; CIA 1995; World Bank 1995b; Goldman 1994; Warmenhoven 1995.

demonstrating and, within weeks, the long-time communist leader (Eric Honecker) was ousted as head of the country. On November 9, the new East German leader, Egon Krenz, opened his country's borders (and wall). The shocking development led to a full-scale party when on the night of November 12, thousands of singing, cheering, and triumphant Germans gathered to see the wall torn down. The scene resembled Times Square on New Year's Eve. Germans climbed on the wall, spray-painted graffiti on it, pounded the concrete in defiance or chiseled out a souvenir. One partier paraded a prized chunk of wall; it contained the word *Freiheit* (Freedom) on it. The scene was nothing short of incredible: Citizens literally helped tear down the wall while East German soldiers stood by and watched the festivities. Another spectator appeared to be Karl Marx himself, whose likeness was carried on a giant banner amid the crowd. Beneath the likeness were these words, "Sorry chaps, it was just an idea."

East European communism was on life support at this point; its death was imminent. The day after the wall was opened, Tudor Zhivkov resigned after thirty-five years in power in Bulgaria. His country had just been rocked by the first public protest in forty years, a protest that attracted 50,000 people. Demonstrations began one week later in Czechoslovakia, including one that attracted a half million people, some carrying signs proclaiming "Dinosaurs, Resign" and "Down with Communism." The country's leader for twenty years, Gustav Husak, quickly obliged. This incredible sequence of events, from Poland to Czechoslovakia, was a complete surprise to almost everyone. But nobody could have been more surprised than Vaclav Havel, the famous Czechoslovakian playwright and popular political activist. In January 1989, he was arrested by the communist government and thrown in prison. Eleven months later, after the fall of communism, he was elected president of the country.

Most communist leaders realized their time was up and stepped down without bloodshed. The lone holdout was the truculent dictator of Romania, Nicolae Ceausescu. He went the hard way. After terrorizing his country for twenty years (his secret police murdered thousands), Ceausescu was taken into custody by his own soldiers. He and his wife (who was also his deputy) were put on trial almost immediately for genocide. After two hours, they were found guilty and sentenced to death. A lottery was held among the soldiers for firing squad duty because so many of them wanted to kill Ceausescu. The Ceausescus were hastily executed immediately after receiving their sentence—on December 25, 1989. Many Romanians considered this act the greatest Christmas gift of all (Watson 1990).

Just a few months before the Ceausescus were executed and buried, another body became the focal point of political activism, this time in Hungary, where citizens had not forgotten an event that occurred three decades earlier. In 1956, Imre Nagy was elected prime minister of Hungary and he promptly led a rebellion against the Soviet Union, which claimed Hungary as one of its colonies. Soviet troops rolled into the country and executed hundreds of "counterrevolutionaries," including Nagy. After he was hanged, his body was wrapped in tar paper, bound with wire, and dumped in a mass grave outside the capital city of Budapest. For over thirty years it was against the law to even lay flowers on his grave. But in 1989, things changed. Nagy's body was exhumed and given a proper funeral before a national television audience. The event became larger than life as Nagy was celebrated as a national hero. His body laid in state in Budapest's Heroes Square; church bells tolled across the country; workers stopped for a minute of silence; and 200,000 people waited for hours to walk past his casket, some placing roses on it. This event, combined with Ceausescu's demise, was hauntingly symbolic of the historic year. A communist dictator was killed and buried in one former communist country, and a champion of democracy was resurrected in another (Meyer 1990).

Why 1989?

Earlier we briefly noted the reasons for the East European revolutions of 1989: economic crisis, abandonment by the Soviet Union, and mass demonstrations. In this section, we elaborate on these points by looking more closely at different East European countries before the fall of communism. We review their relationships with the former Soviet Union and with the West. In line with our theoretical model, our comments show that the European revolutions of 1989 were caused by a variety of economic, political, and social factors, some occurring inside East European countries and some happening outside of them. Revolutions are dramatic sociological events, so it is not surprising that some of the very best academic books have examined the French Revolution (1789), the Bolshevik Revolution (1917), and the Chinese Revolution (1949) (see Skocpol 1979; Goldstone 1991). These revolutions, like those of 1989, allow us "a fascinating, unexpected revealing glimpse into how seemingly stable, enduring social systems fail and collapse" (Chirot 1991, 3).

There are several causes of the revolutions of 1989, no one of which can fully explain them (Chirot 1991). First, economic problems were increasingly prevalent across Eastern Europe. Bulgaria, Poland, and especially Romania were in terrible shape. They were better off than the Third World but far from West European standards. Hungary, Czechoslovakia, and

East Germany were much better off economically although not as developed as West European countries, a fact that was clear to citizens of both East and West.

The basic economic problem was clear: Eastern Europe had centrally planned economies that were modeled after the Soviet Union. One economic policy was especially destructive in the long run: Following the Soviet example, East European governments channeled their money and technology into the development of heavy industries like steel mills, giant electrical plants, and chemical factories. These heavy industries were supposed to stimulate economic growth, reduce dependence on other countries, and provide military hardware for the country. But two problems resulted from this emphasis. First, Eastern Europe lacked the money, technology, and knowledge to modernize their industrial equipment, a problem that became increasingly acute over the years. Heavy industry was inefficient and dirty, resulting in massive air and water pollution that continues to plague the region. Second, Eastern Europe did not have sufficient resources to invest in both heavy industry and the production of consumer goods. Thus, Eastern Europe was short on basic consumer products like washing machines, packaged food, birth control devices, cars (remember the Trabant), and many other goods found across Western Europe. Eastern Europe seemed locked in an earlier stage of industrial development, unable to move into the era of mass consumer production and services, and certainly not into the era of information technology and computers (Rostow 1991). East Europeans were especially frustrated when they compared their lives to their western neighbors, something that was easy to do because many East Europeans received West European television and radio.

Soviet and East European leaders tried to correct the economic situation in the 1970s and 1980s. One plan was to borrow money from the West in order to modernize communist economies. This entire plan may have been a good idea but it was unsuccessful, partly because many old guard East European government officials refused to follow it. They continued to allocate money and other resources to prop up obsolete heavy industries. Moreover, like a number of developing countries, Eastern Europe began to accumulate large debts to the outside world. In response, just as in the developing world, East European governments were required to reduce spending on a wide array of services that were provided free or at low cost to citizens. The money saved from the cuts would then be used to repay the debt. But the cuts were dramatic for citizens who had long depended on the benefits of communism: free education, free health care, free housing, and cheap food. With government cutbacks, citizens suddenly had to pay for all of these services, some of which were very expensive. People were furious; high prices were now combined with a lack of basic consumer products. Strikes, political demonstrations, and other forms of instability began to occur in some countries.

The second cause of the revolutions of 1989 was a complete loss of legitimacy by East European governments (Chirot 1991). East European citizens lost confidence in their governments' ability to deliver services or to act with any degree of moral authority. Repression, secret police forces, and lack of democracy eroded citizens' confidence in the state. Economic problems helped cause, and worsen, this crisis of legitimacy. Such a crisis also opened the way for civil society to oppose repressive governments and offer citizens an alternative institution to the state. In Poland, for instance, the Catholic Church and the Solidarity trade union generated strong opposition to the communist Polish government starting in the late 1970s. Solidarity called for mass strikes in order to cripple the national economy and therefore the government of Poland. Strikers would often start the day by celebrating mass—led by a priest—at their work site. The Church was the moral authority in Poland and continued to undercut the legitimacy of the government. The Polish government had lost all legitimacy by the end of the 1980s, when communists were swept out of office.

The Church was also instrumental in organizing opposition to communism in East Germany and Czechoslovakia. Moreover, churches and other nongovernment organizations remain critically important after the fall of communism. President Havel (the erstwhile playwright) has eloquently discussed the importance of a vibrant civil society to the democratic process. Churches, charities, social organizations, and other institutions take care of people and mobilize them in grassroots activities. In addition, jazz clubs, literary societies, theaters, and other artistic endeavors lead to a more creative and vibrant community of citizens. Civil society is often at odds with dominant central governments because it pulls people together and empowers them. Empowered citizens often want greater independence politically, economically, and intellectually.

A third cause of the revolutions of 1989 occurred when Soviet leader Mikhail Gorbachev called for economic and political reforms throughout the Soviet Union and Eastern Europe (Hanson 1991). He also made it clear that no Soviet troops would be used to put down demonstrations in Eastern Europe. This was a clear break with the past. Soviet tanks had rolled into Hungary in 1956 and Czechoslovakia in 1968 to put down popular uprisings against communist regimes. Before Gorbachev, the Soviet threat to intervene had always loomed in the background to discourage popular revolts. Previous Soviet leaders had also provided billions of dollars in military and nonmilitary assistance to their Eastern European allies. But Gorbachev cut off much aid in an attempt to save the ailing Soviet economy and to force economic and political reforms throughout the communist world.

This entire issue of force and legitimacy can be illustrated with a dramatic story from the revolutionary year of 1989 (Chirot 1991, 15). In October, just weeks before the Berlin Wall was torn down, East German leader Eric Honecker was preparing to put down antigovernment demonstrations with violence. Chinese officials had even visited East German officials to teach them how to deal with prodemocracy demonstrators (recall the murder of Chinese students in the June 4 massacre in Tiananmen Square). Now Honecker was preparing for a crackdown and possible massacre of his own. Soldiers were ordered ready and ambulances and trucks were preparing to carry away dead and maimed bodies in major cities, where demonstrations were most vigorous. But no massacre happened, partly (if not largely) because the Soviets refused to support East Germany, often considered the most orthodox communist regime in Eastern Europe. With no legitimacy and no Soviet support, Honecker could no longer keep up the facade; he was thrown out of office and the Berlin Wall was torn down within weeks. Communism officially ended in East Germany a short time later. Once the Soviets let East Germany fall, it was clear that all East European communist regimes were doomed.

Why was 1989 such a revolutionary year? Because three factors—economic problems, loss of government legitimacy, and withdrawal of support by the Soviet Union—coalesced to create these remarkable and dramatic changes. Some factors were clearly internal and some were clearly external, but they all came together to transform an entire region. It is also interesting to compare the events in Eastern Europe with those in China, where the outcome had been much different despite a similar loss of legitimacy by the Chinese government (Perry 1991). But the Chinese case was not the same, partly because the government was willing to use force to massacre its citizens. The government brought in poor peasant soldiers who were not hesitant to shoot urban students. In Eastern Europe, by contrast, there was a real question as to whether East European soldiers would fire on their fellow citizens. And, once the Soviets refused to become involved, the threat of force became moot. For China, the world can only hope that continued economic reforms will lead to greater democracy and the avoidance of more bloodshed.

With the fall of communism, some people have argued that Europe will become a more united continent. We turn to this topic in the next section.

The Rhetoric Is Unity; What Is the Reality?

Even before the fall of communism, Western Europe was beginning to unite to form a formidable economic and political bloc of countries. After 1989, there was discussion that Eastern Europe would unite with Western Europe to strengthen the entire European community. Although unity sounds like a good idea, it is far from reality in either Western or Eastern Europe.

One Europe?

Have you ever wondered what it would be like for a bunch of countries to merge together to form a single union? Perhaps Canada, the United States, and Mexico could form a miniunion, a North American Union (NAU) that features one monetary system, a common foreign and defense policy, no national borders, a single senate or parliament, one flag, and a single regional anthem. Let's go one step further: Perhaps a citizen of Mexico, Canada, or the United States could freely live, work, or vote in any of the three countries. Each country would keep its own president (or prime minister) and its own national legislature, but they would all have to work with the NAU parliament on a large number of issues. What is your reaction to this proposal? A good idea? A ridiculous notion? Pure fantasy?

It's not a fantasy in Europe. In November 1993, the Maastricht Treaty (named after the Dutch city where it was signed) formally created the European Union (EU), which now includes fifteen countries: Germany, France, Austria, Finland, Sweden, Belgium, Luxembourg, Holland, Britain, Denmark, Italy, Spain, Portugal, Ireland, and Greece. The only West European holdouts are Norway and Switzerland. The EU has a 626-member European parliament that is elected every five years by member countries; a single European passport that allows European citizens to cross the borders of other EU members; a European Union flag (blue with a circle of twelve stars); a European anthem (Beethoven's "Ode to Joy"); and a common economic policy that is supposed to produce a single EU currency by 2002. The overall EU plan is to form a dynamic economic and political bloc of countries that wields substantial clout in the global system.

Despite the rapid development of the EU, it still faces several obstacles that could undermine part or all of the union. One obstacle is economic. Although the EU has enacted a number of economic policies, such as free trade among member countries, it still cannot agree on how to create a single currency. A major problem is that countries with strong economies (like Germany) do not want to see the value of a common currency diminished by countries exhibiting weak economies (like Italy, Portugal, and Greece). Thus, stronger countries continue to pressure weaker countries to implement strict economic policies (for example, cutting budget deficits) that will improve the economic health of the region prior to the creation of a single currency. Weaker countries are complying with some economic directives but it is not clear whether they are willing, or able, to meet all the criteria set forth by Germany and other strong economies. Over time, disagreements on these issues could undermine not only the single currency concept but also other economic policies of the EU (Javetski 1994).

A second obstacle is language. The fifteen EU countries speak a total of eleven different languages, all of which are considered equal by the union. But linguistic diversity also makes it difficult to translate EU meetings (for example, in parliament), write official EU documents, and conduct other EU business. If all languages are considered equal, then which language will be used at any one time? It is unrealistic to expect all documents, treaties, and speeches to appear in all eleven EU languages. Although the EU has not yet taken an official position on this issue, it is likely that its working languages will become German, French, and English, the three most common languages in Europe. (Italian and Spanish might be included.) But designation of EU languages is problematic because it says that some languages are more equal than others. People are understandably attached to their language, possibly causing them to complain that "we are part of a regional union that doesn't even allow us to use our own language."

Language differences are symbolic of an even more serious obstacle to true European unity: national differences among EU countries. Although a common *European* identity and culture does exist to some extent, it is not as strong as national identities, national cultures, or national political systems. People tend to identify more with their national interests than with regional interests. Thus, the balance of power between the European Union and individual EU countries is a very serious issue. On the one hand, all EU members are supposed to follow common economic, environmental, and trade policies. On the other hand, there is no formula for settling political, cultural, or military differences among member countries. Many Europeans believe that such matters belong in the hands of national governments, not a union. And, importantly, all EU members retain national parliaments and a prime minister or president. National disagreements could threaten EU unity on a number of issues. For instance, the two military leaders of Europe, Britain and France, have strongly disagreed over how to handle the conflict in Bosnia, with France favoring a more aggressive military stance against the Bosnian Serbs.

Some observers argue that the EU may become an economic union (although without a common currency), but never a political or cultural union. Political and cultural union runs counter to a strong global trend moving toward nationalism. One of the strongest advocates of this position is John Naisbitt, who states emphatically:

> I feel confident in asserting that the Maastricht Treaty, which seeks to go beyond trade and bind countries politically—moving toward a common foreign policy and defense, as well as a common currency—is doomed to failure. There are many who disagree with me—vociferously. But that is because they do not understand that although people want to come together to *trade* more freely, they want to be *independent* politically and culturally. There will be no real union of Europe. (1994, 10)

Satirical support of this position has been offered by the popular British tabloids, which have promulgated rumors about what EU policies might do to grand Old England. One such tabloid jokingly reported that the EU would mandate a standard EU-sized condom. The tabloid joked that, although the standard condom might be fine for other Europeans, British men would need a larger-sized prophylactic. In fairness to Britain, other countries have also spread "Euromyths" in order to undermine EU proposals (Milbank 1995).

In contrast to those who criticize the EU, others argue that it is expanding at an impressive rate. The number of EU members grew from twelve to fifteen in 1995, when Austria, Sweden, and Finland joined the union. It is possible that ten central and east European countries could join by the end of the century. However, they must reduce their budget deficits and prove that they are stable democracies before being allowed into the club. Thus far, only Poland and Hungary have formally applied for membership, but this number will likely increase in the near future.

An expanded European Union could spread across the continent, creating a dynamic economic region with substantial international clout. Formidable obstacles still remain, though. Central and Eastern Europe are trying to make the difficult transition to capitalism and democracy, and they also bring new languages, new cultures, and new national interests to the European Union. Two astute European scholars note, "A part of Europe's brain will become European, but its body, including the heart, is likely to remain national for a very long time" (Cavazza and Pelanda 1994, 71).

With or without an effective European Union, the continent must take immediate steps to improve its economic standing in the world. We look at strategies for accomplishing this objective in the next section, starting with a focus on Western Europe.

Reviving Western Europe

Europe does need economic revitalization, particularly if it is to compete successfully on the global market. In 1980, Europe accounted for 21 percent of world exports. Today, the figure has declined to about 15 percent. Moreover, Europe has a $90 billion trade deficit with the rest of the world—a sharp increase from the mid-1980s. Although it is beginning to rebound, Europe has just suffered through a rather serious economic recession which has contributed to its highest unemployment levels since World War II. EU unemployment as a whole is close to 11 percent, with the highest rates in Spain (23 percent), France (12 percent), and Italy (12 percent). (The U.S. rate is about 6 percent and the Japanese rate is about 3 percent; Whitney 1995.)

One key to revitalizing European economies involves creating a more hospitable business climate. But, the very high cost of doing business on the continent is a major problem. Compared to their American and Japanese counterparts, Europeans work fewer hours per week, have more time off each year, and receive more pay and other benefits. Data from the early 1990s showed that in terms of pay and benefits, German workers averaged $24.36 per hour; U.S. workers, $15.39; and Japanese workers, $13.20 (Protzman 1992). Labor unions are much more influential in Europe than in other regions, and they remain an effective avenue for improving the lives of European workers. But high wages and generous benefits are also slowing overall European productivity. This is discouraging to foreign investors and to European companies trying to compete in an increasingly competitive global marketplace.

So why not cut labor costs and downsize the workforce? One major reason is because European citizens pay high taxes in exchange for good wages, secure jobs, and extensive government benefits. (We discuss welfare states later in this chapter.) Given high tax rates, a reduction in pay or benefits would be extremely unpopular from a political standpoint. Europeans pay far more in taxes than Americans. For 1993, U.S. tax revenues were less than 30 percent of the size of the total national economy. This rate was 40 percent for Germany; 45 percent for Norway; and 50 percent for Finland, Sweden, and Denmark. Moreover, the top tax rates (for the richest people and businesses) are very high in Europe. The rich pay more than 60 percent of their income in taxes in some European countries, compared with a top rate of less than 40 percent in the United States (Whitney 1995).

High pay and extensive benefits come with a price: Only a limited number of people can be hired without "breaking the bank." By contrast, American companies hire many part-time workers and give them few or no benefits. This is good for business but hurts many individuals who cannot afford the cost of housing or health insurance. And again, this approach would be incredibly unpopular in Europe because people expect substantial benefits in exchange for their taxes. Thus, European leaders are reluctant to insist on substantial cuts in pay and benefits or to advocate part-time work.

Despite this reluctance, some European companies have downsized (usually by not hiring new workers) and governments are beginning to scale back benefits. The giant French automaker, Renault, has eliminated 70,000 jobs around France over the last ten years (Whitney 1995). Germany's largest industrial company, Daimler-Benz, cut 18,000 jobs in 1992 and another 15,000 in 1993. Mercedes-Benz built a factory in the United States, where labor costs are cheaper. And Swedish-built Volvo announced plans to close some factories to save money (Knight 1993). Unless wages, costs, and benefits are reduced, it will simply not be possible for Europe to compete with low-wage economies in Asia and the Americas. European countries are even beginning to use part-time workers to further reduce labor costs. But these controversial strategies raise additional economic and political problems for the fledgling EU. How will the EU handle issues like wage cuts, part-time workers, and unemployment—not to mention a common currency? Europe must decide how to handle these critical issues if the region is going to rebound from recession and compete on the international market.

It will not be easy. Asia and Latin America are experiencing economic expansion and they are relatively united as regions. Europe is formally united through the EU, but whether it is effectively united will be determined in the future.

Moving East

Besides downsizing, West European countries are undertaking other actions to reduce labor costs, some of which are relevant to unity with Eastern Europe. Specifically, West European companies are beginning to invest in Eastern Europe for the same reasons that the United States is investing in Asian countries: cheaper labor. Audi, Volkswagen, Siemens, General Motors Europe, Thomson, and other large multinational corporations based in Western Europe are building plants and investing in Eastern Europe. At the end of 1994, foreign investment in Hungary, Poland, and the Czech Republic totaled $15 billion, and two-thirds of the money was from Western Europe. (In January 1993, Czechoslovakia was divided into the Czech Republic and Slovakia.) Moreover, 40,000 West

European companies have offices in Eastern Europe. This region has a hard-working and well-educated workforce, and it does not have expectations of high wages and large benefits. Thus,

> Manufacturers throughout Europe are reaching the same conclusions. No longer viewing [Eastern] Europe as just a potential market, companies are starting to rely on the region as an alternative manufacturing zone to get around high costs and to battle Asian and U.S. rivals. Indeed, Western Europe's backyard has both Philippine-level industrial wages and well-trained engineers. (Miller 1994, 48)

West European investment in the East does not translate into immediate unity across Europe. In fact, there are several obstacles to significant economic and political unity between Western and Eastern Europe. First, Eastern Europe has a series of new governments that are just getting used to democracy. It is difficult to make the transition to democracy and, until the transition is complete and stable, Western Europe is unlikely to unite with their eastern neighbors in a meaningful way. It is going to be difficult for *West* European countries to unite politically; it is going to be even more difficult for West *and* East European countries to unite politically.

Second, Eastern Europe is still making the very difficult transition from a centrally planned economy to a capitalist one. After 1989, all Eastern European countries experienced economic recession, higher inflation, and higher unemployment, none of which was unexpected. The situation is beginning to improve in some countries, although factories, communication facilities, and other infrastructure need modernizing before Eastern Europe can catch up with the West. As shown earlier in Table 6.1, some East European countries are now experiencing modest economic growth, although they still suffer from high rates of inflation and unemployment. The economic outlook for Eastern Europe will improve substantially if Western Europe continues to pull out of its recession. This could lead to further economic interaction (trade and investment) with Western Europe, which is the main investment and trade partner with Eastern Europe. It is unlikely, however, that Western Europe will want to unify with Eastern Europe until the latter's economies are in better shape.

An instructive lesson is provided by the reunification of Germany, which occurred officially in 1990. East Germany was essentially absorbed by West Germany, meaning that East Germany accepted the democratic structure, currency, and laws of West Germany. Moreover, reunified Germany is allocating substantial resources to the modernization of its eastern factories and infrastructure. Cities in eastern Germany now resemble giant construction zones as new buildings, new homes, new businesses (including fast food chains!), new roads, and new factories are under construction. But rebuilding eastern Germany is expensive, more expensive than originally estimated, perhaps costing as much as $1 billion. West Germans have been assessed additional taxes to finance these changes, eroding the romance of reunification and causing resentment toward the government and even some East Germans. Nonetheless, reunification *is* being accomplished in Germany, but it is slower and more expensive than anticipated. Modernizing the rest of Eastern Europe (not to mention the former Soviet Union) would be a daunting task indeed.

Changes in Eastern Europe also have led to many personal changes for individuals. Prices for food, housing, and other services are higher today than under communism, mainly because communist governments used to subsidize these areas. Workers in their forties and fifties are facing an extremely difficult situation, as many government-supported jobs have been eliminated and workers must be retrained in a new economy. On the other hand, younger workers have more opportunities to work in private business and to make (or lose) a lot of money. Citizens also have the freedom to travel and to vote in open elections. It is inevitable, however, that Eastern Europe will experience greater income inequality in the future, as there will be more people at both ends of the income spectrum. This is the good and bad side of capitalist development. A majority of East Europeans would clearly opt for the new system, despite some of the hardships it imposes.

Change also has its humorous side. German citizens told us a story about a department store sale in the eastern part of the country shortly after unification. The sale was going to last for several days, much like sales in West Germany and the United States. As soon as the sale began, however, people left work, school, and other activities to run to the stores. Business managers and supervisors from the western part of the country were shocked, wondering how people could abandon their responsibilities for a sale that would last several days. But the East Germans were just doing what came naturally to them under the Honecker regime. Under communism, *sales* meant that a few commodities would be available to those who showed up first. To obtain these products, you had to drop everything you were doing and get to the front of the line! The capitalist era means that more commodities will be available (produced by the private market), but they will cost more.

A final impediment to reunification is that Western Europe may continue to treat its eastern neighbors like unequal partners—as a source of cheap production and labor. "Colonies" cannot be seen as equal partners. If Eastern Europe does become part of the European Union, this will help alleviate this problem.

Having long observed the positive aspects of Western Europe, East Europeans hoped that the fall of communism would bring them a better quality of life immediately. Some of the most positive features of the region are exhibited by a small group of countries located in northern Europe and Scandinavia. We examine these countries in the next section.

Welfare States: Benevolent or Burdensome?

Let's play a quick game of word association. When you hear the word *welfare*, what images appear in your mind? Be honest. The word *welfare* has never been more unpopular in the United States than it is today. Many people associate welfare with big government, high taxes, family breakdown, and personal laziness. Conservative (and even moderate) politicians in the United States sometimes accuse their "liberal" opponents of advocating a "welfare state" that involves more taxing and spending. However, compared with European societies, American society has a relatively small national government and low taxes.

European countries often are referred to as welfare states, especially those in northern Europe and Scandinavia, including Norway, Sweden, Finland, Denmark, and the Netherlands. These countries do have relatively big governments and high taxes. They also have high levels of equality, an excellent quality of life, and progressive social policies. Let's look at these issues in greater detail.

One way to examine the size of government is to look at the amount of money a government spends, as a percentage of its total economic output (GNP). Big governments, quite simply, spend a lot of money. Column 1 of Table 6.2 shows that Europe's primary welfare states spend substantially more money than the United States, relative to each country's GNP. Moreover, these countries tend to spend much less money on defense and more on health, education, welfare, and social security relative to the United States.

Not surprisingly, expenditures in welfare-related areas tend to equalize incomes, with the poor getting relatively more income while the rich give up some of their income (through higher taxes). Table 6.3 shows that the poorest 40 percent of the population in these welfare states receive a greater percentage of the national income than those in the United States; and the richest 20 percent receive a smaller share of the national income than those in the United States. Again, as we noted in Chapter 5, Scandinavian countries and Japan are the most equal societies on earth with respect to income distribution.

TABLE 6.2

Government Expenditures in European Welfare States and the United States, 1992

Country	Government Spending as Percent of GNP	Defense Spending as Percent of Total Government Spending	Health, Education, Welfare, and Social Security Spending as Percent of Total Government Spending
Denmark	42.2	5.0	50.9
Finland	39.2	4.3	64.1
Netherlands	52.8	4.6	65.6
Norway	46.4	8.0	59.0
Sweden	47.5	5.5	66.3
United States	24.3	20.6	48.9

Source: World Bank 1994.

TABLE 6.3

Percent of National Income Held by Poorest 40% and Richest 20% of Population, 1992

Country	Poorest 40%	Richest 20%
Norway	19.0	36.7
Sweden	21.2	36.9
Finland	18.4	36.7
Denmark	17.4	38.4
Netherlands	21.3	36.9
United States	15.7	41.9

Source: World Bank 1994.

Another excellent way to assess a society's commitment to quality of life is to look at how it treats children. In a new study of children in industrialized countries, it is shown that the gap between rich and poor children is much worse in the United States than in Europe, especially Scandinavia. Take a close look at the results in Table 6.4. In the United States, the average poor household with four children has an annual income of only $10,923, whereas the average affluent household with four children has $65,536. By contrast, the gap is significantly smaller throughout Europe,

TABLE 6.4

The Gap Between Rich and Poor Children, 1991

	Poor Households with Children*	Affluent Households with Children**
Switzerland	$18,829	$59,502
Sweden	**18,829**	**46,152**
Finland	17,303	41,991
Denmark	17,268	46,326
Belgium	16,679	47,262
Norway	16,575	43,829
Luxembourg	15,396	50,071
Germany	15,257	51,874
Netherlands	14,529	42,616
Austria	14,321	39,911
Canada	13,662	56,174
France	13,003	44,835
Italy	12,552	44,280
Britain	11,581	43,933
Australia	11,512	49,863
United States	**10,923**	**65,536**
Israel	7,871	33,392
Ireland	6,692	27,185

*Households with four children that are poorer than 90% of households in the country.
**Households with four children that are more affluent than 90% of households in the country.
Source: Bradsher 1995.

largely because of generous social programs that redistribute wealth in these societies. In Sweden, for instance, the extremes are $18,829 and $46,152 (Bradsher 1995). The basic lesson of this table is clear: Compared with people in other industrialized countries, the rich are richer and the poor are poorer in the United States.

Some European countries have very strict rules about how you can treat your children. Slapping and spanking are illegal in several countries. Denmark, Norway, Sweden, Finland, and Austria prohibit (by law) the physical punishment of children in the home, in school, or in juvenile correctional facilities. (In the Netherlands, physical punishment can occur in the home but not in the other two locations.) Moreover, Germany, Ireland,

Poland, and Switzerland are also considering severe restrictions on physical punishment of children. By contrast, the United States has no national laws restricting physical punishment of children in these three locations. To the contrary, stories of willful abuse of children by adults and even other children are all too common in the United States. A European-style law restricting punishment of children would meet sharp opposition from many in the United States, who feel that the state has no right to interfere in disciplinary matters inside the home (except in cases of flagrant abuse). Although child abuse does exist in virtually all societies, the rate in Europe is lower than in the United States (UNICEF 1994b).

In addition to progressive policies for children, a number of European countries also exhibit progressive policies for women. Let's consider two illustrative areas. First, Europe's welfare states have substantial governmental representation among women. As Figure 6.1 shows, only six countries in the world have elected parliaments that are at least 25 percent female, and five are the European states under discussion here (the other is the Seychelles, an island off Africa). The U.S. rate is about average in the world: 11 percent of the members of the Senate and House of Representatives currently are women (UNICEF 1994b).

FIGURE 6.1

Percent of Women in National Legislatures, 1993

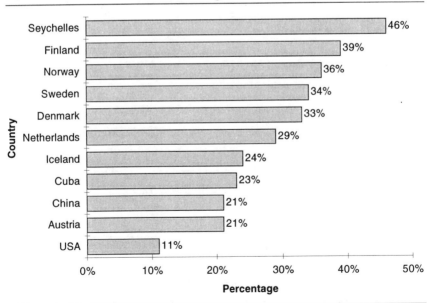

Source: UNICEF 1994b.

While speaking at the Fourth World Conference on Women in China during 1995, Prime Minister Gro Harlem Brundtland, of Norway, reflected on her own five-year tenure in office. She said that it is changing attitudes in Norway and has even prompted a new question around the country. Young Norwegian girls are asking their mothers, "Mommy, is it even possible for a boy to grow up to be prime minister?"

Second, virtually all European countries have relatively good, *paid* maternity-leave policies. Sweden, Finland, and Denmark have the three most generous policies in the world; Norway and the Netherlands also have very good programs (Table 6.5). Many of the other top countries are also in Europe. The United States does not even show up in the table because

TABLE 6.5

Paid Maternity Leave, 1991–1992*

Country	Number of Weeks	Rate of Pay as % of Salary
Sweden	52/65	80%/set payment**
Finland	varies	80%
Denmark	28	100%
Iceland	26	set payment
New Zealand	26	set payment
Italy	22	80%
Greece	21	50%
Norway	6/18	100%/80%
United Kingdom	6/18	90%/set payment
Austria	16	100%
France	16	84%
Luxembourg	16	100%
Netherlands	16	100%
Spain	16	75%
Canada	15	60%
Germany	14	100%
Japan	14	60%
Belgium	14	75%
Ireland	14	70%
Portugal	13	100%
Switzerland	10	varies

*Although the figures shown below are for maternity leave, some countries also allow paid paternity leave.
**A parent can select from two options: collect 80% of salary for 52 weeks or accept a set payment for 65 weeks.
Source: UNICEF 1994b.

it does not have a national policy on paid maternity leave. In 1993, President Clinton signed the Family and Medical Leave Act into law. This act provides workers up to twelve weeks of *unpaid* leave after a birth or family emergency. But it only applies to business or organizations with fifty or more employees (Reskin and Padavic 1994, 162–163).

Finally, the welfare states of Europe are also generous when it comes to giving resources to developing societies around the world. Although the richest countries on earth have set a goal of giving 0.7 percent (less than 1 percent!) of their GNP for Third World development, only four countries have actually done so. Again, as shown in Figure 6.2, they are Denmark, Norway, Sweden, and the Netherlands. The United States, by contrast, is at the bottom of the list, giving less than 0.2 percent of its GNP to other countries in the form of foreign aid.

Although the preceding paragraphs cast welfare states in a positive light, the situation should not be idealized. These states, and the rest of Europe, do have poverty and inequities. They also have growing crime rates. And, as noted earlier, European states are looking for ways to cut government and taxes at a time of economic stagnation and high unemployment.

FIGURE 6.2

Foreign Aid as a Percentage of GNP, 1993

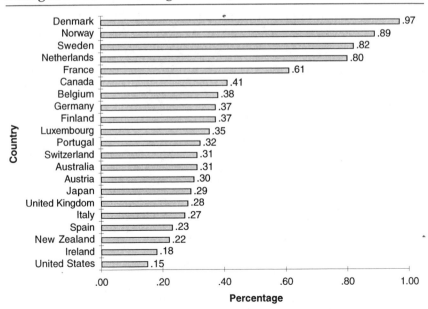

Source: UNICEF 1994b.

But the cuts will not be nearly as severe as in the United States. Many European countries have built an enviable quality of life with substantial government intervention. Europeans believe in government and will continue to desire strong government programs, although with some modifications. Debate over precisely what and where to cut will challenge the EU's degree of economic and political union.

Europe's welfare states clearly invite comparisons and contrasts with the United States. Although the U.S. government has grown over the years, the country's basic philosophy is "antistatist." Americans generally believe in sharp limitations on the role of government, and they would be horrified to pay European-level income taxes. This does not make the American system better or worse than European systems. The systems have different histories, different philosophies, and different pressures. Americans simply cannot understand why Europeans put up with seemingly exorbitant tax rates, which they perceive as a telltale sign that government is running out of control. And Europeans simply cannot understand why Americans tolerate high levels of poverty and resist a national health care plan, both of which influence overall quality of life.

Even if American political philosophies about welfare states changed overnight (which is highly unlikely), it would be difficult to implement such a program in the United States. The U.S. population is large and diverse, with a growing underclass. In order to extend substantial benefits to everyone, it would require a booming economy, higher taxes, and a much stronger central government (the U.S. government is very decentralized by international standards). But, this does not mean that the American system cannot learn from European systems. The Scandinavian emphasis on children and family life is impressive. Norway even has a national holiday in honor of children, a day of great celebration. Americans can learn from these systems, just as these systems are incorporating some of the antistatist measures that Americans welcome.

The quality of life produced by some of Europe's welfare states represents the best of the continent. In the next section, we turn to its dark side.

The Dark Side of Europe

If you visit the Munich headquarters of Germany's far-right Die Republikaner Party, you will encounter a cartoon poster showing an overloaded boat filled with Africans, Arabs, and Russians. The caption reads, "The boat is full" (Morais 1992, 88). It reflects the growing intolerance toward immigrants from the former Eastern bloc, Asia, Africa, and the war zones of the world (for example, the former Yugoslavia). In 1985, 178,000 people immigrated to Europe; by 1991 the number had increased to about 600,000 per year (Morais 1992) and is now more than one million. Combined with economic recession and high unemployment, fear of foreigners has produced an increasing number of ugly incidents throughout Europe.

Attacks on foreigners (including murder) have grown across the continent and much of the violence is directed at ethnic and racial minorities from poor countries (Fekete 1993). Neo-Nazi skinheads and other hate groups have made a resurgence in Germany, France, and other European countries. Moreover, far-right political parties, which often espouse an anti-immigration xenophobic message (that is, fear and hatred of foreigners), are becoming more popular. Although these parties win only a small portion of the vote in most European countries (usually less than 10 percent), their popularity is growing and is not insignificant in some areas. Austria's Freedom Party won almost 23 percent of the national vote in 1994 and the Italian Social Movement (MSI) won more than 13 percent of the national vote the same year (*The Economist* 1994). Both right-wing parties are exerting influence in national politics. Neither Austria nor Italy is becoming a fascist country, but they (and other European countries) are experiencing conservative movements that contain elements of antiforeign hostility. Xenophobia is dangerous. It was one of Adolf Hitler's tools as he rose to power in the 1930s.

In addition to ethnic conflict centering around "outside elements," there is also ethnic conflict from within Europe. In 1993 we were traveling by train from London to Edinburgh, the capital of Scotland. Scotland, of course, is part of Great Britain and is not (yet) an independent country. However, as soon as we crossed into Scotland a very Scottish conductor announced over the speaker, "We are now crossing the *national* border into the country Scotland." There was a defiant and determined tone in his voice. Indeed, Scotland, Wales, and Northern Ireland continue to move toward independence from Great Britain; the Basques fight for self-determination in Spain and France; Czechoslovakia split into the Czech Republic and Slovakia in 1993 because of ethnic issues; and the former Soviet Union continues to disintegrate into smaller and smaller countries.

Are nations going to continue breaking up across Europe? Perhaps. And, if so, are the breakups going to be amiable separations or violent divorces? Events in the former Yugoslavia reveal the worst nightmares that can evolve out of ethnic separation. We turn to this topic in the next section. It is a graphic section that illustrates a contemporary example of genocide.

Lessons Unlearned: The Return of "Little Hitlers"

A young girl (probably under two years of age) peered out of a heavily bombed brick building. An international photographer saw her and took a picture that was distributed throughout the world. The girl's hair was greasy and unkempt, her fingers were skinny, her eyes were dark and hollow, and she was sucking on a bottle of milk. She was straining to look out of an opening that was once a window. The exterior of the building was heavily damaged by bullets, and graffiti was scrawled across the brick. Through all the other yellow paint and bullet holes, two words could be seen: "Dead Zone."

We do not know if the little girl survived, even until the next day. Journalists and politicians seldom follow up on the images of war. And this picture was only one image among many during the war. Others involved trains, emaciated men behind barbed wire, raped women, mass graves, crying children, systematic killing of innocent civilians, and concentration camps. Of course, there were also the usual images that accompany war: blood, bombs, bodies, guns, and limbs. What started the war that the little girl was forced to watch? Short answer: long-established hatreds based on ethnicity, nationality, and religion.

Although these paragraphs could apply to World War II (and many other wars), they are written about the war raging today in the former Yugoslavia. This war is like a horrible, recurring nightmare that reminds Europe of its darkest side: ethnic, national, and religious divisions; genocide; and failure to learn the tragic lessons of the past. European leaders and many others (including President Clinton) desperately want the tragedy to disappear. But it will not. For years, world leaders have gathered around their television sets to "monitor the situation," again demonstrating the willingness of the entire world to watch another episode of genocide. Although everyone claims to hate this show, it is broadcast over and over again in different regions of the world. This is one show that is never canceled.

The conflict in the former Yugoslavia has killed more than 200,000 people in nearly four years, the majority of whom are civilians. It has also created more than 3 million refugees, the worst refugee situation in Europe since the end of World War II (Goldman 1994). But fighting is nothing new in the former Yugoslavia, with wars dating back several centuries (Kaplan 1993). The most recent war began in 1991. To understand the conflict, we need to examine the ethnic diversity of the old Yugoslavia. Take a look at Map 6.2, which shows the territories of the former country: Slovenia, Croatia, Bosnia-Herzegovina, Vojvodina (an "autonomous" region that was really controlled by Serbia), Serbia, Kosovo (another Serbian-influenced "autonomous" region), Montenegro, and Macedonia. The Yugoslavian population was 8 percent Slovene (living mainly in Slovenia), 20 percent Croat (living mainly in Croatia), 36 percent Serb (living mainly in Serbia), and 9 percent Bosnian Muslim (living mainly in Bosnia-Herzegovina). The rest of the population comprised several minority groups (Goldman 1988). The national capital of the former Yugoslavia was Belgrade, located in Serbia, meaning that Serbia retained the primary political and military power in the country.

Some of Yugoslavia's territories were also ethnically diverse. For instance, 12 percent of Croatia's population and 31 percent of Bosnia-

MAP 6.2

Yugoslavia, 1990

Herzegovina's population were made up of Serbs (Goldman 1988). Despite ethnic diversity, Yugoslavia had maintained relative calm since the end of World War II, primarily because of the skillful leadership of its charismatic long-term leader, Marshal Josip Tito. But ethnic tensions remained just beneath the surface. Tito's death in 1980, combined with economic stagnation across Eastern Europe and the breakup of the Soviet Union, brought out all of Yugoslavia's simmering ethnic and economic problems.

One very important problem was the disparity in wealth throughout the country. Basically, the wealth ran from north to south, meaning that the wealthiest area was Slovenia, followed by Croatia. Both of these regions resented having to share their resources with southern republics. Of course, the national government in Belgrade (Serbia) realized that the economic vitality of the northern republics was essential to the Yugoslavian economy. However, as Eastern Europe celebrated its independence in the early 1990s, Slovenia and Croatia decided to join the action and become independent European countries. Their rationale was understandable: Why be part of a troubled country (with serious economic difficulties) when you can improve your situation by joining the rest of Europe? Thus, in 1991, Slovenia and Croatia declared independence from Yugoslavia. They would be their own countries. Belgrade saw its economic power base breaking away and eventually sent troops to Slovenia and Croatia to stop the independence movements. The Serbs left Slovenia rather quickly, deciding to concentrate their efforts on Croatia, where 12 percent of the population was Serbian (Burg 1994; Goldman 1994).

In 1992, the majority of people in Bosnia-Herzegovina also voted for independence, more on political grounds than economic. (Bosnian Muslims were sick and tired of being pushed around by Christian Serbs.) As expected, Serbs living in Bosnia-Herzegovina (Bosnian Serbs) rejected the vote and received strong support for their defiance from the national capital in Belgrade. Belgrade could not afford another breakaway republic and therefore sent substantial military aid to their Serbian comrades in Bosnia-Herzegovina. The well-armed Bosnian Serbs initiated a brutal military campaign to force Muslims out of Serbian areas of Bosnia-Herzegovina and to isolate the region's capital, Sarajevo, which is an ethnically diverse city. Sarajevo, a once beautiful city which hosted the 1984 Winter Olympics, became a killing field.

Bosnian Serb troops began to engage in "ethnic cleansing" throughout Bosnia-Herzegovina, a practice of removing other ethnic groups at all costs. Observers could almost see the steely glare of Adolf Hitler through the haze of death that loomed over the country. Villages and towns were attacked and Muslims were driven out. Some people (including small children) were burned in barns, houses, and buildings. Some Muslim men were captured and sent away on trains to concentration camps, where they were beaten, starved, and sometimes killed. Many governments (including the Bush administration) denied the existence of concentration camps until international photographers took pictures and showed them to the world. Serbs also resorted to another disgusting weapon. Women—especially Muslim women—were systematically raped as a weapon of war. This practice was calculated and unbelievably cruel, considering the sanctity that Islam places on virginity before marriage and fidelity during marriage.

Concentration camps and rape are only part of the Serbian arsenal. Three other tactics are also popular. First, Serbian forces launch missiles, grenades, and bullets at innocent civilians, many of whom are children. This is especially prevalent in Sarajevo, the capital of Bosnia-Herzegovina. The city, surrounded by hills from which the weapons are launched, is an easy target. Thousands of civilians have been killed and maimed while walking (and running) down the street, going to markets, lying in hospitals, and attending schools. The indiscriminant killing violates all international treaties on war. Second, the Serbs often interrupt purely humanitarian aid efforts directed at Bosnia-Herzegovina. A popular tactic is to prevent U.N. airplanes from landing at the Sarajevo airport. The planes carry food, medicine, and other essential supplies for the war-ravaged people of Bosnia. Sometimes the Serbs allow planes to land, but then block trucks from transporting the aid to needy areas. It is bad enough that Serbs target civilian areas; it is even worse that they double the suffering by preventing medicine and food from reaching these same civilians. Further, they often turn off the water and gas lines running into Sarajevo and other areas, interfering with cooking, heating, and basic hygiene.

The third Serbian tactic is especially brazen. The United Nations had designated six small areas throughout Bosnia-Herzegovina as "safe areas." These regions were supposed to be safe havens for Muslim civilians who had become refugees in the war. (The safe areas are shown in Map 6.3. Note also that Serbia has expanded its territory by taking over the previous "autonomous" regions and by forming a federation with Montenegro [compare with Map 6.2].) A small number of U.N. troops were placed in each location to guard civilians against attacks by the Serbs. It did not matter. On July 11, 1995, the Serbs attacked the safe area of Srebrenica, home to nearly 40,000 Muslims, many of whom were women, children, and elderly people. After the attack, the Serbs allowed about half the Muslims to board crowded buses for the very difficult trip to another

MAP 6.3

Former Yugoslavia, 1995

"safe area" called Tuzla. Imagine the scene: hungry and terrified civilians, including many very young children, making the trip north under the watchful eye of the Serbs. Serbian military leaders occasionally boarded the buses to facetiously assure the civilians that nothing would happen to them—never saying anything about those left behind in Srebrenica.

The others were killed, captured, raped, or on the run. (No one knows exactly how many are in each category.) Young Muslim men (of fighting age) were especially sought after by the Serbs. Photographs taken from a U.S. spy plane on July 13 and 14, 1995, showed people crowded into a soccer stadium near Srebrenica. Spy photographs taken a few days later showed an empty stadium, but freshly dug earth next to the stadium. It is estimated that at least 2,000 bodies rest under the soil. Eyewitnesses who managed to escape from the Serbs report that men were taken in groups of twenty to twenty-five from the stadium and machine-gunned to death. The United Nations estimates that 4,000 to 6,000 Muslims are still missing from various assaults in the region. It is not likely that they will be found above ground.

But other atrocities were reported by refugees fleeing the terror of Srebrenica and other regions during the four-year war: more rapes, beatings, eye gougings, ears and noses sliced off, and testicles crushed. Other reports claim that some Muslims were beheaded and that their heads were placed on stakes to remind Muslims who was in charge. Other reports told of women forced to drink the blood dripping from their sons' slit throats. Although television cameras did not capture these events on film, it is certain that some of them occurred and that all of them are very possible.

Adolf Hitler is not around to direct the genocide in the former Yugoslavia. He is not needed. He is replaced nicely by Bosnian Serb leader Radovan Karadzic, Bosnian Serb General Ratko Mladic, and Serbian President (in Serbia) Slobodan Milosevic. The first two have already been found guilty (in absentia) of "genocide and crimes against humanity" by the United Nations International Tribunal for the Former Yugoslavia, a world court held in the Netherlands during July 1995. It was the first such tribunal since the famous Nuremberg and Tokyo trials following World War II. An international warrant has been issued for the arrest of Karadzic and Mladic, meaning that they are wanted by the entire world for their crimes. If they leave their country, they will probably be arrested and sent to the Netherlands to stand trial. Dusan Tadic, another Serb convicted of war crimes in 1995, was apprehended while traveling in Germany. He is now in a Netherlands prison cell awaiting trial. The official charge: "the collection and mistreatment, including killing and rape, of civilians within and outside the Omarska [concentration] camp" located in Bosnia-Herzegovina. (This information was supplied by the United Nations.)

The Western reaction to the fall of Srebrenica was swift . . . and mild. Two things happened. First, the United Nations ordered Western allies (the United States and Western Europe) to conduct an air strike against the Serbs. The planes flew over and destroyed *two* Serbian tanks. The Bosnian Muslim prime minister was so unimpressed with the retaliation that he termed the action a "so-called air-strike" (*The New Republic* 1995a, 7). Second, world leaders in Washington and elsewhere condemned the Serbian attack on a safe area but then equivocated on its meaning. Michael McCurry, White House press secretary, expressed support for the U.N. mission in Bosnia and noted that it "helps keep the citizens of Bosnia alive." But, in what may be the understatement of the year, he admitted that "with respect to the protection of this particular eastern enclave [Srebrenica], it has not been a good day" (7). In Bosnia, the chief U.N. spokesperson, Lieutenant Colonial Coward (yes, that is his real name), stated, "It's still a fine judgment as to whether or not the Bosnian Serbs' intent is to continue" (7). The mystery was solved several days later when the Serbs rolled into a second "safe area" called Zepa. (Quick, turn on the television sets; it's time for another episode of genocide!) Spy planes continued to "monitor the situation" several thousand feet above the ensuing carnage. It is symbolic of how far away world leaders wanted to be from the entire situation.

The Roller Coaster of War

In early August 1995, shortly after the two safe areas fell, the war in Bosnia-Herzegovina took a dramatic turn. As the Serbs drove north toward a safe area called Bihac, near the Croatian border, the relatively strong (but recently quiet) Croatian army launched a vigorous assault. They retook territory in Croatia previously captured by Serbs and expelled Serbian civilians from the Croatian area Krajina. Suddenly, another round of ethnic cleansing was under way, but this time Croats were driving out Serbs. Up to 150,000 Serbian refugees were forced out by jubilant Croatian forces who, along with Croatian citizens, jeered and taunted the Serbian civilians. They threw rocks at the Serbs' cars fleeing the area, dragged civilians from their cars and beat them, and killed an undetermined number of people. Although the brutality apparently did not match the Serbian raid on Srebrenica, it is all becoming relative. Some contended that "it serves them right" after hearing that Serbian civilians were on the run, for a change. But hungry and injured Serbian children certainly looked a lot like hungry and injured Muslim and Croatian children.

As Serbian refugees were fleeing Krajina, television cameras captured a bizarre, almost surreal scene and showed it to the world. U.S. Ambassador to Croatia, Peter Galbraith, showed up on the scene to try to comfort the expelled Serbian civilians. Galbraith chastised the Croatian government for permitting the harsh treatment of Serbian civilians. Dressed in a coat and tie, Galbraith approached many war-torn Serbs who were dirty and exhausted by the ordeal. One Serb, sitting in his car in the thirty-mile caravan of cars, explained in broken English that he had just left his dead relatives behind in Krajina. He started to say more when his voice broke before the cameras, he looked away and said, "You know, we are just so hungry." The ambassador jumped on the back of a tractor and rode with the refugees for an hour. Why? His ride, he said, was intended as "an act of solidarity and a warning that the international community was watching" (Bonner 1995). The key word was *watching*, a point no doubt noted by Croatian President Franjo Tudjman as well as by Karadzic, Mladic, and Milosevic. Ethnic cleansing and watching go hand in hand, a fact understood by Big Hitlers and Little Hitlers alike.

Just two weeks later, the United States tried to present a peace proposal to the combatants in the former Yugoslavia. (We talk about possible solutions to the war in Chapter 8.) Three American diplomats arrived at an airport far north of Sarajevo. Heading into the city to begin their meetings, they traveled along a dangerous mountain road littered with burned out vehicles. For some still unexplained reason, their armored car veered off the road and careened down an embankment and into a ravine, killing the diplomats. It was yet another haunting symbol of how easily the peace process is sidetracked in the former Yugoslavia, and how many lives have been consumed by the conflict. One of the dead diplomats, Robert Frasure, received a heart-wrenching eulogy from his 16-year-old daughter. Standing before her father's flag-draped coffin back in the United States, Sarah Frasure bravely talked about never again receiving driving lessons from her father or going fishing with him or eating his pancakes on Sunday morning. In closing, she shared, "One question I will always ask myself is, 'Why'? I know I will never have the answers to my questions" (*Washington Post* 1995, A15). Thousands of families in the former Yugoslavia—Muslim, Croat, and Serb alike—could say the same.

Only days later on August 28, 1995, yet another Serbian-launched mortar shell fell into the heart of a Sarajevo market, killing thirty-five people and injuring eighty others. Many of the casualties were children and old people. Blood, limbs, and death were everywhere. Some bodies literally fell apart as they were picked up by family members and rescue officials. International reporters helped civilians and rescue workers load injured people into cars for the drive to the hospital. One driver, a reporter for the Reuters news agency, told about two of his "passengers." A little girl, obviously in shock, quietly said to her mother, "Mommy, I lost my hand. Where is my hand?" The girl's mother could be forgiven for not seeing the problem. Her face was covered with blood and one eye was hanging out of its socket. Their nightmare was not over: The Serbs later delivered a mortar shell blast to the hospital, hitting some victims of the market disaster a second time. Mladic and Karadzic were working overtime to live up to their status as international criminals.

This time, however, the attack on Sarajevo was handled differently by the international community. Three and a half years after the genocide began and at least two years after the international community *threatened* to discipline the Serbs, the United States and other Western allies launched punishing bombing raids against Bosnian Serb positions around Sarajevo and other areas of Bosnia-Herzegovina. Wave after wave of bombers destroyed Serbian military headquarters, ammunition depots, antiaircraft equipment, bridges, and communication facilities. Muslim civilians in Sarajevo were literally cheering in the streets as they watched the jets scream overhead on their way to strike Serbian targets. Two weeks and nearly 1,000 bombs later, U.S. warships launched thirteen sophisticated cruise missiles toward Serbian antiaircraft targets in the center of the country. Western allies mandated that one condition be met before the bombing would stop: All of the Serbs' heavy weaponry (for example, tanks and large mortar launchers) must be moved outside of a $12\frac{1}{2}$-mile radius around Sarajevo, thereby keeping the city safe from shells directed at civilians.

Several days later the Serbs finally complied with this order and removed their heavy weapons from around Sarajevo. As we complete this book, the situation remains very uncertain. On the positive side, Sarajevo is experiencing its first peace in many months, allowing relief planes to bring badly needed food and medicine into the city. Peace talks, led by the United States, have also started among the Bosnian Serbs, the Bosnian Muslims, the Croats, and the Serbian Serbs. The road to peace will be long and hard, and may not be completed at all. But at least the international community seems to have finally taken an active interest in the process. On the negative side, however, the fighting has not ended in the former Yugoslavia. Taking full advantage of Serbian losses at the hands of Western bombers, Bosnian Muslim and Croatian troops continue to recapture territory previously taken by Serb forces. Moreover, it is clear that many atrocities have been committed against Serbian civilians in the process. Peace negotiations hopefully will end this killing soon, but no one can predict future events in the former Yugoslavia.

Some readers may wonder why we have devoted so much space to the conflict in the former Yugoslavia. The reason is because so few people have told the story. We want people to know something about the war in Bosnia specifically, but also something about genocide in general. As in Bosnia, genocide has a history, it has a number of horrible events and massacres, and it presents the world with a series of choices about whether to intervene. For years, Western politicians displayed an astounding lack of willingness to get involved in a situation of genocide. We again repeat a well-known adage: Those who don't know history are bound to repeat it. Europe and other regions of the world seem to fail their history lessons over and over again. We revisit this topic near the end of the book.

Europe in Theoretical Perspective

World-system and modernization theories normally are used to discuss the plight of developing regions, not regions as developed as either Eastern or Western Europe. However, these theories are still useful for explaining some aspects of developed regions and countries. As seen in Chapters 4 and 5, for instance, several European nations once colonized substantial portions of the world. In fact, the seventeenth, eighteenth, and nineteenth centuries could well be called the European centuries. But Europe was weakened during the twentieth century by two world wars and overextended colonial empires. It could be argued that Western Europe, in a new search for cheaper wages, is now treating Eastern Europe as an informal colony. Although this might well be an exaggerated description, it still underscores the fact that Europe is losing ground in the international economy and needs cheaper wages to compete with Asia and the Americas. Europe's global position is also dependent on its ability to modernize its institutions, especially in the east. To compete in the international economy, Eastern Europe must continue to modernize its factories and to change its legal and political systems to promote democracy.

Like other regions, Europe can be understood only by focusing on phenomena at the international, regional, national, and local levels. Europe's position in the world economy clearly is slipping relative to other regions, especially Asia. The continent is trying to respond by constructing an economic and political union across Western Europe and, eventually perhaps, across all of Europe. National- and local-level factors will affect the prospect for unity, however. For example, strong nationalist movements—which often have local origins—could interrupt regional movements and even promote disunity and violence in some countries. Europe is still an ethnically diverse continent and such diversity will pose a challenge to regional unity. As has occurred in other areas (for example, Asia), it is very possible that some form of economic consolidation could coexist with political fragmentation. Of course, coexistence has limits; economies clearly are interrupted when violence breaks out.

National- and local-level factors in Europe have produced some of the best and worst features in the entire world. On the positive side, countries in Scandinavia and northern Europe have produced an enviable quality of life. They have also been global leaders in terms of children's rights and social and political progress for women. Beyond European borders, these welfare states have been generous contributors to other countries, enhancing civil society in developing regions. On the negative side, countries experiencing ethnic conflict, most notably the former Yugoslavia, have produced some of the most horrible atrocities known to humans. Rape, torture, murder (even of young children), concentration camps, and mass graves remind Europe and the entire world of Nazi Germany and similar eras. Not as many people are dying today as during the Nazi era, but how many have to die to create a holocaust?

The revolutions of 1989 underscore the capacity of Europe to create dramatic change. Ending communism was a long struggle that included some incredible acts of leadership and courage. Lech Walesa and Vaclav Havel stood up to the Polish and Czechoslovakian governments, respectively, risking their lives and eventually becoming presidents of their countries. Many other less famous Europeans also engaged in a struggle that changed the face of the world. This spirit will be needed as Europe confronts its current challenges: the European Union, slow economic growth, unemployment, government spending cuts, political divisions, ethnic conflict, and new democracies. It is not so much a matter of whether Europe can overcome these problems to become *the* global economic and political leader. It is more a matter of whether Europe can simply remain a major economic and political player on the world stage. Asia and the Americas are economically stronger than Europe, and the United States is the political leader of the Western world. We next turn to the Americas.

MAP 7.1

7

The Americas: Reinventing Ourselves

In June 1992, more than 35,000 people from 178 nations including 118 heads of state, converged on Rio de Janeiro, Brazil, for the United Nations Conference on the Environment and Development (UNCED), better known as the "Earth Summit." The Earth Summit attracted not only world leaders and diplomats, but representatives of the world's indigenous peoples, scientists, industrialists and workers, environmentalists, feminists, artists and musicians, and ordinary people. George Bush, the self-proclaimed "Environmental President," hedged and vacillated before bowing to world pressure to attend the conference. Consisting of more than 400 official and unofficial events, the labyrinthine, twelve-day spectacle was the largest and most complex conference—on anything—ever held to that point in time. A five-week preparatory meeting in New York a month before produced 24 million pages of paper, ironic for a conference organized to help save the world's environment.

An event as colossal as the Earth Summit would have been inconceivable prior to the events of 1989. With the collapse of communism in the Soviet Union and Eastern Europe, a fundamental shift in global power from an East-West axis to one that runs North and South took place. The conference's main theme of *sustainable development* cogently expressed the issue that both unites and divides the rich, industrial North and the poor, developing South: How can a society, rich or poor, chart a course of development and economic growth that does not do irreparable damage to its environment? The sheer scale of the Rio conference was a clear indication that the answer to this question could no longer be provided by single nations; rather, it requires international cooperation of an unprecedented scale. Although the Earth Summit of 1992 did not necessarily provide conclusive answers to the global environmental crisis, it began to ask the right questions. The conference's daunting mission was succinctly expressed by Spain's Prime Minister Felipé Gonzalez: "Five hundred years ago men set out to discover the size of the earth. At this meeting we discovered its limits" (Brooke 1992).

It is no coincidence that the world's first major international conference on the environment in twenty years was held in Brazil, a country with the second largest economy in the Americas (behind the United States), but also a microcosm of many of the environmental ills of the global village. Under the motto "Develop Now, Distribute Later," the "Brazilian Miracle" of the 1970s fueled annual rates of economic growth as high as 14 percent, but also resulted in one of the most unequal distributions of income in the world. About 70 percent of Brazil's 157 million people live at or near the poverty level (Serrill 1992). With a population of 12 million, Rio de Janeiro is the twelfth largest city in the world but only the second largest in Brazil (São Paulo has almost 20 million people). Decades of shameless development have destroyed about 160,000 square miles of Brazil's Amazon rain forest—an area about the size of Iraq (Serrill 1992). Rapid industrialization with little attention to the environmental impact has spawned appalling levels of air and water pollution and contributed to global warming. Currently, Brazil is sixth in the world in per-capita emissions of greenhouse gases, a by-product of industrialization and modern living. The question "What is a sustainable level of development?" is particularly acute for Brazil and is likely to have sweeping economic, social, and political implications throughout the Americas.

Today the tension between *development* and *environment* looms as perhaps the most polarizing inequality between the rich countries of the industrialized North (the United States, Canada, Western Europe, and Japan) and the poor countries of the developing South (most of the countries in the tropics or the Southern Hemisphere). No region of the world more typifies this tension and the shifting axis of power between North and South than the hemisphere of the Americas. So we devote the first section of this chapter on the Americas to an examination of the environmental crisis and its importance for North-South inequality.

The Road to Rio: Environmental Apocalypse Now?

Consider the following facts. With just about one-quarter of the world's population, the North consumes about 70 percent of the world's energy, 75 percent of its metals, and 85 percent of its wood (Begley 1992). The United States alone, with less than 5 percent of the world's population, consumes almost one-quarter of the world's energy and produces more than one-fifth of its carbon dioxide, a major contributor to global warming (Elmer-Dewitt 1992). Also, by some estimates a child in the North consumes 125 times as much as a child in the South. The consumption of such vast resources by the industrialized North contributes to deforestation, desertification, air and water pollution, global warming, and the destruction of the ozone layer, all of which pose serious environmental threats to all countries.

Take a moment to think about your everyday lifestyle. If you are a typical citizen of the United States, you are surrounded by electronic appliances: televisions, radios, refrigerators, stoves, microwave ovens, air conditioners, computers, VCRs, coffeemakers, and other conveniences of the electronic age. We require tremendous resources to manufacture, consume, and dispose of the things we use to make our lives comfortable, from houses to toys to automobiles. On a worldwide scale there is about 1 automobile for every 11 persons (Wright 1995, 285); in the car-crazy United States, there is 1 automobile for every 1.8 persons (U.S. Department of Transportation 1993)! All told, the average U.S. citizen consumes about ten times as much energy as a citizen in the rest of the Americas (excluding Canada) and about twenty times as much as the average African. Moreover, U.S. citizens today use about 50 percent more energy per capita than they did in 1950.

There are two messages hidden in these statistics. The first one is obvious: If measured by sheer consumption, U.S citizens *on average* enjoy a considerably more affluent lifestyle than much of the rest of the world, and that lifestyle is more affluent than a generation or two ago. The second message is less obvious: All this consumption puts a tremendous strain on global resources and is seriously endangering the *global* environmental situation.

The situation is serious enough to call for dramatic action. But what action? The rich countries of the North are genuinely concerned about the environment, but not enough to sacrifice their affluent lifestyles to save a rain forest in Honduras. They look alarmingly at the rates of population growth in many of the developing regions and counsel Third World leaders about the strain such a volume of people will put on an already overburdened environment. The poor countries of the South have seen their countries pillaged by multinational corporations for cheap agricultural products and raw materials to satiate the North's quest for consumerism. Now, many citizens of these countries are demanding that their resources be used for their own internal development, and they argue that the North's admonishments to take environmental caution are hypocritical. For example, they point out that the United States has deforested 90 percent of its own forests over the last 200 years. The 1992 Earth Summit represented a forum for all nations of the world to exchange views and propose solutions toward the common goal of sustainable development.

Let's review some of the environmental issues that motivated the Earth Summit. These do not necessarily represent an exhaustive list of environmental problems, but do introduce some of the main themes.

Deforestation and Biodiversity

Did you ever stop to think about the ecological impact of the hamburger? Alan Durning, a researcher for Worldwatch Institute, has done precisely that and much of the following account is taken from his insightful analysis (1991). The environmental impact of cattle grazing is bad enough for the United States (about 85 percent of the rangeland in the U.S. West is overgrazed and about 10 percent has been turned into deserts), but its impact on countries that export beef to the United States and other countries is devastating. For instance, the United States imports only 0.5 percent of its beef from Central America, but that tiny percentage has contributed to a tragic deforestation of many rain forests in the region. To produce one quarter-pound hamburger imported from Latin America requires the clearing of six square yards of rain forest. Over the past three decades, the small Central American nation of Costa Rica has produced many millions of quarter pounders. Costa Rica once contained one of the richest rain forests in the world with perhaps 5 percent of all plant and animal species on earth. But the country experienced explosive growth in its cattle industry between the mid-1960s and mid-1980s, exporting as much as two-thirds of its beef to countries like the United States. The rate of beef export has slowed in recent years, but in the aftermath about 83 percent of the Costa Rican rain forests has been destroyed. Rain forests in the nearby countries of Honduras, Nicaragua, and Guatemala are also in serious jeopardy.

Meat consumption is a primary cause of deforestation. But a meat-centered diet is a luxury available to only about one-quarter of the world's population. The United States leads the world in meat consumption, averaging about 270 pounds of meat (beef, veal, poultry, and pork) per person annually. What would happen if Third World countries began to emulate the U.S. appetite for meat? Alan Durning shudders at the thought:

> The logical extension of this trend—a world where everyone eats as much meat as Americans—is a recipe for ecological disaster. Supporting the world's current population of 5.3 billion people on an American-style diet would require as much energy as the world now uses for all purposes, as well as two-and-a-half times as much grain as the world's farmers produce. How many planets would it take to feed the world's projected future population of 10 billion people on the American ration of eight ounces of grain-fed meat a day? (17)

At the root of much of the deforestation problem in South and Central America is the unequal distribution of land. About 93 percent of the arable land in Latin America is controlled by only 7 percent of the landowners. These large landowners gobble up ever-larger parcels of land to produce crops and livestock for export. Most of the remaining 93 percent of landowners are subsistence farmers who work small, marginal plots of land and barely grow enough to feed themselves and their families. Every year, using self-defeating "slash-and-burn" methods, they push deeper into the forests to find better places to grow crops or raise livestock. Others, for lack of a better means of income, burn the forests to produce charcoal for sale as cooking fuel. Satellite photographs taken over Brazil's Amazon forest show the scale of deforestation and have actually spotted burning forest fires. Developers and miners inflict further damage on the forests as they build roads, mines, dams, and railroads (Bunker 1985). Deforestation is clearly a global problem. Each year, the world loses about an acre of forestland per second, an area about the size of the state of New York . Since 1972, we have lost an area about one-third the size of the continental United States to deforestation.

Closely linked to the deforestation crisis is the problem of biodiversity, which refers to the diversity of plant and animal species in the rain forests. About one million species of plants, insects, and animals have been identified by biologists, but there may be 10 million different species—or more—in the world's rain forests that have yet to be documented. The ecosystem of the many rain forests is so fragile that the loss of one species might trigger a chain reaction throughout other species.

You might be shocked to learn how many of the products you use originate in the world's rain forests, including fruit and vegetable juices, spices, food colorings, vitamins, pesticides, natural rubber, and waxes. Perhaps most important, literally hundreds of drugs have been derived from tropical plants, ranging from diosgenin in Mexican yams used in antifertility drugs to vincristine and vinblastine found in the rosy periwinkle to fight some types of cancer (Myers 1983). Plant species as yet undiscovered may hold the cure for cancer, AIDS, or other deadly human diseases. Pharmaceutical companies, which might someday develop these cures, have a vested interest in slowing down the rate of deforestation. One U.S. company, Merck Sharp and Dohme, is paying Costa Rica about $1 million for the rights to chemically prospect a segment of its remaining forests for plants that may have pharmaceutical value. The company will share royalties with a Costa Rican nonprofit corporation if successful products are developed (Begley 1992, 39). Although this serves as one model of North-South cooperation to achieve sustainable development, such efforts need to be undertaken on a wider scale.

Global Warming and Ozone Depletion

Two other environmental issues that sharply divide the North and South are global warming and ozone depletion, both of which are products of industrialization and modern living. Global warming occurs when carbon dioxide, methane, and other gases accumulate in the earth's upper atmosphere and trap the sun's heat close to earth, leading to gradual but permanent increases in temperature. This process often is called a *greenhouse effect*, because the sun can go through the gases on its way to the earth's surface, but the reflected heat cannot escape through the layer formed by the gases. One of the biggest culprits in global warming is carbon dioxide, the main waste gas of automobiles and factories. Worldwide emissions of carbon dioxide have almost quadrupled since 1950 (Wright 1995, 606) and the North produces ten times as much carbon dioxide as the South.

Climatologists have documented an increase in the world's average annual temperature in the last century of about 1 degree Fahrenheit, a trend that coincides with increased emissions of carbon dioxide. Some project that if current trends continue, the world's temperature might rise three to five degrees over the next fifty to sixty years. We should point out that scientists disagree over these projections and their possible implications, but there is a growing scientific consensus that we should take global warming seriously (Stevens 1995b). Even a tiny increase in average temperature might have devastating effects on the world's environment: changes in climate (for example, more hurricanes), decreasing crop yields, and melting of polar ice caps, which would cause rising sea levels and flooding of coastal areas throughout the world.

Does this sound far-fetched? Try telling that to the Alliance for Small Island Nations, a group of thirty-seven island nations at the Earth Summit who voiced concerns about how global warming might affect sea levels. Scientists have shown that some U.S. beaches are disappearing at the rate of two to three feet per year and that most East coast beaches could be gone in twenty-five years. By the year 2100, rising sea levels near low-lying river delta regions from New Orleans to Shanghai could endanger tens of millions of people or force them to become environmental refugees (Stevens 1995b, A5).

The depletion of the ozone layer of the earth's atmosphere is also a serious concern. The ozone is a thin layer of gas in the upper atmosphere that permits the sun's heat to penetrate to the earth's surface but filters out about 90 percent of the sun's harmful ultraviolet rays. Excessive exposure to ultraviolet rays would lead to numerous ill effects including skin cancer, cataracts, and damage to the immune system in humans; altering photosynthesis in plants and lowering crop yields; and disrupting the food chain in the oceans.

The ozone layer is destroyed by ozone-destroying chemicals, particularly chlorofluorocarbons (or CFCs), which have been used in refrigeration, air conditioners, aerosol sprays, foam, and cleaning agents since the 1930s. Once CFCs reach the ozone, a complex chemical reaction occurs in which chlorine atoms attack and break down ozone molecules. The atmospheric life of most common CFCs is seventy-five years or longer; in that time a single chlorine atom can destroy about 100,000 ozone molecules. Due to the earth's prevailing winds and other climactic conditions, CFCs tend to concentrate at the North and South poles. The heaviest concentration is over Antarctica where perhaps 50 percent of the ozone has been lost, creating a hole about the size of Alaska.

The world might be fortunate that the worst ozone problem is over the most unpopulated region of the earth, but it's beginning to creep farther north. In Chile's southernmost city of Punta Arenas, people are taking precautions. Children are kept indoors from mid-morning to mid-afternoon and soccer practice has been moved from mid-afternoon to later in the day (Lemonick 1992, 62). Adults and children wear wide-brimmed hats and other protective clothing when they must be out in the sun. In the north, a broader but less concentrated patch of CFCs has developed over Canada, the northeastern United States, Europe, and Russia. While the northern patch is not as dangerous as the one in the south, it will threaten larger populations if it becomes more serious.

Thankfully, some progress is being made to slow the production of CFCs. Only two years after scientific documentation of the ozone hole over Antarctica, the world's industrial powers met in Montreal, Canada, to discuss the problem. In a model of environmental cooperation, the meeting passed the Montreal Protocol of 1987, which proposed a phaseout of CFC production and a switch to safer chemical substitutes. The industrialized nations that crafted the Montreal agreement and a followup pact in 1990 are on target to phase out CFCs by the year 2000. (In a rare act of unanimity, the U.S. Senate passed a law requiring an accelerated phaseout of CFCs by a 96–0 vote.)

Unfortunately, strategies to end CFC production have led to further conflicts between developed and developing countries. Developed countries have called on every nation around the world to end CFC production, but the poor developing countries have asked, "How can we possibly acquire the money, technology, and expertise required to produce alternatives to CFCs?" The situation is especially frustrating to developing countries because they are just beginning to enjoy the "benefits" of CFCs by acquiring air conditioners and other products that emit the harmful chemicals. Developing countries also see the stance taken by developed countries as hypocritical. Developed countries have been the primary users of CFCs and now, having found alternative chemicals, they insist that developing countries get their houses in order too, knowing full well that poor countries cannot do so without substantial assistance from the North. Without a global effort, world production of CFCs will not be halted by the year 2000. Moreover, if by some miracle CFC production does end by that year, ozone depletion will get worse before it gets better because of the atmospheric life of the estimated 20 million tons of CFCs already in the atmosphere.

Overpopulation and "Megacities"

In the time it takes you to read this sentence, 18 new babies will be born and 6 people will die around the world, adding 12 more people to the world's population. This translates into 93 million new people per year. Population growth is a major contributing factor to the world's environmental crisis as societies strain to meet the needs of so many people. The current world population is about 5.6 billion people with over three-quarters of it in the developing world. But world population is still on the rise and projected to grow to about 10 billion people by the middle of the next century. At least 95 percent of new population growth will occur in poor countries that can least afford more people to feed, clothe, and educate.

As discussed earlier, the fastest growing region of the world by far is Africa, where women are still bearing about 6 children each. Asia and Latin America have reduced their fertility rates to just more than 3 children per woman, but their youthful populations will continue to grow for decades to come. For instance, Mexico has made tremendous strides to reduce its fertility rate from 6.7 children per woman in 1970 to 3.2 in 1994, but its population will still double in the next thirty-five years. By contrast, the populations of Europe, the United States, Canada, and Australia have fertility rates at or below 2.1; their populations will grow slightly into the next century and then start declining after 2025.

Can the planet sustain a near-doubling of its population in the next fifty-five years? What will the quality of life be like for people who live in rich and poor countries? Several scenarios exist. According to Donella Meadows of Dartmouth College, coauthor of *Beyond the Limits* (1992), the planet could support about 8 billion people at the standard of living of Western Europe in 1990.

But this optimistic scenario rests on several shaky assumptions. First, population growth must be curbed immediately, but draconian population control measures can have very negative social consequences, especially for women (recall China's one-child policy). Second, it assumes that societies of the North can curb their insatiable appetite for growth and accumulation of consumer goods. Third, it assumes that poor countries of the South can raise their standard of living without ravaging their own environments (the Earth Summit's goal of "sustainable growth"). Fourth, it assumes that developing countries can manage economic growth internally to create a more equitable distribution within their own societies. Fifth, and most important, this scenario assumes a rational allocation of resources among countries that is not impeded by trade barriers, wars, ethnic conflict, religious and ideological divisions, political corruption, or multinational greed. All of these assumptions fly in the face of past experience and existing social structures within both rich and poor societies. A much more likely scenario, unfortunately, is a world population that exceeds 10 billion by the middle of next century, with increasing polarization between the haves and have nots and continued environmental degradation.

About the turn of the century, the world will pass a demographic milestone: For the first time in history, more people will live in cities than in rural areas (Linden 1993). Much of this is due to the inexorable growth of cities in the developing world—growth spurred by overpopulation combined with extreme land inequality that pushes more people into large cities. In Latin America, newly arrived peasants congregate in squatter settlements or shantytowns on the outskirts of major cities in the hope of finding work. Many Third World urban dwellers live without running water, electricity, or basic sanitation facilities. And they put a tremendous strain on sewage, transportation, education, and health services.

How big will cities get? As seen in Table 7.1, the United Nations projects that by the year 2010 the world will have 26 *megacities,* urban agglomerations with more than 10 million people; 22 of these will be in poor countries of the world. (By comparison, the world's only megacity in 1950 was New York City.) Another 33 cities will contain between 5 and 10 million people, 27 of them in poor countries. The emergence of megacities will exacerbate a range of existing urban problems including social unrest, crime, racial divisiveness, poverty, deteriorating infrastructure, poor sanitation, and pollution. In addition, new health problems are introduced by crowding so many people into urban slums. Epidemiologists fear that megacities will serve as a breeding ground for new and more virulent strains of disease that may spread quickly through large numbers of people. In 1992 a cholera epidemic swept through several Latin American cities killing 4,000 and hospitalizing more than 400,000 people in just a few months (Linden 1993).

TABLE 7.1

Megacities Projected to Have More Than 10 Million People
by 2010 (population figures below are in millions)

Urban Agglomeration	1950	2010
Tokyo, Japan	6.9	28.9
São Paulo, Brazil	2.4	25.0
Bombay, India	2.9	24.4
Shanghai, China	5.3	21.7
Lagos, Nigeria	0.3	21.1
Mexico City, Mexico	3.1	18.0
Beijing, China	3.9	18.0
Dacca, Bangladesh	0.4	17.6
New York, United States	12.3	17.2
Jakarta, Indonesia	1.5	17.2
Karachi, Pakistan	1.0	17.0
Metro Manila, Philippines	1.5	16.1
Tianjin, China	2.4	15.7
Calcutta, India	4.4	15.7
Delhi, India	1.4	15.6
Los Angeles, United States	4.0	13.9
Seoul, South Korea	1.0	13.8
Buenos Aires, Argentina	5.0	13.7
Cairo, Egypt	2.4	13.4
Rio de Janeiro, Brazil	2.9	13.3
Bangkok, Thailand	1.4	12.7
Teheran, Iran	1.0	11.9
Istanbul, Turkey	1.1	11.8
Osaka, Japan	4.1	10.6
Moscow, Russian Federation	5.4	10.4
Lima, Peru	1.0	10.1

Source: United Nations 1993.

Overpopulation and overurbanization in developing countries also
have important consequences for countries of the North. As living conditions in the South deteriorate, Third World populations increasingly look
to the rich countries of the North as safe havens with new opportunities

for jobs, housing, and education. Between 1991 and 1993, about 1.25 million *legal* immigrants to the United States came from Mexico, more than the next fourteen countries combined. Thousands more come through U.S. borders *illegally* every year to seek a better life for themselves and their families. This has prompted politicians in border states like California, Texas, and Florida to propose drastic measures to curtail the flood of illegal immigration from the South. In conclusion, overpopulation and other aspects of the environmental crisis are not simply "somebody else's problem" but are international problems that require global solutions.

The Lessons of Rio: Is Sustainable Growth Possible?

The 1992 Earth Summit in Rio de Janeiro gave the world an early glimpse at the possibilities of global diplomacy in the post–Cold War era. But it also revealed the perils of brokering international agreements on intractable problems like environmental degradation. One of the key accomplishments of the summit was the signing of a global warming treaty that *recommends* the curbing of greenhouse gases. The United States signed the treaty only after stipulations about specific targets for carbon dioxide emissions were dropped. But the United States refused to sign a second treaty that would require nations to share profits and technology with nations whose plant resources they use. Several other nonbinding agreements were made and an international watchdog committee was set up to monitor how well nations adhere to the agreements.

The most sweeping nonbinding agreement, the controversial "Agenda 21," provides guidelines on sustainable development in almost every area of the environment and stipulates that countries of the North should provide foreign aid to the South to subsidize development in an environmentally sound manner. Industrialized countries signed Agenda 21 only after developing countries dropped their demands for specific aid targets.

What Can One Person Do?

Ultimately, the environmental crisis will probably not be resolved by international treaties and financial aid packages alone, but rather must be addressed by grassroots efforts of people in all parts of the world. A popular automobile bumper sticker slogan says, "Think Globally, Act Locally." Here is a story about one remarkable person who has done just that in a quest for solutions to environmental problems. The following account is drawn from an article by James Hope (1995).

Dave Deppner was a prosperous and bored poultry farmer in Ohio when he answered his true calling to become a Peace Corps volunteer in 1972. Assigned to work in the Philippines, he learned about a "miracle tree," the *leucaena leucocephala*, which had been transplanted from the tropics of the Americas by Spanish explorers. The "Ipil-Ipil tree," as the Filipinos called it, had some amazing qualities that enabled it to restore land destroyed by clear-cutting. The tree is easy to plant, virtually indestructible and can grow to a height of twenty-four feet in its first year. Its thick canopy of leaves and elaborate root system create an ideal ambiance for other surrounding plants. Its roots actually build and enrich the topsoil by bringing nutrients up to the surface. Hardwoods indigenous to the local area begin to return on their own and soil erosion is significantly reduced. In one year, a single acre of Ipil-Ipil trees can produce about 18.5 cubic yards of clean-burning firewood and over seven tons of animal forage more nutritious than alfalfa meal. Incredibly, the trunks of the Ipil-Ipil grow back faster after every cutting. In addition, scientists have identified twenty-eight products that can be derived from the Ipil-Ipil, ranging from vitamin supplements to a substitute for coffee.

Dave Deppner knew a good thing when he saw one. Like a modern-day Johnny Appleseed, he began traveling throughout the Americas and other developing regions spreading the gospel of the Ipil-Ipil tree. After working for various nongovernmental organizations involved in developing countries, Deppner started his own organization called "Trees for the Future" in 1989. His strategy is to visit rural villages afflicted by deforestation, convince a few families to plant the new tree, and then let the results speak for themselves. When neighbors see the value of the miracle tree, they can use the tree's seeds to plant their own. With a staff of only six people and a huge international network of volunteers, Trees for the Future has planted 40 million trees—most of them Ipil-Ipil—in eighty-nine countries. A lot of people in the poor countries are glad Dave Deppner gave up poultry farming.

A Question of Sovereignty

At the root of environmental degradation and so many other problems in Latin America lies the question of sovereignty, that is, the ability of the Latin American state to operate independent of internal and external influences. Although formal colonialism ended during the nineteenth and early twentieth centuries in Latin America, these countries' independence is still threatened by a variety of factors, some internal and some external. Externally, they have experienced economic domination by multinational corporations and rich countries of the North. Internally, they have faced political and social upheavals, government corruption, and military coups.

In 1971 comedian Woody Allen directed and starred in the hilarious movie *Bananas* that lampooned the lack of sovereignty of the Latin American state. The movie depicted a chaotic political situation in the fictional South American country of "San Marcos." After a bizarre set of events, including a right-wing military coup, an armed invasion by the United States, then a takeover by a leftist guerilla movement, the movie's central character, a gullible American college dropout named Fielding Melish (played by Woody Allen), finds himself installed as president of San Marcos by a counterrevolutionary faction. This movie parodies just about everything, but especially the weakness and transitory nature of Latin American governments, disparaged by some as "banana republics." *Bananas* caricatures Latin American politics but is a sadly accurate portrait of the dilemma of some Latin American states.

Life imitates art. The landlocked South American country of Bolivia could easily have been the model for *Bananas.* In the 170 years since its independence from Spain, Bolivia has endured 77 different governments—most of them military regimes—and more than 150 coups or attempted coups (Nash 1992). Since 1982, the country has made halting economic progress under civilian rule and free-market economic policies, but frequent rumblings from factions within the military are a constant reminder that democracy has a fragile presence in Bolivia. Bolivia's experience, although a bit unique, is just one illustration of the constant threat to Latin American sovereignty.

Outside Influences

In one of the scenes from *Bananas,* a plane is flying U.S. troops to the country of San Marcos to quell the latest uprising. Here is the dialogue between two of the troops on the plane:

> First Soldier: Any word on where we're heading for?
> Second Soldier: I hear it's San Marcos.
> First Soldier: Are we fighting for or against the government?
> Second Soldier: The CIA's not taking any chances this time. Some of us are
> for and some of us are gonna be against them.

A key factor intruding upon the sovereignty of countries in the Americas is the economic and military presence of the hemisphere's only superpower, the United States. Since 1823, when U.S. President James Monroe proclaimed U.S. opposition to European encroachment in the Western Hemisphere—a proclamation the world came to know as the Monroe Doctrine—U.S. influence in the region has been virtually unchallenged by other superpowers. World-system theorists have long argued that multinational corporations headquartered in the United States have left a legacy of underdevelopment and dependency in Latin America. Today, despite some strides toward economic autonomy, the countries of the Americas are still economically linked to the United States. Figure 7.1 shows the percentage of exports from selected countries in the Americas to the United States. (A similar picture exists with respect to imports from the United States.) These data show that the United States is the major trading partner of many countries in the Americas and an important partner for most of the rest. The conspicuous exception to this pattern is Cuba, whose communist government under Fidel Castro has been the target of a U.S. trade embargo since 1961. These trade data underscore the significance of U.S. economic interests in the region.

To make the Americas safe for multinationals, the United States has frequently intervened in the domestic affairs of Latin American countries,

FIGURE 7.1

Percent of Exports to the United States from Countries in the Americas

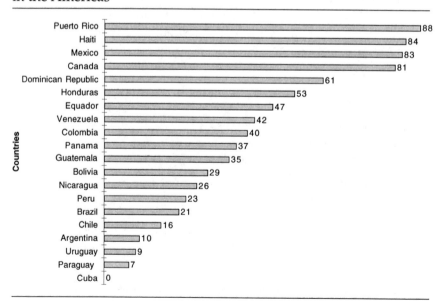

Source: United Nations 1994.

sometimes resorting to military force. This century has been punctuated with periodic episodes of open U.S. military intervention in the Americas: Haiti, 1917 and 1994; Nicaragua, 1909 and 1927; Cuba, 1933 and 1962; the Dominican Republic, 1965; Grenada, 1983; and Panama, 1989. In addition, the United States has never hesitated to offer covert support, military assistance, or foreign aid to reward its friends and punish its enemies in the region. In the Cold War era, the United States justified intervention by claiming that it needed to root out communism in the Western Hemisphere. U.S. involvement in civil wars in El Salvador and Nicaragua in the 1980s under President Ronald Reagan were cases in point.

Between 1979 and 1992, the United States poured more than $6 billion in aid into El Salvador to fend off an insurrection against the government headed by José Napoléan Duarte, a political centrist and U.S. ally. Duarte's regime had been installed when two previous governments, both with substantial military influence, failed to consolidate control of the country. Duarte's government gained some legitimacy by promising an aggressive agricultural reform package. The most essential part of the program called for redistributing land from the export agriculture sector to small landholders, but not surprisingly the plan encountered stiff opposition from the agricultural elite and was never implemented. The failure of agricultural reform and the rising expectations of El Salvador's professionals and middle-class workers incited demonstrations and strikes which were countered by government repression and assassination of opposition leaders. Popular opposition against the Duarte regime coalesced under a leftist revolutionary confederation called the Farabundo Marti Front for National Liberation (FMLN). A bloody civil war ensued between Salvadoran government forces and the guerilla forces of the FMLN in which 75,000 people were killed and more than one million civilians were displaced from their homes. Although unspeakable atrocities were committed by both sides, a United Nations-sponsored commission determined that most of the human rights violations were committed by Duarte's U.S.-financed government forces. At the height of the conflict, the army, the security police, and government death squads conducted mass executions and beheadings.

One unnamed volunteer for the El Salvador Commission on Human Rights, standing beside a wall of pictures showing mutilated victims of government hit squads, summed it all up: "I think the photographs show more than anything I can say. They are images I can never forget. We have to show this and try to make sure that it never happens again" (Annenberg/CPB Project 1993a).

But it did happen again—right next door in Nicaragua. In Nicaragua, the political situation was reversed, but the human experience of civil war was starkly similar. Here U.S. policies were directed not at propping up a government it liked but in deposing one it disliked (*Bananas?*).

A bit of the history of the Nicaraguan situation is necessary. For most of this century, Nicaragua has been strategically important to the United States because of its proximity to the Panama Canal, the key waterway linking the Atlantic and Pacific oceans. While the Panama Canal was under construction in the early 1900s, Nicaraguan President José Santos Zelaya stated his intentions to build a Nicaraguan canal, which would have threatened U.S. control of the sea lanes in the region. This prompted the United States to support a conservative uprising against Zelaya. Between 1909 and 1933, U.S. marines occupied Nicaragua and tried to install a regime sympathetic to U.S. interests. Augusto César Sandino led a guerilla movement against U.S. occupation forces until he was assassinated by the head of the Nicaraguan National Guard, Anastasio Somoza García in 1934. By 1937, Somoza had emerged as Nicaragua's strong man, taking over the presidency with the blessing of the United States.

For four decades, Somoza and his sons ruled the country with an iron hand but Sandino's revolutionary spirit remained alive in the hearts of Nicaraguans for years. In 1979 a broad coalition of opposition groups bearing his name, the Sandinista National Liberation Front (FSLN), overthrew the Somoza dictatorship and took control of the country. In 1984, the Sandinistas consolidated their hold on power with a decisive electoral victory. But the United States refused to recognize the legitimacy of the Sandinistas and sought to destabilize their government. Fearing that a permanent Sandinista victory might allow communism to gain a foothold in Central America, the United States covertly but actively provided arms and military assistance to Contra rebels trying to overturn the Sandinistas. The infusion of U.S. aid fueled a bloody, ten-year civil war that cost thousands of lives and left the economy in a shambles. By 1990, U.S. intervention in Nicaragua had taken its toll. U.S.-backed conservative forces mounted an electoral challenge to the Sandinistas and gained political power.

By 1989, the specter of communism in Europe had faded and public pressure in the United States to disengage from the conflicts in Central America was mounting. In the 1990s, both Nicaragua and El Salvador have teetered toward economic recovery and a fragile coexistence between government and opposition forces. In El Salvador, the withdrawal of U.S. support forced the Salvadoran government to make peace with the FMLN. The 1992 treaty ending the twelve-year civil war in El Salvador was viewed as nothing short of a revolutionary victory by the FMLN and was celebrated with great fanfare throughout the country. The agreement called for voluntary disarmament of the guerilla groups of the FMLN, prosecution of officers in the Salvadoran military who committed atrocities, agrarian and economic reforms, and full political participation. The FMLN has made the transition to an opposition political party, but other guerilla groups remain active in the countryside. In 1993, the Salvadoran legislature reneged on a key promise of the peace agreement by granting amnesty to public officials and military officers linked to human rights violations. The United States under President Clinton, in a reversal of its former policy, has tried to link future aid to El Salvador with the dismissal of the worst offenders.

In Nicaragua, a conservative, ten-party political coalition called the National Opposition Union (UNO) rules the country, and the Sandinistas are one of several opposition/revolutionary parties. The ruling coalition faces pressure from all sides: the Sandinistas and other opposition parties, the workers' movement, former Contras who are angry at continued Sandinista influence in the army and police, and factions of the business community who are disillusioned with the slow pace of economic recovery. Nicaragua has one of the highest rates of debt per capita in the world, which has discouraged foreign investment and led to government austerity measures. These, in turn, have hurt the most vulnerable sectors of society. In the case of both El Salvador and Nicaragua, combined external and internal threats to sovereignty have left the state weakened and ill-equipped to reconcile the various economic, social and political divisions in their countries.

Ironically, followers of the left (world-system theorists) and right (modernization theorists) cheer recent events in Central America, although they offer very different interpretations of the situation. On the one hand, world-system advocates have long argued that the United States exploits other countries in the Americas. The exploitation has lessened in recent years, they assert, because internal armed movements fought for a fundamental restructuring of the system. Without these guerilla forces, Latin American countries would remain lackeys of the imperial United States. On the other hand, modernization advocates reject this view. They applaud U.S. foreign policy for standing up to communism in the Americas. Only after communism fell around the world did these countries begin to experience more peace and prosperity. Both sides will continue this debate well into the future.

Don't Blame the United States for Everything

Sometimes the greatest threat to sovereignty comes from within. Such is the case of Colombia. Colombia is one of the oldest democracies in the Americas but also a country rich in the tradition of violence. Since its independence from Spain in 1910, Colombian society has been torn by six civil wars driven primarily by ideological battles between the country's two rival political parties (the Liberals and Conservatives) about the course of economic development. Typically, these conflicts have ended by a settlement among elite factions of the two parties, but have left fundamental problems of social and economic development in Colombia unresolved. The most recent of these civil wars, "La Violencia," lasted from 1948 to 1957 and took the lives of more than 200,000 people (Walton 1984), a scale of death comparable to that of the contemporary crisis in the former Yugoslavia. La Violencia was ended by a deal between the two party elites known as "The National Front" which amounted to a sixteen-year power-sharing arrangement between Liberals and Conservatives that left other political groups out in the cold.

One by-product of the continuing Liberal-Conservative stranglehold on power has been a stunted pattern of development in Colombia that favors the cities and the export sector of commercial agriculture. As a result, vast regions of the country, particularly in the Andes Mountains, have been ignored by the state and remain underdeveloped. In many parts of rural Colombia, people struggle on a daily basis just to make ends meet. Many of these people are not touched by the daily decisions of the two mainstream parties in the Colombian capital of Bogota. The state ignores them and they ignore the state. In the vacuum created by the absence of state authority in the rural regions, armed guerilla groups have emerged to function as a virtual state within a state. They enforce their own laws, collect their own taxes, and wage war against outside aggressors—mainly the Colombian state. Parts of the Colombian countryside have experienced a more-or-less constant state of war between guerilla groups and the state for over thirty years. Not unique to Colombia, this internal challenge to the state is replicated in other Andean countries like Peru and Bolivia.

One means by which guerilla groups gain popular support in their home regions is by promoting an alternative path to economic development—the cultivation of crops that drive the international drug trade. The Andes Mountains provide an ideal climate for growing marijuana and coca, which is used in the manufacture of cocaine. Poor Andean families cannot afford to contemplate the ethical ramifications of growing coca. On the streets of New York or Los Angeles, Colombian cocaine might destroy lives; but in Colombia, the coca plant sustains life. Poor Andean farmers grow coca for the same reasons growers in Colombia's commercial agricultural sector feed the North's more "legitimate" addictions to coffee or tobacco—because they are assured a cash return for their crop. Guerilla groups provide protection and facilitate the processing and trafficking of cocaine to the drug centers of Medellín and Cali where it enters the smugglers' pipeline. Drug rings in these two cities, and in numerous other smaller cities in Colombia, traffic drugs from Colombia, Peru, Bolivia, and Panama to destinations in North America and Europe. U.S. officials often criticize Colombian authorities for allowing the production of huge quantities of cocaine, but Latin American producers are simply following the most basic rules of economics. As long as U.S. customers continue to demand cocaine, poor Latin American farmers will continue to supply it.

Many critics of U.S. drug policy argue that the U.S. government has directed too much effort at cutting the supply of the drugs coming from Latin America. In 1989 under President George Bush, the U.S. launched a major campaign to reduce the volume of cocaine from Latin America by 50 percent over a ten-year period. The United States provided hundreds of millions of dollars of aid to countries in the Andean region in the form of guns and military helicopters to fight cocaine production at its source. Colombia, whose elections had been marred by political assassinations of antidrug candidates, was very willing to accept the aid. Colombia promised to extradite drug traffickers to the United States for prosecution. But this new scheme only made things worse; the violence escalated and the drug wars spread throughout the nation. In the eyes of many Colombians, the U.S. policy of extradition had created another war and posed an even more serious threat to the sovereignty of the Colombian state. In 1990, a new Colombian government reversed the policy of extradition and embarked on a policy of negotiated surrender of drug traffickers. Many guerillas, tired of the drug wars, turned in their arms and gave the new government a chance, but many guerilla groups continued to fight.

The drug wars have had differing twists in the two major drug centers of Colombia. In Medellín, touted as the drug capital of the world in the 1980s, powerful drug rings enforced a harsh justice against transgressors almost in defiance of state authority. Armed gangs murdered journalists, judges, politicians, and informants who attempted to get in their way. In 1992, more than 5,000 murders occurred in Medellín—sometimes at a rate of fifteen or twenty per day—and were shielded by a code of silence so that authorities found it difficult to arrest and convict the perpetrators (Annenberg/CPB Project 1993b). The kingpins of the Medellín drug rings even tried to run for political office (some were even elected!), and they sometimes assassinated candidates who opposed them. Their brazen public image eventually exposed their leadership to the wrath of Colombian authorities, and in 1993 Medellín drug boss Pablo Escobar (coincidentally, congressional representative from a Medellín suburb) and several of his lieutenants were killed by state authorities. At his funeral, large crowds turned out to mourn Escobar and proclaim him a modern-day Robin

Hood (Martz 1994, 134). The Medellín drug ring, which was responsible for about 80 percent of the cocaine reaching the United States in the 1980s (*The Economist* 1994/1995), was crippled by the purge of its leadership but not put out of business.

For the time being, the center of the world's drug trade has shifted to Cali, the Colombian city that now supplies about 80 percent of the world's cocaine (*Time* 1994). In Cali, traffickers are more sophisticated, preferring to set up legitimate, parallel business operations as fronts for their drug operations. These entrepreneurial connections have permitted them to quietly gain access to the inner circle of the Cali business community where authorities have found it difficult to root them out. The Cali ring has also funneled money into national political campaigns to gain influence with elected officials. Under U.S. pressure, Colombian officials recently dealt a major blow to the biggest ring in Cali by apprehending six of their leaders, but numerous smaller rings in Colombia seem to be filling the void in cocaine production (Schreiberg 1995).

Today, the Colombian drug trade is thriving despite government efforts. The drug trade is such a strong force in the Colombian economy that it will not soon disappear. As one recent article concludes, "Less than two decades after large-scale exports of cocaine from Colombia began, the country's drug business now seems too big, too diversified, and too clever for law enforcement efforts to have more than a marginal effect on its viability" (*The Economist* 1994/1995, 22). Conservative estimates of the Colombian drug profits for 1993 are between $20 billion and $25 billion (Martz 1994). Drug entrepreneurs now control about one-third of the agricultural land in Colombia, mostly in the highlands of the Andes. Amazing as it may sound, profits from the sale of drugs represent a significant portion—maybe as much as half—of the country's total accumulation of capital (*The Economist* 1994/1995, 24). Thus, nearly half of the country's economy is an underground economy, one not officially recognized by the government. Finally, one growing economic problem is that dependence on the drug trade is causing a misallocation of resources that could be used for more profound forms of economic development.

Despite these problems, one hopeful sign for Colombia is that its legal private economy is thriving, growing at a rate of 5 percent per year. The political situation is relatively stable. Recent discoveries of oil in the Cusiana oilfields should triple Colombia's oil production in the next few years, making Colombia the second leading oil producer in Latin America behind Venezuela. But the drug trade will continue to dominate the Colombian economy for a long time to come, posing a constant internal threat to the sovereignty of the Colombian state, a threat—it should be remembered—that is driven by rising levels of cocaine consumption in the rich countries of the North.

The Enduring Character of Democracy

One of Latin America's most remarkable features is that, despite interruptions from inside and outside of the region, its countries have marched toward democracy during the last twenty years. The "Map of Freedom" shown in Chapter 2 (Map 2.2) looked much different two decades ago, when democratic regimes were rare. Although democracy has not yet swept across the southern portion of the Americas, it is moving in that direction, opening the door to new possibilities for women's groups and other groups in civil society (Noonan 1995). Newly emerging democracies in Africa often look to Latin America as examples representing the promise of democracy. But Latin America has several advantages that Africa lacks, namely, more economic growth, more overall development, less ethnic conflict, a longer period of independence, more political parties, and a longer history of democratic movements.

Some of Latin America's economic success is derived from the fact that it is part of the Americas, a region that is consolidating economically. We turn to this issue in the next two sections, starting with North America and then moving south.

Economic Consolidation in the Americas

NAFTA: North America, Inc.

In the previous chapter, we tantalized you with the idea of a North American Union that would rival the European Union of Western Europe. Although the notion of total *political* unity under a single government, flag, and regional anthem may be unrealistic for the foreseeable future, major strides have been made toward *economic* unity—not just in North America, but throughout all the Americas.

The most publicized move toward economic consolidation in the Americas is NAFTA, the North American Free Trade Agreement, which went into effect on January 1, 1994. This agreement between Canada, the United States, and Mexico significantly reduces tariffs (taxes) and trade barriers among these three countries, creating a virtual free trade zone among 376 million people with a combined economy of about $6.8 trillion.

(The U.S. economy accounts for about 87 percent of the total.) For the United States, NAFTA fortifies trade relationships with its two biggest trade partners in the Americas (Figure 7.1). Mexico is better situated to attract investment from, and to gain freer access to, the United States and Canada. Canada, which had already negotiated a bilateral trade agreement with the United States in 1988, now gets new investment opportunities in Mexico (but not without great concern about what free trade will mean for its own sovereignty and national identity).

Although NAFTA does not eliminate all trade barriers—each country is permitted to protect some key industries—the relaxation of tariffs spurred sharp increases in trade among all three partners in the first year of the agreement. In the first eight months of the program, U.S. and Canadian companies invested $2.8 billion in Mexico, accounting for 55 percent of all direct foreign investment in Mexico (Harbrecht 1994). U.S. exports to Mexico increased so much during the period that Mexico surged past Japan as the second largest consumer of U.S. goods (Canada is first). NAFTA also helped increase foreign investment from outside countries seeking to gain the benefits of reduced tariffs in the North American market. For example, Japanese automaker Toyota announced a $450 million expansion of a plant in Ontario to make Corollas which it can then sell tariff-free to all three North American countries (Harbrecht 1994).

Critics of NAFTA argue that free trade will mean the loss of U.S. jobs to Mexico, where average pay is about one-sixth the U.S. rate. Ross Perot, the on-again, off-again independent candidate for U.S. president in 1992, warned that if NAFTA were passed we would hear a "giant, sucking sound" of U.S. jobs leaving for Mexico. (Perot has never been accused of shrinking from hyperbole to make a political point.) Although some jobs in vulnerable sectors have been lost to Mexico, the expected mass migration of U.S. jobs to Mexico has not occurred, at least for now. Several factors have curbed the tendency of U.S. employers to move jobs to Mexico in the first two years of NAFTA. First, although Mexican workers' services are cheaper than U.S. workers', automation makes U.S. workers more productive. But the productivity gap between U.S. and Mexican workers is narrowing as Mexican plants are modernized and Mexican workers receive necessary training on new equipment. Second, lower tariffs have allowed many employers to maintain higher-cost U.S. facilities because of offsetting reductions in the costs of exporting to Mexico. For instance, U.S. automaker Ford actually increased its exports of U.S.-made cars to Mexico from 1,200 in 1993 to about 30,000 in 1994 because of reduced tariffs (Harbrecht 1994).

Third, and perhaps most important, a stunning sequence of domestic problems that besieged Mexico from 1994 to 1995 tempered the enthusiasm of U.S. investors in the country. First, a guerilla uprising of the poor, indigenous population in the southern state of Chiapas, initiated on the very day that NAFTA took effect, provoked heavy government retaliation and killed hundreds. Under the banner of the Zapatista National Liberation Army (named for Emiliano Zapata, a national hero of the region in the Mexican Revolution of 1910), the rebellion focused worldwide attention on the millions of Mexican peasants who were largely excluded from the state-led drive to modernization. A shaky cease-fire ending the two-month revolt brought state commitments of political and economic reform and a promise to study the impact of NAFTA on Indian communities in Chiapas. Second, the assassination of presidential candidate Luis Donaldo Colosio Murrietta, the handpicked successor of Mexican president Carlos Salinas de Gortari, rekindled concerns among investors about the political stability of the Mexican republic. Although officials later determined that Colosio's assassination was not politically motivated, it still cast doubts on whether Mexico's ruling Institutional Revolutionary Party (PRI) would retain its sixty-five-year control of the country. President Salinas chose reform-minded Ernesto Zedillo Ponce de León as the new PRI candidate and he was elected by the slimmest majority since the PRI took power.

A third factor is most problematic for proponents of NAFTA. One of the first acts of newly elected President Zedillo in 1995 was to devalue the Mexican peso. Specifically, he devalued the peso in order to make the Mexican currency worth *less* compared to other world currencies. Why? To stimulate exports to the United States and jump start the sagging Mexican economy. Let's take a closer look at how currency devaluation works in the Mexican case. Before devaluation of the peso, an American tourist in Mexico could exchange $100 for about *350 pesos*, enough to buy an elegant dinner for two at one of Mexico City's finest restaurants. But after the 1995 devaluation, the tourist could exchange the same $100 for about *550 pesos*, enough to buy the same dinner *and* tickets to the theater. American tourists love devaluation for obvious reasons: They can buy more with less. Mexican businesses also benefit because their products seem cheaper to foreign consumers who then buy more Mexican goods. Devaluation should increase the flow of goods from Mexico to the United States because Mexican products suddenly are cheaper across the border. However, manufacturing businesses in the United States dislike this arrangement, because it means that Mexican products may displace U.S. products and U.S. jobs.

The devaluation scheme has worked, at least for Mexico. In 1994, before devaluation, the United States sold Mexico $1.4 billion more in products than Mexico sold to the United States; in 1995, after devaluation, the situation totally changed: Through September, Mexico sold the United States $15 billion more in goods than the United States sold to Mexico! This reversal of fortunes has flooded the U.S. market with Mexican products, taking perhaps 100,000 jobs away from U.S. workers who normally make these same products for the U.S. market (Myerson 1995). Can you hear the giant, sucking sound? Critics of NAFTA, especially Ross Perot and Pat Buchanan, are practically screaming "I told you so!" They insist that closer economic ties between the United States and Mexico will continue to drag the United States down to the status of a Third World country. By contrast, proponents of NAFTA caution against hysteria. They believe that this is a short-term blip on the screen prompted by the unusual action of devaluation. They further argue that the Mexican economy will recover and be stronger than ever. A revitalized Mexican economy would ultimately have a greater demand for U.S. products, thereby creating jobs for U.S. workers (Myerson 1995). Which side is right? The simple truth is that it is too early to draw any definitive conclusions about the effects of NAFTA.

Despite its obvious problems and negative impact for some sectors of the U.S. economy, there are three primary reasons the United States decided to pursue the NAFTA agreement. First, it is clear that while the United States is still a major player in the world economy, it is not the dominant force that it once was. As we saw in earlier chapters, Asia is posing a severe competitive threat to U.S. business interests and Europe is trying to do the same. Consider the graph in Figure 7.2, which shows the regional distribution of the "Global 500," the top 500 corporations in the world, from 1962 to 1993. This graph shows that the number of firms headquartered in the Americas (mainly the United States) has been cut sharply from 313 in 1962 to 173 in 1993. Europe, with a balanced mix of firms from Germany, the United Kingdom, France, and several other countries, has held steady in the 140 to 170 range over most of this thirty-one-year period. But Asia (primarily reflecting growth in Japan) has almost quintupled its number of Global 500 firms from 32 to 157 in the same period. Today, there is a virtual parity among these three regions of the world in Global 500 representation, with Africa and Australia far behind on this indicator. In the face of an economically unified Asia and perhaps Europe, NAFTA provides a first step toward consolidating the economic markets of the Americas.

Second, changes in the global economy are being driven primarily by the constant search for cheaper sources of quality labor. Joining NAFTA

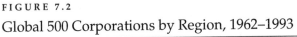

FIGURE 7.2

Global 500 Corporations by Region, 1962–1993

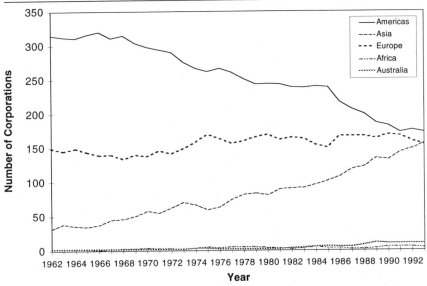

Source: Fortune Magazine, annual directories, most recently under the title "The Global 500."

gives U.S. businesses freer access to the youthful Mexican labor force which, as global corporations are discovering, is resourceful, motivated, and cheap. In 1993, average hourly wages of Mexican industrial workers were much lower than wages for comparable workers from the four little dragons of Asia: $2.89 per hour in Mexico compared to $5.62 in Hong Kong, $5.45 in South Korea, $5.56 in Singapore, and $5.49 in Taiwan (International Labour Office 1994). Joining NAFTA gives the United States an inside track to this cheap, well-motivated source of labor in Mexico. U.S. labor unions oppose NAFTA for this very reason. They see this cheap labor as a severe threat to the security of U.S. jobs.

The third major factor pushing the United States to join NAFTA is the need to grow new consumer markets for U.S. goods. Mexico is a huge potential market of more than 90 million people with the largest middle class in Latin America. About three in ten Mexican households—and 58 percent of all households in Mexico City—qualify as "middle class" consumers, potentially hungry for mass-produced consumer goods. Another 12 percent of Mexican households qualify as upper-middle or upper class, potential buyers of high-end consumer goods such as cars, refrigerators, and fashionable clothing (Walker 1995). Competition from Asia and Europe, access to cheap labor in Mexico, and an emerging middle-class consumer market in Mexico—these are the primary motivations for U.S. interest in the NAFTA pact.

Moving South

Ambitious economic pacts may be new to North America, but they are old news in the southern portion of the Americas. In fact, South America is wondering why there is any debate at all over NAFTA. After all, South America has already decided in favor of economic consolidation with two major agreements of their own. The first of these, MERCOSUR (Mercado Comun del Cono Sur, or the Southern Cone Common Market), is a pact that unites Brazil, Argentina, Paraguay, and Uruguay. These four countries combine for about 200 million people (more people than the EU) and a market size of about $630 billion. Brazil and Argentina are the leading industrial powers in South America with highly competitive industries in textiles, automobiles, consumer goods, and chemicals. In the past decade, they have laid aside long-standing political rivalries between their two countries for the sake of economic consolidation. Argentina, the smaller and richer of the two (in terms of average income), gains freer access to Brazil's huge consumer market. Brazilian firms will be able to undertake joint ventures with Argentine firms in similar industries. Uruguay, the smallest member of the pact, offers a highly educated workforce, a modern services and financial sector, and a strategic location between the two larger partners. Uruguayans hope their capital city Montevideo becomes a major hub of finance and transportation linking the pact. Landlocked Paraguay is the poorest country in the group and for many reasons has the most to gain by economic union with stronger partners. It offers a source of cheap labor and a strong agricultural sector.

To enhance free trade between member countries, MERCOSUR began lowering its tariffs for member countries in stages in 1991 and achieved almost total elimination of tariffs by early 1995. In these four years, MERCOSUR has enlarged the volume of trade among the four countries from $2.7 billion to $12 billion. MERCOSUR is also implementing lower common tariffs for most products imported from the rest of the world, making these four countries attractive trade partners compared to higher-tariff regions of the world. In the next decade, MERCOSUR plans to emulate the European Union by developing a common economic policy and currency (Long 1995).

The second major South American free trade bloc—the Andean pact—includes most of the other major economies on the continent: Colombia,

Venezuela, Ecuador, Peru, and Bolivia. They combine for about 100 million people and $200 billion in combined market size. These countries have also achieved a virtual free trade zone internally and have lowered tariffs for exports from outside. Although the Andean pact is significantly smaller than MERCOSUR, many foresee a union of these two blocs to create a South American Free Trade Agreement, SAFTA, by the year 2005 (Long 1995).

In addition to NAFTA and the two major South American free trade blocs, there are more than twenty other free trade arrangements in the Americas. One pact links Caribbean nations (CARICOM), and most of the others are bilateral arrangements among small clusters of nations (such as one linking Mexico with Chile, Costa Rica, and Bolivia). Virtually every country in the hemisphere, with the exception of Castro's Cuba, is getting in on the action. The interconnections among various countries are growing so complex that the possibility of a unified "Free Trade Area of the Americas" may not be as far-fetched as it sounded when President George Bush proposed the idea in 1990.

One intriguing player in the free trade sweepstakes is Chile. In the early 1980s, under the military dictatorship of Augusto Pinochet Ugarte, Chile was an economic basket case with soaring unemployment, an escalating debt crisis, and a glut of imports that put hundreds of Chilean companies out of business (Smith 1994). But Chile found democracy in 1988. The country voted to end the Pinochet dictatorship and elected a civilian government that advocated free-market economic policies. In the short period of civilian rule, Chile has turned its economic fortunes around to the point that it is now one of the most prosperous nations in South America, with a lot of capital to invest in foreign ventures. The skyline of Santiago, the capital, is outlined with gleaming new office towers, hotels, and apartment buildings.

One sign of Chile's new prosperity is that everyone wants to include the country in its trade bloc. In fact, Chile could be the linchpin that ultimately forges an economic integration of all the Americas—or beyond. Currently, Chile sends about 41 percent of its manufactured exports to MERCOSUR and 31 percent to NAFTA, making it a likely candidate for both trade blocs (Smith 1994, 52). In fact, Chile was courted as a fourth member of NAFTA until President Clinton decided that the package was already difficult enough to sell to the Congress without Chile. The door may be open to including Chile in the future, but the courtship with NAFTA has cooled. Chile has also been courted by MERCOSUR and the Andean pact, but so far has not joined either. However, it has entered into bilateral agreements with several South American countries which could give it many of the advantages of pact membership. In addition, Chilean investors have been buying up controlling interests in Argentine firms in order to strengthen their foothold in MERCOSUR (Smith 1992, 51). In 1994, Chile joined the Asia-Pacific Economic Cooperation (APEC) trade bloc, giving it freer access to Asian markets. Currently, Chile and Bolivia seem likely to join MERCOSUR. If this happens, then the eventual inclusion of the countries in the Andean pact to create a SAFTA seems assured.

Today, economic integration across the Americas and between the Americas and other regions of the world seems more possible than it did a decade ago. MERCOSUR seems to be taking the lead in these efforts, first by trying to forge links with the Andean pact to create a unified SAFTA, and second by initiating talks with Europe's Economic Union—with whom MERCOSUR countries already have major trade links—about lowering economic barriers between these two blocs. The addition of Chile with its links to APEC would give MERCOSUR inroads to the Asian bloc. With respect to NAFTA, MERCOSUR's strategy seems to be to build its strength and to wait for NAFTA to come calling. The feeling is that NAFTA cannot afford to ignore such a dynamic and growing economic bloc to its south, especially one that has built bridges to trade blocs in other regions of the world.

Why Integration Now?

A decade ago the economic integration of the Americas might have seemed like a pipe dream, but today it seems inevitable. You're probably asking, if economic consolidation is such a great thing, why did it take so long to start happening in the Americas? The reasons for this trend are complicated, but we can isolate four contributing factors.

First, the ending of the global Cold War between the East and West has eased the heavy-handed presence of the United States in the Americas. Now the United States is less likely to view every internal problem of Latin American countries as a harbinger of Soviet-sponsored communism. The winding down of the civil wars in Nicaragua and El Salvador was no surprise in the wake of the Soviet Union's disintegration and the fall of communist states in Eastern Europe. Now Cuba, the former Soviet client state, stands alone and largely insignificant in the hemisphere as the last remnant of Cold War hostilities. Mexican novelist Carlos Fuentes observed, "The fact that we can see the problems in their proper perspectives rather than through the mask of anti-communism or pro-communism is the beginning of the resolution of those problems on their real terms" (Golden 1992, 1, 5).

Second, across Latin America, authoritarian military regimes have given way to democratically elected civilian governments. Although military-civilian relations remain strained in some countries, viable democratic institutions are beginning to take root in Latin America and seem unlikely to disappear soon. Most Latin American countries continue to face sporadic internal threats to the sovereignty of the state from armed guerilla groups—from the drug gangs of Colombia and Panama, to the Chiapas in Mexico, to the Shining Path (an ardent communist organization) in Peru. Some of these openly revolutionary movements have an ethnic dimension, others are purely ideological. But importantly, in the absence of heavy-handed interference by the United States, most Latin American countries have steered a moderate course between the extremes of left and right, and a tone of civility has been restored to Latin American politics.

Third, most newly elected regimes have instituted free-market economic policies while successfully wrestling with a range of economic and political problems. Economically, they have been successful for the most part in bringing the debt crisis of the 1980s under control, lowering inflation rates, and privatizing many inefficient state-run industries. All of these steps have made Latin America more attractive to foreign investors. They also have begun to address political problems such as building democratic institutions, eliminating corruption in the government and judiciary, and managing internal threats to sovereignty from the military and guerilla groups. Importantly, the free-market policies have encouraged trade among countries in the Americas and with other countries in the world.

Fourth, despite persistent poverty in many countries of the Americas, experts view it as having tremendous potential for economic growth in the future—perhaps greater than the former socialist economies of Eastern Europe and the dynamic economic bloc in Asia. About 27 percent of Latin American households have a purchasing power greater than or equal to a lower-middle-class household with a $20,000 income in the United States. This is the highest percentage of any region of the world outside the established market economies of the North (Walker 1995, 44). As shown in Figure 7.3, many Latin American countries are becoming middle-class societies, but this assertion must be balanced against the sobering reality that more than half of the households in these countries remain at or near a subsistence-level income. Middle-class consumers attract foreign investors and create large internal markets that can nurture democracy. By contrast, most African countries have a "middle class" that is less than half the size of most Latin American countries, making self-starting national development difficult.

FIGURE 7.3

Percent of Population in Each Social Class, 1994

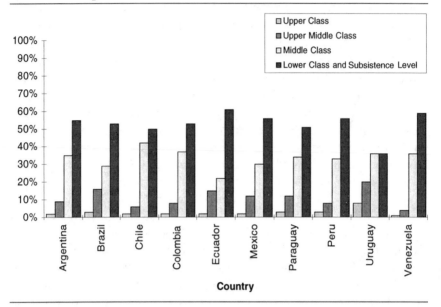

Source: Walker 1995.

All of these factors contribute to the new economic dynamism in the Americas and the trend toward economic consolidation. What direction this consolidation will take in the future is anybody's guess. Will there be a single Free Trade Area of the Americas in your lifetime? What are the implications of such economic consolidation for the restructuring of jobs and the nature of inequality within and among countries? Can the tremendous potential for economic growth in the Americas be accomplished in an environmentally sound manner? These are questions that world leaders and ordinary citizens will be wrestling with in the next decade. What contribution will you make to this debate?

The Americas in Theoretical Perspective

The Americas is a region that is undergoing dramatic changes across a spectrum of economic, political, and environmental issues. In a sense, the Americas is reinventing itself. These changes necessitate new theoretical approaches to understand the problems of development. World-system theory gives some insight into the historical circumstances at the root of underdevelopment in Latin America. The legacy of European colonialism has left its mark on Latin American development in the form of distorted economies, authoritarian military regimes, and subjugation of indigenous populations. Neocolonialism, particularly the heavy-handed economic and military presence of the United States in the region, further stunted economic and political democracy in the region for decades. But recently, democracy has been breaking out all over the region. World-system theory is poorly equipped to account for these developments and it cannot explain how the new civilian governments have managed to cope with the seemingly intractable economic problems of debt and inflation.

Modernization theory seems to offer insight into the internal sources of Latin America's newfound dynamism. The synergy in Latin America does not rest on adoption of Western strategies for development, but on charting a new Latin American course of development. Although persistent problems of poverty, inequitable distribution of wealth, and government corruption will not disappear overnight, Latin American countries are discovering an economic autonomy and self-sufficiency unprecedented in the past. Not coincidentally, the strongest manifestation of this new autonomy is among countries with the weakest economic ties to the United States in terms of trade relations—Chile and the countries of the MERCOSUR bloc (Figure 7.1).

But modernization theory also is lacking because it does not anticipate the new interconnections among societies in the Americas. Countries in the Americas are charting their own unique path to development in the 1990s, but it is a path that is steered by the new wave of economic consolidation. The pattern of economic consolidation in the Americas is a unique one, with more than twenty separate trading blocs operating like little engines of economic growth throughout the hemisphere. But like Asia, economic growth in the Americas in the past decade has come largely as a result of trade *among* nations within the region.

Although countries in the Americas have not experienced as much political disintegration as Africa or parts of Europe, they have encountered continuous threats to the sovereignty of the state. Armed guerilla groups espousing extreme views of the left or right pose a constant internal threat to the state. In some cases, such as Colombia, Peru, and Bolivia, guerilla groups have established a virtual state within a state in rural regions of the country that nurture the drug trade. In some Latin American countries, fidgety generals lurk in the background as a constant reminder of the possibility of military coups should civilian governments stumble. Amid chronic problems of poverty and past government corruption, which seem almost endemic to Latin America, civilian governments struggle to find a way to create democratic institutions.

Against seemingly insurmountable odds, the countries of the Americas must navigate a course of sustainable development, a path of economic development that does not inflict irreparable harm on the environment. The global environmental crisis, which is brought clearly into focus in the Americas, is a complicated result of internal and external factors. And, as the Earth Summit clearly demonstrates, such problems will not be remedied by individual countries acting unilaterally. Hopefully, the new spirit of economic cooperation in the region will lay a foundation for cooperation on environmental matters so that the goal of sustainable development can become a reality for the entire region.

8

Creating a Better World

Summarizing Trends and Changes

Internationally oriented social scientists have an exciting job because the world is constantly changing. Asia is growing stronger and more dominant in the global economy. The Americas are also doing well, with substantial economic growth and democratization across much of Latin America. However, growing inequality in both North and South America threatens the quality of life for many citizens. Europe is experiencing economic stagnation. The European Union could help change this situation, but differences across the continent threaten any real unity. Africa continues to decline in almost every respect. With only a few bright spots, this fascinating continent is in danger of being forgotten by much of the world.

These four world regions, though unequal, are very interconnected in the global village. Asia, Europe, and the Americas invest in and trade with each other, and Africa provides substantial raw materials to the rest of the world. Computers, fax machines, and information technology make it possible for people in one area to communicate in seconds with people in another region. Here is a story that illustrates this point. Several years ago a graduate student who works with us was conducting research in East Africa. She was scheduled to travel by train into a relatively remote area that did not have reliable telephone service. We did not know the exact day that she would travel, but we knew it would be sometime during a particular week. Suddenly, though, we heard on the news that the country had experienced a terrible train wreck in the region she was scheduled to visit. Hundreds were reported dead. Needless to say, we were very worried and wanted information on the accident as quickly as possible. Thus, we logged onto the Internet to an on-line service that provides information about the specific country in question. Within seconds, we found a report telling us that the train was *leaving* the area of concern, not *entering* it, meaning that our student could not have been on board. Without the Internet, we would not have received any information about this student for several days.

Global communication and technology also create inequality, however. For instance, the United States is by far the leading producer of computer software in the world. This means that the predominant international language of computing (and the Internet) is English. Although many countries and institutions are working to convert software into local languages, they will have a difficult time keeping up with the rapid changes in software technology. Thus, the gap between those with and without vital information on education, business, and other topics will grow dramatically in future years. The have-nots are poor countries that cannot afford new technology or lack the capacity to translate it into a widely understood language. The bottom line is this: Economic inequality is a major global problem; technological inequality is a major global crisis.

Because we have stressed the interconnected character of the world throughout this book, you might have questions about several countries and regions that have received little coverage thus far. What about Russia? What about Israel, Egypt, and the whole "Middle East"? What about Iran, Iraq, and the Persian Gulf region? What about Australia? What about other Asian countries that were not discussed? All of these regions are important and have been the source of numerous articles and books. Unfortunately, this introductory book can cover only a limited amount of material and we have selected four regions, and particular countries within the regions. But readers can take the principles presented in this book and apply them to other areas. Global studies are always fascinating because there is so much to study. We hope you study some of the areas we have discussed as well as many other regions.

Creating Positive Changes

Several years ago during a class in social change, a student raised his hand and said: "I'm so frustrated. We have studied so many issues and problems during this course, but I don't know what can be done to solve them. Is it all hopeless?" It was a great question and prompted us to add an entire section to the course called "Creating Positive Changes." We elaborate on these changes in this chapter. Our purpose is *not* to push a particular agenda or ideology; instead, it is to discuss a wide range of options that might be used to change the world. We start by presenting solutions proposed by world-system and modernization theories. Then we discuss a variety of strategies available to regions, countries, communities, and individuals.

Solutions Proposed by World-System and Modernization Theories

World-system theorists often propose fairly radical solutions to global problems, most of which are unrealistic. According to this theory, the major cause of global inequality and many other problems is exploitation of poor countries by rich countries. Thus, the primary solution to these problems involves a fundamental and complete transformation of the world economic and political structure. Some call this a transformation to a New International Economic Order (NIEO). Strong advocates of this position even see the necessity of a new world government to promote greater equality:

> We propose a new world political system in which economic and human rights of citizens are guaranteed by a limited federal world state. Such a state would be constitutionally limited from imposing cultural conformity upon citizens or nation-states. It would, however, have certain powers to prevent international war by exercising judicial and military control over conflicting parties, and it would have the power to levy [taxes] to guarantee a basic income for individuals. (Bornschier and Chase-Dunn 1985, 154)

Although their proposals are vague, world-system theorists basically call for a redistribution of income from rich countries (and people) to poor countries (and people), a redistribution enforced by some type of world government. Considering the global trend toward political fragmentation, it is unlikely that there will be a move toward any type of single state. (Recall the problems associated with political unity in Europe or solutions to ethnic fighting in many regions of the world.)

If world-system theory errs on the side of proposing an overly ambitious agenda for social change, modernization theory errs by proposing virtually no agenda. According to this perspective, poor countries will automatically develop when they adopt free markets, democratic systems, and Western values. Rich countries can expedite the development process by giving foreign aid and technical assistance, both of which supposedly will help create "modernizing institutions" (for example, schools) that produce development (Inkeles and Smith 1974; Delacroix and Ragin 1978). Moreover, modernization theory sees no reason to redistribute wealth; poor countries will magically rise to the level of developed nations as they become increasingly modern.

Unfortunately, neither modernization nor world-system theory is particularly useful for creating positive social changes. World-system theorists throw up their hands in frustration over the lack of an NIEO, and modernization theorists simply wait for development to evolve. Next, we discuss specific solutions to global problems that are not shaped by ideological or political agendas.

Global, Regional, National, and Community Solutions

Realistic solutions to global problems can be considered at each of these levels. We will look briefly at several possibilities under each category.

Global. Three global actions to create positive changes could be undertaken. First, wealthy countries could give more foreign aid to developing nations, especially to basic needs such as nutrition, health care, clean water, family planning, and education. Data for 1990 show that the richest countries around the world gave about $40 billion in official nonmilitary development assistance. Only 6.3 percent of this money, just $2.5 billion, went to improve basic needs. UNICEF asks rich countries to give 20 percent of their aid to basic needs, which would result in more than $8 billion per year being allocated to the most important aspects of life (UNICEF 1993, 3).

Second, wealthy countries and financial institutions could "forgive" or substantially renegotiate the more than $1 trillion in debt owed to them. As we noted earlier, much of this debt will never be repaid. Thus, it would make sense for all parties (including banks) to write off at least some of the debt. This would give indebted countries additional funds to improve basic needs. It would also eliminate the structural adjustment programs (SAPs) that create such great hardships on poor citizens and children throughout the developing world. Debt forgiveness packages could even include a stipulation that some of the money saved be used for development projects.

Third, wealthy countries could provide technical assistance to developing countries, especially by providing computers, computer training, and computer software. Without access to such technology, poor countries will fall increasingly farther behind in almost all respects. Universities in rich countries should also be encouraged to increase exchange programs and other initiatives that will train both foreign faculty and students in new forms of computer and information technology.

Regional. Regional efforts to create positive changes sound like a great idea and have been attempted all over the world. Some have included formal agreements such as NAFTA, the EU, and OPEC. Others are largely unofficial and market-driven, such as Asia's cooperative regional effort. But regional initiatives have been difficult to sustain because of political, economic, and ethnic differences. The EU is finding this out now and OPEC found this out in the 1980s. They are not alone. In Africa, for instance, a number of regional plans have been attempted over the last forty years. In 1957, Ghana became an independent country and its first president, Kwame Nkrumah, called for Pan-Africanism, a proposal to create a "United States of Africa." Nkrumah wanted all African countries to unite in order to make the continent more self-reliant and less dependent on the West. It was a great concept and has produced numerous proposals since that time (Liebenow 1986).

One set of proposals called for the continent's raw material producers to come together to demand higher prices for their products. All coffee producers were supposed to agree on a price and a set of rules for trading with developed countries; all tea, sugar, and mineral producers were supposed to do the same. These raw material associations would withhold any trade with the developed world until their price demands were met. This may have been a good idea, but it failed miserably. The raw material producers could not agree on prices and plans, and a number of them faced political and military instability, making regional cooperation next to impossible. Moreover, most African countries are so dependent on one or two products for export that they are in no position to bargain. If they withhold their coffee from the world market, for instance, they will effectively have nothing to trade and therefore become even poorer. It is a very precarious situation.

To succeed, regional efforts normally require at least two ingredients. First, a region needs sufficient money and other resources to exert some influence in the world. This is why Asia has been so successful. The region has money, technology, and skilled personnel, all of which give it substantial clout in the international marketplace. By contrast, Africa has little bargaining power or leverage in the world and, consequently, the world's second largest continent is increasingly ignored by many people. Second, a region needs skilled diplomacy in order to formulate creative solutions to the many obstacles that can derail official or unofficial alliances. This may seem like an obvious point, but it is one that has been ignored by many world leaders. Without skilled diplomats and creative initiatives, regional efforts do not last long.

National. National governments can also undertake a number of useful initiatives to help themselves, despite their poverty. In addition to obvious things like not killing their citizens, developing countries could undertake three actions that might create positive social change. First, they need to implement reforms that will encourage foreign banks and governments to forgive at least some of their debts. Fewer government employees, a crackdown on wasteful spending, and a well-organized development plan would help convince lenders that countries are serious about reform. These reforms would help save money for debt repayment and they would also help prevent a new round of debt in the future. Importantly, though, in contrast to those who call for mass cuts in all government spending, developing countries should maintain spending for basic needs and a social safety net. This will only be possible, however, if other types of spending are reduced.

Second, because of their limited resources, it is essential that developing governments work closely with nongovernment organizations (NGOs) in civil society to help promote development. Governments can provide money, cars, tools, personnel, and information to various development organizations. Unfortunately, many governments interfere with NGO efforts because they feel threatened by the goodwill generated through nongovernment efforts (Ndegwa 1996). Governments are worried that people will follow community leaders more than government leaders. Without a vibrant civil society, however, many poor countries will not achieve any level of development in the near future.

Third, governments need to work together to formulate regional solutions to development problems. As noted earlier, regional efforts are difficult but not impossible. Recently, for instance, twelve southern African countries met in Johannesburg, South Africa, to construct policies for the Southern African Development Community (SADC). These countries pledged to trade more with each other, ease travel restrictions between countries, and create a single currency. Does this sound like Europe or South America? The discussion may be in the right direction, but such proposals will be difficult to bring to reality because most of the twelve countries are extremely poor. South Africa's economy, for instance, is four times larger than the other eleven members combined. South Africans are, on average, thirty-five times richer than Mozambicans, the region's poorest citizens (*The Economist* 1995). Regional plans work best when there are several strong players who can bring valued resources to the group. Nonetheless, the SADC's proposals are a good start. A *group* of national governments exerts far more power and influence than a single government standing alone.

Community. Finally, community and local efforts by nongovernment organizations are some of the best ways to reduce inequality and create positive social changes. While professors and policy makers debate the merits

of various theories, there are many selfless individuals and groups working in towns, villages, and other communities around the world. Some
projects are based locally, meaning that people from the communities
direct them. Local religious organizations work with the poor; local
women's organizations help empower women and teach them marketable
skills; local charitable organizations work with street children to provide
them with food, shelter, and basic education; and the list goes on and on.
Other organizations operate in local communities but are based outside
the area, usually in wealthy countries. Most are international charities or
relief organizations like CARE, Save the Children Foundation, the Red
Cross, the Salvation Army, AmeriCares, Doctors without Borders, and
OXFAM. These groups have performed outstanding work providing immunizations, helping refugees, fighting poverty, planting crops, and assisting disaster victims.

Although nongovernment organizations have saved and improved
countless lives, they often face two difficult constraints. First, lack of
money, technology, and other resources is a major problem, especially for
local organizations that are not associated with an international NGO. To
overcome this problem, it would be helpful if (1) local groups could form
an alliance with an international group, or (2) foreign aid were given directly to poor communities in the developing world, not to national governments that might divert the money elsewhere (for example, to military
budgets). Second, nongovernment organizations are forced to work within
a given structure over which they have little control. Governments,
armies, and armed gangs have interrupted many projects in developing
countries. For instance, the International Red Cross has consistently had
their humanitarian efforts sabotaged in the former Yugoslavia; and Doctors without Borders and OXFAM have been harassed and threatened in
refugee camps across the Rwandan border in Zaire. Nongovernment organizations do not have military forces and do not hold political office.

We have presented a number of ideas that can be used to create positive social changes in the world, many of which will reduce global and
national inequality. No proposal is easy, but many are possible and some
have been accomplished in various regions around the world. The most
successful development efforts combine initiatives from at least two of the
four levels discussed here: global, regional, national, or community. We
conclude this section with an example that illustrates this point.

The Undugu Society ("Brotherhood Society" in the Swahili language)
is a local NGO in Kenya devoted to helping street children in urban slums
(Ndegwa 1996). It was started by a Dutch Catholic priest named Arnold
Grol in 1973. The initial one-person operation has grown substantially

since that time. It now has a professional staff of more than 140 social workers, advisers, office personnel, and nurses. It also has an annual budget of about $1.4 million. The Undugu Society utilizes its resources well to provide innovative social service, educational, and job-training opportunities for street children. For example, each year the society teaches basic education skills to 700 slum and street children, pays school fees for another 300 children in regular schools, and trains 60 to 70 children for jobs in the informal sector such as automobile repair and carpentry. The money for these programs comes from a variety of sources. About half of its funding is generated through commercial activities in Kenya: Undugu fixes motor vehicles, sells products, and provides consulting services to various business. And about half of its resources come from outside of Kenya, including foundations in Germany, Holland, and the United States (Ndegwa 1996). Without outside assistance, the Undugu Society could not provide nearly as many services for children.

Forcing Change from the Outside: What Is Justified?

The world has seen an increasing number of mass tragedies in recent years, some of which were discussed in this book. In the 1990s alone, armed conflict has directly contributed to the deaths of about 1.5 million people in Somalia, Rwanda, and the former Yugoslavia. All three crises lead to the same question: Should the United States and other countries intervene militarily to try to stop the bloodshed? It is a question that will be asked with increasing frequency in future years, as the world faces more tragedies born out of poverty, population growth, government instability, and ethnic hatred. Therefore, when talking about potential solutions to global problems, we need to focus on this issue. Because of our earlier presentation on the former Yugoslavia and the timeliness of this issue, we will use this conflict to make broader points.

There are two good arguments against military intervention and two good arguments in favor. You can consider the arguments and then make up your own mind. Let's consider the case against involvement. First, most wars do not threaten the national interests of the United States and most other countries of the world. Moreover, the wars include intense ethnic hatreds that have been around for centuries. So why should the United States, Europe, the United Nations, or any other body become involved in these tangled messes? Yes, people are dying; yes, the wars are bad; yes, people are suffering; but no, it is not the responsibility of other nations to intervene in the conflict. Let the local people (and people in surrounding areas) settle their own disputes. Western soldiers should not have to die in order to settle disputes that do not directly concern them.

Second, military intervention might stop the killing, but it does not lead to long-term solutions. In Somalia, for instance, intervention by U.S. and other forces stopped much of the killing and enabled starving people to eat, at least for a few months. This is an example of *peacekeeping*. But peacekeeping does not build governments, which is a job for citizens of the local country. Somalia has literally not had any government for years, primarily because the warring factions cannot agree on how to select one. Somalia's inability to form a government, combined with increasing attacks on foreign soldiers, clearly signaled an end to the usefulness of peacekeepers in Somalia, who then pulled out. Three years after the pull-out, the killing continues and Somalia still has no government. Some people therefore argue that outside intervention was a waste of time, money, and lives.

However, there are at least two arguments in favor of intervention by U.S. and other outside forces. First, some observers make a *moral* argument for involvement. How, they ask, can the United States (now the only superpower in the world) and its allies stand back and allow genocide or other major conflicts to continue? This view argues that the powers of the world must act to prevent mass killing, thereby sending a strong message to other despots around the world. Of course, a counterargument is: How can the United States and its allies police every situation of genocide and near genocide?

But many people, both conservative and liberal, have advanced the moral argument for intervention in the former Yugoslavia. Conservative columnist George Will has written eloquent columns about the need for U.S. intervention. Vaclav Havel, the president of the Czech Republic, has spoken directly to President Clinton about the moral imperative of immediate action. And the *New Republic* magazine, a left-of-center publication that would like to support a Democratic president, has run a series of blistering editorials against President Clinton's reluctance to become involved in Bosnia-Herzegovina. In part, one stated:

> Since the United States is the only power in the world that can stop the ethnic cleansing, the United States is responsible if the ethnic cleansing continues. Well, not exactly the United States. The American president is an accomplice to genocide. Not so the American people. The president of the United States does not have the right to make the people of the United States seem as indecent as he is . . . more and more Americans want to know why we are standing around and doing nothing. (1995b, 7)

Second, if the moral argument is not persuasive, then a *political* argument for involvement may be more compelling. In the former Yugoslavia, for instance, if war had spread north toward Europe or south toward Greece, then it is clear that the European community and the United States would have become immediately interested in the conflict. When a country's national interests are threatened, then it often becomes involved in war. When Iraq threatened Western oil supplies in the Persian Gulf, the United States and its allies launched operation Desert Storm to stop it. Absent a clear threat to national interests, however, some people argue that war is not justified. This attitude infuriates those who make a moral argument for intervention to stop mass killing. What is more important, they ask, protection of oil wells or human beings?

Since the start of the conflict in the former Yugoslavia, numerous peace proposals have been discussed and then dismissed by one side or the other. The United Nations has also placed thousands of peacekeeping forces (mostly from Europe) on the ground throughout Bosnia-Herzegovina. As of August 1995, about 20,000 such troops were in the region. Although these troops were armed, they were not equipped to repel attacks by the large Serbian army, as the assaults on Srebrenica and Zepa showed. The North Atlantic Treaty Organization (NATO), a military alliance made up of Europe and the United States, threatened the Serbs repeatedly, but assumed a very limited military role until September 1995, when the bombing of Serbian positions began. Lack of involvement by NATO was due to two major factors: (1) Europe disagreed over what to do, with France calling for aggressive military action and Britain calling for little more than U.N. peacekeeping efforts (so much for a unified Europe); and (2) the U.S. president and other American politicians were unwilling to take a lead role in initiating a military campaign in the former Yugoslavia. This is an important point because about 90 percent of NATO jets are American jets flown by American pilots.

As noted in Chapter 6, peace talks are again under way to negotiate a settlement in the former Yugoslavia. The current peace initiative calls for Bosnia-Herzegovina to be divided into two sections: 51 percent of the land for the Muslims and Croats (mainly Muslims) and 49 percent for the Bosnian Serbs. Obstacles to the plan remain formidable, however. What sections of the country will each group receive? How will large groups of people be moved safely into new settlements? Who will police the division of territory and the movement of people? How will violations of the treaty be handled? What role will the United States, Europe, the United Nations, and NATO have under the new arrangements? How will past atrocities be prosecuted? Will convicted murderers (for example, Karadzic and Mladic) be allowed at the peace table? And the list goes on and on.

Regardless of how the negotiations proceed, three enduring lessons have already been learned from the war in the former Yugoslavia. First, genocide is effective when unchecked by outside forces. Even if the Serbs settle for 49 percent of Bosnia-Herzegovina, they will have won in some respects. They will get to keep half of what used to be Bosnia-Herzegovina, even though they slaughtered thousands of people in "winning" the territory. Still, it may be the best solution at this point. Three years ago NATO probably could have stopped the genocide, but, instead, world leaders decided to watch. This emboldened the Serbs and allowed them to build up their military forces throughout the country. Now, almost four years later, it is difficult to roll back much of what has already been done. Thus, dividing Bosnia-Herzegovina in half looks like a positive development today; but three years ago it would have seemed intolerable.

Second, limited military campaigns such as the one launched by NATO can work effectively under some circumstances. This does not mean that NATO or any other military alliance should use force—or threaten to use force—as a first resort. But military action should always remain an option if it can save lives in the long run. History teaches us that genocide is not stopped by negotiation alone. NATO bombing was an important factor facilitating the peace process in the former Yugoslavia. Future Yugoslavias will again compel the Western world to decide whether to use military force to stop mass killing.

Third, although a peace plan would be a welcome relief in the former Yugoslavia, it will not bring back to life the 200,000 people killed by the war or ease the incredible suffering of more than 3 million refugees. In addition to the physical damage, the psychological and emotional toll on children, raped women, and other victims of atrocities committed by the Serbs, Croats, and Muslims is incalculable. World leaders will eventually want to take credit for negotiating an end to the conflict, but it will not erase this suffering. Watch the 1996 presidential campaign in the United States: *If* peace has been achieved in the former Yugoslavia, the American administration will not want voters to forget this fact or that the administration was successful in bringing all parties to the peace table. Still, Americans might want to ask one additional question of their leaders: What took so long?

In closing this section, we want to recount one happy moment amid the suffering caused by the war in Bosnia. U.S. Air Force Captain Scott O'Grady, who was shot down in the summer of 1995 while flying a surveillance mission over Bosnia-Herzegovina, was rescued after surviving several days in the Bosnian wilderness, surrounded by Serbian forces. The rescue by U.S. helicopters was dramatic and Captain O'Grady was welcomed home as a genuine American hero. It was a small moment of celebration during a tragic war. President Clinton was so happy that he admitted to smoking a celebratory cigar.

Ironically, exactly fifty years earlier another world leader lit up a victory cigar. The prime minister of England, Winston Churchill, was celebrating a victory in World War II. He had just helped stop fascism; he had just helped stop Hitler; he had just helped stop genocide. Although Churchill lived in a different era and faced different circumstances from Clinton, it is unlikely that anyone would confuse the two cigar-smoking leaders on the issue of stopping tyrannical forces.

Creating Positive Social Changes: What Individuals Can Do

What can one individual do to change the world, even a small piece of it? Throughout this book we have seen examples of individuals who do make a difference, some on a large scale and others on a small scale. Nelson Mandela, Lech Walesa, and Vaclav Havel helped transform entire governments. Wang Weilin stood up to a column of tanks and thereby became an international symbol of courage, determination, and democracy. Dave Deppner planted trees in deforested regions of the developing world. Wangari Maathai established an environmental movement in Africa that raised awareness on the continent and beyond. And Father Arnold Grol started an organization that has saved and empowered thousands of poor Kenyan street children who otherwise would have faced destitution.

This movement to change the world has even captured the efforts of presidents after they leave office. By all accounts, President Jimmy Carter was humiliated and depressed following his landslide defeat in 1980 at the hands of Ronald Reagan. He did not know what he would do with the rest of his life. But he did not brood over his defeat for long. One year after leaving office he started the Atlanta-based Carter Center at Emory University. It is a nonprofit organization that brings people together to promote peace, resolve conflict, foster democracy, and fight disease around the world. The center now has thirteen core programs in more than thirty countries, including the United States. One program has monitored multiparty elections in Haiti, Ghana, Mexico, Panama, Paraguay, Guyana, Zambia, Nicaragua, and the Dominican Republic. Another has helped resolve civil conflicts in the Sudan, Bosnia, Liberia, Ethiopia, Haiti, and the Korean peninsula. A third program is especially impressive. Working with various partner organizations, the Carter Center is now leading a campaign to eradicate Guinea worm disease from the face of the earth. This painful disease, which is caused by drinking water contaminated with fleas carrying the Guinea worm larvae, has crippled and debilitated adults and children in nineteen countries. To avoid the disease, people are taught how to filter water to eliminate the fleas. Since the campaign began in 1986, there has been a 95 percent drop in the number of cases of Guinea worm. If the disease is eradicated within the next couple of years, as expected, it will be only the second disease (after smallpox) that has been completely eliminated.

In addition to these (and other) activities, Jimmy Carter is a volunteer in his community. He builds houses for Habitat for Humanity, participates in church-related projects, and works for many charitable causes throughout the country. He also writes books on peace and conflict resolution: Some have been for scholars and world leaders; some have been for the general public; and others have been for students, including a current project that explains the importance of peace to children. At seventy-one, Jimmy Carter has earned the right to enjoy a long retirement reflecting on his many accomplishments. But he is busier than ever. Regardless of what people thought of President Carter, former President Carter is widely regarded as one of the nation's greatest ex-presidents precisely because of his efforts in civil society.

But you don't have to be a former president or a famous person to make a difference. The vast majority of positive social changes in the world are created by people who are not widely known. They volunteer to teach people to read; they visit senior citizens who are alone; they counsel distressed people; they coach youth sports; they serve food in shelters; they join the Peace Corps; they host foreign exchange students; they build homes, schools, and community centers in poor countries and the United States; they plant trees; they educate people about environmental issues; they give money to charity; they visit the terminally ill in hospitals; they teach people to grow food; they stand up to institutions (and governments) that are unjust; they join community development projects; they perform music and make art; they empower others.

In summary, individuals can do four things to help change both developing and developed countries. First, they can learn more about global problems. People can take courses on global issues, read books and magazines on various topics, talk to people from other countries, and travel when possible. We hope you know more about the world than when you started this book. We also hope you go on and learn even more about the world. Education, both formal and informal, has always been one key to positive change.

Second, people can give money to worthwhile causes and organizations. Most American charitable contributions go to activities in the United States. In 1990, for instance, only 4 percent of charitable contributions were allocated to international development assistance or emergency relief (Calhoun, Light, and Keller 1994, 470). Thus, more people might consider giving to organizations and institutions that focus their efforts on Third World development (for example, CARE). Many of these organizations are highly responsible and allocate more than 85 percent of their contributions directly to programs that help people. Before giving money to an organization, however, it is a good idea to ask what percentage of the funds go for this purpose. If the amount is under 85 percent or not provided at all, it is probably a good idea to look for another charity. In addition to giving money to private charities, American citizens can also encourage their government to give more money to the developing world. As discussed earlier, the United States gives only a miniscule amount of its wealth to foreign aid around the world.

Third, people can volunteer in one of the many activities mentioned earlier. Thousands of committed individuals have volunteered for the Peace Corps and other development organizations. College students are some of the most active and very best volunteers anywhere. If it were not for the thousands of student volunteers across the country, far fewer people would benefit from the many projects sponsored by civil society. Although volunteerism cannot take the place of all government programs, it can make a real difference in many lives.

Fourth, people who build coalitions and put aside ideological differences can be very effective at creating social changes that reduce inequality. Have you listened to any radio talk shows lately? A common characteristic is that each one pushes an ideological viewpoint. Conservative talk shows advance only conservative points of view and liberal talk shows advance only liberal points of view. People are divided into conservatives or liberals, Republicans or Democrats, black or white, and good people or bad people. Divisions are easy because they place people into comfortable categories, namely, "us" and "them." In reality, though, people usually categorize others out of fear and ignorance.

But great changes occur when people put aside differences and find the best solutions to problems. To eradicate smallpox, for instance, thousands of people, dozens of countries, hundreds of organizations, and many different types of governments all worked together for over a decade. Literally every case of smallpox throughout the world had to be found and vaccinated. People were dispatched into the most remote villages to track down every last case of the disease. The project could easily have been derailed along the way if conservative and liberal groups had refused to work together, or if governments with opposite ideologies had not cooperated with the program. But people and organizations set aside differences to reach a common goal. As a result, a disease that had been a scourge for centuries was eradicated from the face of the earth, saving millions of people around the world.

We conclude this book with a story. In October 1991, the African country of Zambia held its first democratic elections in twenty-seven years. President Kenneth Kaunda had been the country's only head of state since 1964, and he had finally acceded to multiparty elections. To ensure a fair election, outside observers (headed by Jimmy Carter) were brought in to monitor every polling location in the country. Citizens were allowed to cast their vote until 6 P.M., just a few minutes before sunset and then darkness. After the polls closed, a religious-like atmosphere enveloped the polling sites as each ballot box was locked and then sealed with wax dripping from a lighted candle. Election officials and monitors leaned reverently over each ballot box and watched the wax seal harden as darkness descended on polls across the country. The burning candles provided the only light in remote areas of the country that did not have electricity. Ballot boxes were then loaded into vehicles and driven on very poor roads to the capital city of Lusaka, where the ballots would be counted in a central location. As the boxes were being placed onto a truck in one remote location, a Zambian observer quietly reflected on the meaning of democracy, "Yesterday 8 million Zambians followed their leaders. Today, we changed that and became the leaders." It was an inspiring statement for all people interested in changing their world.

References

Adamson, Peter. 1990. "Giving Children a Future." In *World Summit for Children*, edited by UNICEF (pp. 1–5). New York: United Nations.

Africa Demos. 1994. A Bulletin of the African Governance Program. Vol. III, No. 3. September. Atlanta: The Carter Center.

Allen, Thomas (Ed.) 1995. *Offerings at the Wall.* Atlanta: Turner Publishing, Inc.

Andrews, Edmund. 1995. "Japan's Job Market Shocks Collegians." *New York Times*, September 5, p. C2.

Annenberg/CPB Project. 1993a. "Fire in the Mind." *Americas*: Part 9 (video).

Annenberg/CPB Project. 1993b. "Get Up, Stand Up." *Americas*: Part 8 (video).

Ballinger, Jeff. 1993. "The New Free Trade Heel: Nike's Profits Jump on the Backs of Asian Workers." In *Global Issues 93/94*, edited by Robert Jackson (pp. 46–47). Sluice Dock, Guilford, CT: The Dushkin Publishing Group.

Banister, Judith. 1987. *China's Changing Population.* Stanford: Stanford University Press.

Barnathan, Joyce. 1993. "China: The Emerging Economic Powerhouse of the 21st Century." *Business Week*, May 17, pp. 54–65.

———. 1994. "China: Is Prosperity Creating a Freer Society?" *Business Week*, June 6, pp. 94–99.

Begley, Sharon. 1992. "Is It Apocalypse Now?" *Newsweek*, June 1, pp. 36–43.

Bello, Walden, and Stephanie Rosenfeld. 1990. *Dragons in Distress: Asia's Miracle Economies in Crisis.* San Francisco: Institute for Food and Development Policy.

Blank, Renee, and Sandra Slipp. 1994. *Voices of Diversity.* New York: American Management Association.

Bollen, Kenneth, and Robert Jackman. 1989. "Democracy, Stability, and Dichotomies." *American Sociological Review 54*, 612–621.

Bongiorno, Lori. 1995. "The Business Week 1000." *Business Week*, March 27, pp. 96–165.

Bonner, Raymond. 1995. "The Serbs' Caravan of Fear." *New York Times*, Week in Review, August 13, p. 3.

Bornschier, Volker, and Christopher Chase-Dunn. 1985. *Transnational Corporations and Underdevelopment.* New York: Praeger.

Boswell, Terry, and William Dixon. 1990. "Dependency and Rebellion: A Cross-National Analysis." *American Sociological Review 55*, 540–559.

Bradshaw, York. 1993. "State Limitations, Self-Help Secondary Schooling, and Development in Kenya." *Social Forces 72*, 347–378.

Bradshaw, York, Claudia Buchmann, and Paul Mbatia. 1994. "A Threatened Generation: Impediments to Children's Quality of Life in Kenya." In *Troubling Children: Studies of Children and Social Problems*, edited by Joel Best (pp. 23–45). Hawthorne, NY: Aldine de Gruyter.

Bradshaw, York, and Elvis Fraser. 1989. "City Size, Economic Development, and Quality of Life in China: New Empirical Evidence." *American Sociological Review 54*, 986–1003.

Bradshaw, York, and Bruce Fuller. 1996. "Policy Action and School Demand in Kenya: When a Strong State Grows Fragile." *International Journal of Comparative Sociology* (Forthcoming).

Bradshaw, York, Paul Kaiser, and Stephen Ndegwa. 1995. "Rethinking Theoretical and Methodological Approaches to the Study of African Development." *African Studies Review 38*, 39–65.

Bradshaw, York, Young-Jeong Kim, and Bruce London. 1993. "Transnational Economic Linkages, the State, and Dependent Development in South Korea, 1966–1988: A Time-Series Analysis." *Social Forces 72*, 315–345.

Bradshaw, York, Rita Noonan, Laura Gash, and Claudia Buchmann. 1993. "Borrowing Against the Future: Children and Third World Indebtedness." *Social Forces 71*, 629–656.

Bradsher, Keith. 1995. "Low Ranking for Poor American Children." *New York Times*, August 14, p. A7.

Bratton, Michael. 1989. "The Politics of Government-NGO Relations in Africa." *World Development 17*, 569–587.

Brauchli, Marcus. 1995. "China's Economic Role in Asia Is Burgeoning." *Wall Street Journal*, July 24, p. A1.

Brauchli, Marcus, and David Hamilton. 1995. "Watch Out, Investors: Asia's Hot Spots Are Flaring." *Wall Street Journal*, August 18, p. A6.

Brinton, Mary. 1993. *Women and the Economic Miracle: Gender and Work in Postwar Japan*. Berkeley: University of California Press.

Brooke, James. 1992. "U.N. Chief Closes Summit with an Appeal for Action." *New York Times*, June 15, p. A12.

Brown, Lester et al. 1990. *State of the World 1990*. New York: Norton.

Buchmann, Claudia. 1996. "The Debt Crisis, Structural Adjustment and Women's Education: Implications for Status and Social Development." *International Journal of Comparative Sociology* (Forthcoming).

Bunker, Stephen. 1985. *Underdeveloping the Amazon: Extraction, Unequal Exchange, and the Failure of the Modern State*. Urbana: University of Illinois Press.

Burg, Steven. 1994. "Why Yugoslavia Fell Apart." In *Russia, The Eurasian Republics, and Central/Eastern Europe*, edited by Minton Goldman (pp. 291–297). Sluice Dock, Guilford, CT: The Dushkin Publishing Group.

Butler, Steven. 1995. "Vietnam's Next Crusade." *U.S. News and World Report*, May 1, pp. 55–62.

Byrne, John. 1991. "The Flap over Executive Pay: Investors, Employees, and Academics Are Asking How Much Is Enough?" *Business Week,* May 6, pp. 90–110.

———. 1994. "That Eye-Popping Executive Pay." *Business Week,* April 25, pp. 52–101.

———. 1995. "CEO Pay: Ready for Takeoff." *Business Week,* April 24, pp. 88–116.

Calhoun, Craig, Donald Light, and Suzanne Keller. 1994. *Sociology.* 6th ed. New York: McGraw-Hill.

Carter, Jimmy. 1993. *Talking Peace: A Vision for the Next Generation.* New York: Dutton Children's Books.

Cavazza, Fabio Luca, and Carlo Pelanda. 1994. "Maastricht: Before, During, After." *Daedalus* (Spring), 53–80.

Center for National Security Studies. 1995. Recent Trends in Domestic and International Terrorism. Public Report, Washington DC, April 26.

Central Intelligence Agency. 1995. *The World Factbook.* Washington, DC: CIA.

Chase-Dunn, Christopher. 1989. *Global Formation: Structures of the World-Economy.* Cambridge: B. Blackwell.

China International Economic Consultants. 1985. *The China Investment Guide.* Hong Kong: Longman.

Chirot, Daniel. 1977. *Social Change in the Twentieth Century.* New York: Harcourt Brace Jovanovich.

———. 1986. *Social Change in the Modern Era.* San Diego: Harcourt Brace Jovanovich.

———. 1991. "What Happened in Eastern Europe in 1989?" In *The Crisis of Leninism and the Decline of the Left: The Revolutions of 1989,* edited by Daniel Chirot (pp. 3–32). Seattle: University of Washington Press.

———. 1994a. *How Societies Change.* Thousand Oaks, CA: Pine Forge Press.

———. 1994b. *Modern Tyrants: The Power and Prevalence of Evil in Our Age.* New York: The Free Press.

Cole, Jeff. 1995. "Jet Makers, Once Keen for a Giant Aircraft, Are Drawn to a Fast One." *Wall Street Journal,* June 12, pp. A1, A9.

Cornia, Giovanni Andrea, Richard Jolly, and Frances Stewart (Eds.). 1987. *Adjustment with a Human Face.* 2 vols. New York: Clarendon Press.

Daily Nation (Nairobi newspaper). 1993. "Time to Focus on the Dying Child." Editorial. June 16, p. 6.

Delacroix, Jacques, and Charles Ragin. 1978. "Modernizing Institutions, Mobilization, and Third World Development: A Cross-National Study." *American Journal of Sociology 84,* 123–150.

Dicken, Peter. 1992. *Global Shift: The Internationalization of Economic Activity.* 2d ed. New York: Guilford Press.

Durning, Alan B. 1991. "Fat of the Land." *World Watch,* May/June, pp. 11–17.

The Economist. 1994. "The Rise of the Outside Right." October 15, pp. 68–70.

———. 1994/1995. "Colombia's Drug Business." December 24/January 6, pp. 21–24.

———. 1995. "Southern Africa Dreams of Unity." September 2, p. 35.

Elmer-Dewitt, Philip. 1992. "Rich vs. Poor." *Time,* June 1, pp. 40–65.

Engardio, Pete. 1993. "Asia's Wealth: It's Creating a Massive Shift in Global Economic Power." *Business Week,* November 29, pp. 100–108.

———. 1994. "Rising from the Ashes: Can Free Markets Turn Vietnam into a Tiger?" *Business Week,* May 23, pp. 44–48.

Farnsworth, Clyde. 1995. "Quebec Separatists Split on Timing and Terms of Referendum." *New York Times,* April 18, p. A7.

Fekete, Liz. 1993. "Jeux Sans Frontieres: It's a Lock-Out." *New Statesman & Society,* November 5, pp. 23–26.

Firebaugh, Glenn. 1992. "Growth Effects of Foreign and Domestic Investment." *American Journal of Sociology 98,* 105–130.

Firebaugh, Glenn, and Frank Beck. 1994. "Does Economic Growth Benefit the Masses? Growth, Dependence, and Welfare in the Third World." *American Sociological Review 59,* 631–653.

French, Howard. 1995a. "Mobutu, Zaire's 'Guide,' Leads Nation into Chaos." *New York Times,* June 10, pp. A1, A6.

———. 1995b. "Out of South Africa, Progress." *New York Times,* July 6, pp. C1, C5.

Fuller, Bruce. 1991. *Growing-up Modern: The Western State Builds Third-World Schools.* New York: Routledge.

Gibbs, Nancy. 1994a. "Why? The Killing Fields of Rwanda." *Time,* May 16, pp. 57–63.

———. 1994b. "Cry the Forsaken Country." *Time,* August 1, pp. 28–37.

Gladwell, Malcolm. 1995. "The Plague Year." *The New Republic,* July 17, pp. 24, 38–46.

Glain, Steve. 1995. "For South Korea Firms, Speaking Too Freely May Carry Steep Price." *Wall Street Journal,* August 18, pp. A1, A10.

Golden, Tim. 1992. "Sweeping Political Changes Leave Latin Poor Still Poor." *New York Times,* May 30, pp. 1,5.

———. 1995. "In Mexico, Both Army and Rebels Say They're in Control." *New York Times,* February 24, p. A3.

Goldman, Minton. 1988. *The Soviet Union and Eastern Europe.* 2d ed. Sluice Dock, Guilford, CT: The Dushkin Publishing Group.

———. 1994. *Russia, the Eurasian Republics, and Central/Eastern Europe.* 5th ed. Sluice Dock, Guilford, CT: The Dushkin Publishing Group.

Goldstone, Jack. 1991. *Revolution and Rebellion in the Early Modern World.* Berkeley: University of California Press.

Government of Kenya and UNICEF. 1992. *Children and Women in Kenya: A Situation Analysis 1992.* Nairobi: Regal Press.

Griffiths, Ieuan. 1993. *The Atlas of African Affairs*. 2d ed. London: Routledge.

Gugler, Josef. 1988. "Overurbanization Reconsidered." In *The Urbanization of the Third World*, edited by Josef Gugler (pp. 74–92). New York: Oxford University Press.

Gurr, Ted Robert. 1993. *Minorities at Risk: A Global View of Ethnopolitical Conflicts*. Washington, DC: United States Institute of Peace Press.

Hanson, Stephen. 1991. "Gorbachev: The Last True Leninist Believer?" In *The Crisis of Leninism and the Decline of the Left: The Revolutions of 1989*, edited by Daniel Chirot (pp. 33–59). Seattle: University of Washington Press.

Harbrecht, Douglas. 1994. "What Has NAFTA Wrought? Plenty of Trade." *Business Week*, November 21, pp. 48–49.

Harden, Blaine. 1990. *Africa: Dispatches from a Fragile Continent*. Boston: Houghton Mifflin.

Harris, Philip, and Robert Moran. 1991. *Managing Cultural Differences*. Houston: Gulf Publishing.

Hope, James. 1995. "Johnny Ipil-Seed." *Ohio*, August, pp. 15–16.

Hyden, Goran. 1983. *No Shortcuts to Progress: African Development Management in Perspective*. Berkeley: University of California Press.

Hyden, Goran, and Pauline Peters. 1991. "Debate on the Economy of Affection: Is It a Useful Tool for Gender Analysis?" In *Structural Adjustment and African Women Farmers*, edited by Christina Gladwin (pp. 301–335). Gainesville: University of Florida Press.

Inkeles, Alex, and David Smith. 1974. *Becoming Modern: Individual Change in Six Developing Countries*. Cambridge: Harvard University Press.

International Labour Office. 1994. *Yearbook of Labour Statistics, 1994*. 53rd ed. Geneva, Switzerland: International Labour Organisation.

Javetski, Bill. 1994. "Europe: Unification for the Favored Few." *Business Week*, September 19, p. 54.

Jenkins, J. Craig, and Augustine Kposowa. 1990. "Explaining Military Coups D'état: Black Africa, 1957–1984." *American Sociological Review 55*, 861–875.

Kaiser, Paul. 1996. *Culture, Transnationalism and Civil Society in Africa: A Study of the Aga Khan and His Followers in Tanzania*. Boulder, CO: Greenwood Press.

Kamm, Henry. 1995. "In Prosperous Singapore, Even the Elite Are Nervous about Speaking Out." *New York Times*, August 13, p. A6.

Kaplan, Robert. 1993. *Balkan Ghosts: A Journey Through History*. New York: Vintage Books.

Knight, Robin. 1993. "Push Comes to Shove: Western Europe Is Ailing, Angry and Afraid of the Future." *U.S. News and World Report*, June 14, pp. 53–64.

Kristof, Nicholas. 1995a. "Japan's Schools: Safe, Clean, Not Much Fun." *New York Times*, July 18, pp. A1, A4.

———. 1995b. "Where a Culture Clash Lurks Even in the Noodles." *New York Times*, September 4, p. A4.

Lamb, David. 1985. *The Africans*. Rev. ed. New York: Random House.

———. 1988. *The Arabs: Journeys Beyond the Mirage*. New York: Vintage Books.

Lele, Uma. 1991. "Women, Structural Adjustment, and Transformation: Some Lessons and Questions from the African Experience." In *Structural Adjustment and African Women Farmers*, edited by Christina Gladwin (pp. 46–80). Gainesville: University of Florida Press.

Lemonick, Michael D. 1992. "The Ozone Vanishes." *Time*, February 17, pp. 60–63.

Lenski, Gerhard, Jean Lenski, and Patrick Nolan. 1991. *Human Societies: An Introduction to Macrosociology*. New York: McGraw-Hill.

Liebenow, J. Gus. 1986. *African Politics: Crises and Challenges*. Bloomington: Indiana University Press.

Linden, Eugene. 1993. "Megacities." *Time*, January 11, pp. 28–38.

Livernash, Robert. 1992. "The Growing Influence of NGOs in the Developing World." *Environment*, June, pp. 12–20, 41–43.

London, Bruce. 1987. "Structural Determinants of Third World Urban Change: An Ecological and Political Economic Analysis." *American Sociological Review* 52, 28–43.

London, Bruce, and Bruce Williams. 1990. "Multinational Corporate Penetration, Protest, and Basic Needs Provision in Non-Core Nations: A Cross-National Analysis." *Social Forces* 66, 747–773.

Long, William R. 1995. "Look, Out, NAFTA! Latin Trade Bloc Is Growing." *Los Angeles Times*, January 24, p. H2.

Martz, John D. 1994. "Colombia: Democracy, Development, and Drugs." *Current History*, March, pp. 134–137.

Mazrui, Ali. 1986. *The Africans: A Triple Heritage*. Boston: Little, Brown.

McFadden, Robert. 1993. "Blast Hits Trade Center, Bomb Suspected; 5 Killed, Thousands Flee Smoke in Towers." *New York Times*, February 27, pp. A1, A22.

Meadows, Donella, Dennis Meadows, and Jorgen Randers. 1992. *Beyond the Limits: Confronting Global Collapse, Envisioning a Sustainable Future*. Mills, VT: Chelsea Green.

Meyer, Michael. 1990. "The Tumult of the Tomb." *Newsweek*, June 26, p. 45.

Migdal, Joel. 1988. *Strong Societies and Weak States: State-Society Relations and State Capabilities in the Third World*. Princeton: Princeton University Press.

Milbank, Dana. 1995. "Will Unified Europe Put Mules in Diapers and Ban Mini-Pizza?" *Wall Street Journal*, June 22, pp. A1, A9.

Miller, Karen Lowry. 1994. "Europe: The Push East." *Business Week*, November 7, pp. 48–49.

Morais, Richard. 1992. "People in Glass Houses Throwing Stones." *Forbes*, May 25, pp. 84–94.

Myers, N. 1983. *A Wealth of Wild Species: Storehouse for Human Welfare*. Boulder, CO: Westview Press.

Myerson, Allen B. 1995. "Out of a Crisis, an Opportunity." *New York Times*, September 26, pp. C1, C4.

Naisbitt, John. 1994. *Global Paradox.* New York: William Morrow.

Nash, June, and Maria Patricia Fernandez-Kelly. 1983. *Women, Men, and the International Division of Labor.* Albany: State University of New York Press.

Nash, Nathan. 1992. "Army Unrest Stirs Bolivia, the Land of Coups." *New York Times,* June 3, p. A12.

Ndegwa, Stephen. 1996. *The Two Faces of Civil Society: NGOs and Politics in Africa.* West Hartford, CT: Kumarian Press.

Neff, Robert. 1995. "Japan's New Identity." *Business Week,* April 10, pp. 108–112.

The New Republic. 1995a. "It Has Not Been a Good Day." July 31, p. 7.

———. 1995b. "Accomplices to Genocide." August 7, p. 7.

New York Times. 1994. "Movement for Sovereignty Is Growing in Hawaii." June 5, Section 1, p. 36.

Noonan, Rita. 1995. "Women Against the State: Political Opportunities and Collective Action Frames in Chile's Transition to Democracy." *Sociological Forum* 10, 81–111.

Ojwang, J. B., and J. N. K. Mugambi (Eds.). 1989. *The S. M. Otieno Case: Death and Burial in Modern Kenya.* Nairobi: Nairobi University Press.

Perry, Elizabeth. 1991. "Intellectuals and Tiananmen: Historical Perspective of an Aborted Revolution." In *The Crisis of Leninism and the Decline of the Left: The Revolutions of 1989,* edited by Daniel Chirot (pp. 129–146). Seattle: University of Washington Press.

Preston, Richard. 1994. *The Hot Zone.* New York: Random House.

Protzman, Ferdinand. 1992. "German Companies Finding Low-Cost Locations in U.S." *New York Times,* May 26, pp. D1, D3.

Reskin, Barbara, and Irene Padavic. 1994. *Women and Men at Work.* Thousand Oaks, CA: Pine Forge Press.

Rostow, W. W. 1960. *The Stages of Economic Growth: A Noncommunist Manifesto.* Cambridge: Cambridge University Press.

———. 1991. "Eastern Europe and the Soviet Union: A Technological Time Warp." In *The Crisis of Leninism and the Decline of the Left: The Revolutions of 1989,* edited by Daniel Chirot (pp. 60–73). Seattle: University of Washington Press.

Rueschemeyer, Dietrich. 1991. "Different Methods, Contradictory Results? Research on Development and Democracy." *International Journal of Comparative Sociology 32,* 9–38.

Rueschemeyer, Dietrich, Evelyne Huber Stephens, and John Stephens. 1992. *Capitalist Development and Democracy.* Chicago: University of Chicago Press.

Sassen, Saskia. 1994. *Cities in a World Economy.* Thousand Oaks, CA: Pine Forge Press.

Schreiberg, David. 1995. "Birth of the Baby Cartels." *Newsweek,* August 21, p. 37.

Serrill, Michael S. 1992. "Brazil's Two Faces." *Time,* June 8, pp. 74–77.

Shaoyu, Xu. 1988. "Trends and Differences in China's Fertility Rate." In *New China's Population,* edited by China Financial and Economic Publishing House (pp. 15–31). New York: Macmillan.

Shenon, Philip. 1994. "Hunt in Forests of Borneo Aims to Track Down Natural Drugs." *New York Times,* December 6, p. B9.

Skocpol, Theda. 1979. *States and Social Revolutions: A Comparative Analysis of France, Russia, and China.* Cambridge: Cambridge University Press.

Smith, David. 1991. "Method and Theory in Comparative Urban Studies." *International Journal of Comparative Sociology 32,* 39–58.

Smith, Geri. 1992. "The New World's Newest Trade Bloc." *Business Week,* May 4, pp. 50–51.

———. 1994. "Why Wait for NAFTA?" *Business Week,* December 5, pp. 52–54.

Stevens, William. 1995a. "The 25th Anniversary of Earth Day: How Has the Environment Fared?" *New York Times,* April 18, pp. B5–B6.

———. 1995b. "Scientists Say Earth Warming Could Set Off Wide Disruptions." *New York Times,* September 18, pp. A1, A5.

Thiong'o, Ngugi wa. 1965. *The River Between.* London: Heinemann.

Timberlake, Michael, and Jeffrey Kentor. 1983. "Economic Dependence, Overurbanization and Economic Growth: A Study of Less Developed Countries." *Sociological Quarterly 24,* 489–507.

Time. 1994. "Birth of a 'Narcodemocracy.' " April 11, p. 19.

Trompenaars, Fons. 1994. *Riding the Waves of Culture: Understanding Diversity in Global Business.* Burr Ridge, IL: Irwin Professional Publishing.

Ungar, Sanford. 1985. *Africa: The People and Politics of an Emerging Continent.* New York: Simon & Schuster.

United Nations. 1993. *World Urbanization Prospects: The 1992 Revision.* New York: United Nations, Department of Economic and Social Information and Policy Analysis.

———. 1994. *1993 International Trade Statistics.* New York: United Nations.

United Nations International Children's Emergency Fund (UNICEF). 1990. *The State of the World's Children 1990.* New York: Oxford University Press.

———. 1991. *The State of the World's Children 1991.* New York: Oxford University Press.

———. 1992. *The State of the World's Children 1992.* New York: Oxford University Press.

———. 1993. *The State of the World's Children 1993.* New York: Oxford University Press.

———. 1994a. *The State of the World's Children 1994.* New York: Oxford University Press.

———. 1994b. *The Progress of Nations.* New York: UNICEF.

———. 1995. *The State of the World's Children 1995.* New York: Oxford University Press.

Updike, Edith Hill. 1995. "The Dashed Dreams of Generation X." *Business Week*, August 7, pp. 38–39.

U.S. Bureau of the Census. 1993. *Statistical Abstract of the United States: 1993.* 113th ed. Washington, DC.

———. 1994. *Statistical Abstract of the United States: 1994.* 114th ed. Washington, DC.

U.S. Committee for Refugees. 1994. *World Refugee Survey 1994.* Washington, DC: U.S. Committee for Refugees.

U.S. Department of Transportation. 1993. *Highway Statistics 1992.* Washington, DC: U.S. Department of Transportation.

U.S. Government Printing Office. 1964. *Public Papers of the Presidents of the United States: John F. Kennedy.* January 1 to November 22, 1963. Washington, DC.

———. 1989. *Public Papers of the Presidents of the United States: Ronald Reagan.* January 1 to July 3, 1987. Washington, DC.

Vogel, Ezra. 1991. *The Four Little Dragons: The Spread of Industrialization in East Asia.* Cambridge: Harvard University Press.

Walker, Chip. 1995. "The Global Middle Class." *American Demographics*, September, pp. 40–46.

Wallerstein, Immanuel. 1974. *The Modern World System I.* New York: Academic Press.

Walton, John. 1984. *Reluctant Rebels: Comparative Studies of Revolution and Underdevelopment.* New York: Columbia University Press.

Walton, John, and Charles Ragin. 1990. "Global and National Sources of Political Protest: Third World Responses to the Debt Crisis." *American Sociological Review 55,* 876–890.

Ward, Kathryn (Ed.). 1990. *Women Workers and Global Restructuring.* Ithaca: Industrial and Labor Relations Press, Cornell University.

Warmenhoven, Henri. 1995. *Western Europe.* 4th ed. Sluice Dock, Guilford, CT: Dushkin Publishing Group.

Washington Post. 1995. "Tears and Tributes for a Fallen Envoy." August 23, p. A15.

Watson, Russell. 1990. "The Last Days." *Newsweek,* January 8, pp. 16–23.

Wells, Ken. 1995. "South Africa Lags in Foreign Investment." *Wall Street Journal,* August 21, p. A6.

Whiting, Robert. 1990. *You Gotta Have Wa.* New York: Macmillan.

Whitney, Craig. 1995. "Jobless Legions Rattle Europe's Welfare States." *New York Times,* June 14, p. A3.

Whyte, Martin King, and William Parish. 1984. *Urban Life in Contemporary China.* Chicago: University of Chicago Press.

Williams, Michael, and Jathon Sapsford. 1995. "Japan's Slow Response to Bank Crisis Shows Its Big, Basic Problems." *Wall Street Journal,* June 14, pp. A1, A8.

Wimberley, Dale. 1990. "Investment Dependence and Alternative Explanations of Third World Mortality: A Cross-National Study." *American Sociological Review 55,* 75–91.

World Bank. 1993. *World Development Report 1993.* New York: Oxford University Press.

———. 1994. *World Development Report 1994.* New York: Oxford University Press.

———. 1995a. *World Development Report 1995.* New York: Oxford University Press.

———. 1995b. *World Bank Atlas.* Washington, DC: World Bank.

World Trade. 1995. "China: People Patterns." May, p. 12.

Wright, John W. 1995. *The Universal Almanac 1995.* Kansas City, MO: Andrews and McMeel.

WuDunn, Sheryl. 1995. "Erosion in Japan's Foundation: Real Estate Crash Threatens the Entire Economy." *New York Times,* October 4, pp. C1, C3.

Index